TERRORISM
PVT LTD

TERRORISM
PVT LTD

Dr NC Asthana, IPS

Manas Publications
(We Convert Fighters into Writers)
New Delhi - 110 002 (INDIA)

MANAS PUBLICATIONS
(We Convert Fighters into Writers)
(Publishers, Library Suppliers, Importers & Exporters)
4402/5-A, Ansari Road (Opp. HDFC Bank)
Darya Ganj, New Delhi - 110 002 (India)
Phones: Off.: 011-23260783, 23265523, Res.: 011-23842660
E-mail: manaspublications@gmail.com
manaspublications@yahoo.com
Website: www.manaspublications.in

ISBN 978-81-7049-543-7

₹ 995

Designed at
Manas Publications

Printed in India at
R.K. Printers, Delhi
and published by Mrs Suman Lata for
Manas Publications, 4402/5-A,
Ansari Road (Opp HDFC Bank),
Darya Ganj, New Delhi - 110 002 (INDIA)

Preface

After every bomb blast or some other form of terrorist attack, we and our friends in the West claim to have solved the case, arrested the accused, including the mysterious 'masterminds', exposed their trans-national network and busted the terror 'modules' – yet the attacks continue to take place with frightening regularity, year after year! Why? Obviously, something is seriously amiss somewhere. There has to be a grave flaw in our understanding of terrorism. It is fashionable in the academic circles to speak of the so-called 'root causes' of terrorism. Unfortunately, terrorism is too complex and diverse a phenomenon to speak easily of causes or root causes. As such, there cannot be a formula (Condition 'a' + Grievance 'b' + Group Dynamic 'c' + Ideology 'd' = Terrorist Violence) that applies to terrorism and provides its root causes for the governments to address. Fact is, root causes are necessary only in so far as the susceptibility for the emergence of individuals or groups likely to use terrorism as a tactic is concerned – but they are not sufficient causes. Terrorism has resulted from a complex interplay of myriad forces, the situation being unique to most places. The primary requirement, the *conditio sine qua non*, of tackling terrorism is therefore an understanding of terrorism in all its complex dimensions.

This treatise provides, for the first time, a rare and comprehensive insight into the entire subject of terrorism including radicalization; Salafism/Wahabism; jihad; the formation, evolution, ideology, morphology and methodology of important terrorist groups like the ISIS (Islamic State of Iraq and Syria), Lashkar-e-Taiba, and Jaish-e-Muhammad; financing of terrorism; combating financing of terrorism; how terrorists procure their arms and ammunition; Pakistan's state sponsoring of terrorism; and how we must prepare for the worst-case scenarios, among other things.

Terrorists measure their success in terms of how effective they have been in creating havoc, a general feeling of insecurity and a loss of confidence in the government besides taxing the resources of the government in chasing shadows – the physical damage caused in terrorist strikes is basically a bonus. Humans have an in-built dread of the unknown and the uncontrollable. The fear that they can strike you anytime and anywhere makes them appear larger than life. We are, therefore, obliged to live in an insecure world. The sinister forces that make the world insecure, however, are neither immutable nor insurmountable. Terrorists seek to elicit a certain type of response from their targets. If the targets of terrorism are fully aware of the perceptions that eventually lead to the response that corresponds with the purpose of the terrorists, they can be made to alter their perceptions and respond in a different way. The mere act of doing this will be tantamount to a defeat of the terrorist because then he would have failed in eliciting the desired response from the target.

Fascinated by the live coverage of anti-terrorist operations, most people come to nurse a fond misconception that terrorism is essentially a tactical problem – that is, if you have a large number of smartly-dressed commandos laden with the latest military gadgets, the problem would be solved in no time. Yet another group of people starts placing an implicit trust in draconian laws. For them, terrorism is essentially a police problem and if more resources are allocated to the police and the domestic intelligence machinery, the menace would be over. They are all dangerous misconceptions. The failure of the Western world in rooting out terrorism, in spite of enacting draconian laws like the Patriot Act, is all but lost – there have been nearly 50 incidents of terrorist attacks in the USA since 9/11 mounted by Muslims which targeted Americans/Jewish persons specifically; including Omar Mateen's rampage shooting in an Orlando nightclub that killed 49 and injured 53 (June 2016); the San Bernardino shooting by Syed Farook and Tashfeen Malik that killed 14 and injured 22 (December 2015); the Boston Marathon bombing that killed three and injured over 260 (April 2013); and Maj Nidal Malik's rampage shooting in Fort Hood that killed 14 (November 2009); to name a few. The laws could not deter those terrorists. European countries have suffered the worst with the Berlin Christmas market attack (12 killed, 56 injured, December 2016); the Nice, France truck attack (87 killed, 434 injured, July 2016); the Brussels bombings (35 killed, 340 injured, March 2016); the November 2015 Paris attacks (137 killed, 368 injured); and the Norway attacks (77 killed, 319 injured, July 2011) that rattled the Continent; harsh laws like the UK's Counter-Terrorism and Security Act; France's sweeping surveillance law; Germany's Act to Amend the Crime of Preparation of a Serious Violent Offence Endangering the State; and EU Framework Decision on Terrorism, etc notwithstanding. The pre-emptive neutralization strategy, which the Israelis pursue for the Palestinians, could, at best, be used against citizens of other countries, not against citizens of one's own country as the rest of the world faces. It needs no particular illumination that the world as a whole has been barking up the wrong pole.

Victory against terrorism can be achieved only if we have completely understood the entire phenomenon of terrorism, replete with all its complex facets. The motivation of the terrorists, the intrinsic weaknesses of the targets, the intrinsic strength of the way of the terrorist, and the follies of the approach that a nation or nations persisted with so far. It is the most vital step towards shaping and implementing appropriate policies and actions. A nation where people do not understand this, continues to respond in a knee-jerk fashion; take wasteful decisions; exert itself disproportionately; expend its resources disproportionately; and thus 'exhaust' itself – with little tangible results in sight. If any nation has floundered in its "war against terrorism", it is because it has never had a serious and honest-to-God analysis of terrorism besetting it, and hence the need of this book.

Being in government service means that I have not commented on any matter of Government policy of India. In this book, therefore, wherever I have spoken of India, it refers to India as a nation and not the Government of India – what our imperatives must be if we have to survive the menace of terrorism; that should be the concern of every citizen.

Terrorist attacks unleash a plethora of reactions from amongst the common people, the media, the security forces, the intelligence agencies and the political leaders – some of them amusing; some outrageous, some funny, some hopelessly stupid, some un-cogitated, and some simply knee-jerk reactions. Most self-styled experts on TV, media, and in the academia are desperately anxious to present a magic wand solution to terrorism, or some single 'silver bullet' of counterterrorism, within the one minute allotted to them. Had life been so simple, nations of the world would not have been battling terrorism for decades in spite of having spent trillions of dollars! As Lt Gen Asad Durrani, a former chief of the ISI, described it very astutely in his article "CT Made Easy" in *The Dawn* newspaper (March 30, 2017) of Pakistan,

> "Nothing comes close to a non-remedy to fight the menace of terrorism than our latest gimmick – 'the terrorists have

> been brainwashed, so let's read to them another narrative.' Anyone who believes that those committed to a cause deeply enough to blow themselves up could be 'reprogrammed' by a *mantra*, obviously has no idea what 'de-radicalization' entails."

Complex problems demand complex solutions. There is no running away from complexity. And for that we require in-depth knowledge first.

The extremely authentic knowledge presented in the book is backed by a formidable array of as many as 370 sources and authorities cited in the bibliography. In order to maintain the continuity of narrative and ease of reading, I have avoided giving footnotes. However, the bibliography has been arranged alphabetically and any authority cited in the book anywhere can be easily located in the bibliography.

The hallmark of the book is its comprehensiveness. As a responsible citizen, it is your duty to be well-informed so that your reactions to any developments on matters related to national security are guided by reason and not by emotions. After all, it is the common man whose perceptions eventually guide national policies, albeit imperceptibly. It is therefore imperative that your perceptions are not derived from the half-baked, hurried scramble dished out daily on TV or in the media. Whether you are a lay man, a student, a homemaker, a media person, a policy-maker, or a man in the armed forces, the comprehensive knowledge contained within the pages of this book will set you free from the tyranny of the ignorant.

New Delhi

Dr NC Asthana

Declaration: In terms of Rule 6 of the All India Service (Conduct) Rules, 1968, I hereby declare that the views and opinions expressed in the book are my own, and not those of the Government of India. That the views and opinions expressed are my own means that they are my personal intellectual creations and are not endorsed in any way by the Government of India or the official position held by me. It is further certified that, in terms of Rule 7 of the All India Service (Conduct) Rules, 1968, there is nothing in the book which has the effect of an adverse criticism of any current or recent policy or action of the Central Government or a State Government; or which is capable of embarrassing the relations between the Central Government and any State Government or which is capable of embarrassing the relations between the Central Government and the Government of any Foreign State. Precisely for this reason, any policy of the Central Government or any State Government of India has not been discussed at all in the book. As for the foreign governments mentioned in the book, all the information/facts given in this book pertaining to them have been in the public domain since long and I have elaborately cited the sources/references. I have only collated and processed information available in the public domain and presented it in a logical, systematic manner with only explanatory comments of mine so as to make them clearer for the reader.

Dr NC Asthana

Contents

1

ISIS: Ideology, Morphology and Methodology

NOMENCLATURE, IDEOLOGY AND OBJECTIVES

From ISIL to IS to Daesh to ISIS

The group had called itself first by the name of *'Al-Dawla Al-Islamiya fil Iraq wa Al-Sham'*. *Al-Dawla*, *daulah* or *daulat* means a State. The term *Al-Sham* was commonly used during the rule of the Muslim Caliphs from the 7th century to describe the area between the Mediterranean and the Euphrates, Anatolia (in present day Turkey) and Egypt. On the other hand, the British had, in the imperial past, been using the term 'Levant' (from the Italian word Levante, meaning 'rising', implying the rising of the sun in the east) to describe the eastern part of the Mediterranean, with its islands and the countries adjoining – that is, somewhat similar to *Al-Sham*. The name of the organization was therefore translated in English first as 'Islamic State in Iraq and the Levant' (ISIL).

However, since June 2014 the organization declared the creation of a Caliphate and shortened its name to *Ad-Dawla Al-Islāmiya*. This was translated as 'Islamic State' (IS). May be they made that change in name to correspond with their expansionist ambitions.

Since many people who have not studied the history of the Middle East and the Ottoman Empire, were not familiar with the word Levant, a popular version of the name became ISIS – Islamic State in Iraq and Syria. *Sham* has been historically understood as the area that was dominated by Damascus, an important regional centre, and hence the association of the word with modern Syria. This was more easily understandable as people could easily identify with the names of the places and also because those were the places where the organization was operating.

Many people objected to the use of the word 'state' in its name because it was felt that it accorded the group some sort of unintended legitimacy. Such people invented the name *Daesh* for it. *Daesh* is essentially an Arabic acronym formed from the initial letters of the group's previous name in Arabic *'Al-Dawla Al-Islamiya fil Iraq wa Al-Sham'*. Although it does not mean anything as a word in Arabic, it sounds unpleasant and hence it serves to delegitimize the group's claims. In this book, I have, however, stuck to the name ISIS for the simple reason that it is more popular in India and more people understand it.

Ideology of the ISIS

Ideologically, the ISIS subscribes to Salafism/Wahabism of the type that has had been advocated earlier by the Al-Qaida and the Taliban among others. The ISIS have not bothered to invent something new in ideology neither they have discovered any new facet of extremist views. However, this does not mean that they are obliged to always think in sync with, or necessarily cooperate with each other. Anti-Americanism has been, of course, a common feature of most of the Muslim terrorist organizations even if they do not ascribe to Wahabism/Salafism. As such,

Wahabism/Salafism need not be described as the only source of all evil. Later in the book, we have discussed Wahabism and Salafism in greater detail and hence we are not discussing them here further.

Vision, Ambition and Objectives

The ISIS differs from other terrorist organizations in one important aspect. And that is its proclaimed objective. The ISIS, from the beginning, has declared itself a 'state' and a sort of transnational Islamic Caliphate the extent of which is not confined to their place of origin. In other words, they are looking for an eventual conquest of the world. Terrorist organizations generally do not bother with holding territory and administering it. (The Taliban were the first exception to it. The LTTE had tried for it and had failed miserably. We have discussed it in detail later in the book.)

Their ambitions of an Islamic Caliphate actually extend beyond the areas of what was once called *Bilad Al-Sham*, a Rashidun, Umayyad and later Abbasid Caliphate province. (*Bilad* means a group of cities or states.) This is called Greater Syria in English and includes modern Iraq, Syria, Lebanon, Israel/Palestine, Jordan, and even Kuwait. According to its vision, the Caliphate in Greater Syria will be the core of an extensive Islamic Caliphate. It will include the countries of the Middle East; North Africa; parts of Iran, Pakistan and Afghanistan (Khorasan); European countries that were conquered from the Muslims in the past (Spain, the Balkans); and other Muslim countries (Turkey, the Caucasus). Since the ISIS does not recognize modern nation-state boundaries to have any significance in its scheme of a theocratic state, its vision includes an Islamic takeover of the entire world (and symbolically, "the occupation of Rome", the symbol of Christianity) – quite a grandiose scheme! That was reflected in the tape distributed by

Abu Bakr Al-Baghdadi shortly after the declaration of the Caliphate.

In terms of aspirations, they seek to take "their version of the faith" back to the days of its medieval glory when under the banner of the Crescent, the Islamic *shamsheer* had dazzled the world. The period of the first four Caliphs of Islam, Abu Bakr (incidentally, whose name was adopted by Abu Bakr Al-Baghdadi), Umar, Uthman/Osman and Ali (632-661), was politically the most cohesive period in the history of Islam and is called its Golden Age.

The Arabic title given to the rulers who came after the death of the Prophet Muhammad (SAW-PBUH) in 632 AD, was *Khalifat Rasul Allah*, ie "substitute for the messenger of Allah" or, in its short form, Caliph ('substitute'). The necessity of the concept of a 'substitute' arose because no mortal could succeed him. The Caliphate, in simple terms, means establishing a single Muslim Theocracy, elimination of various modern nation States (the fruit of the 'imperialist plot'), subjecting all Muslims to a single accepted and agreed-on ruler, and eliminating the 'infidel regimes' in Arab and other Muslim countries. The theocracy is supposed to be governed in accordance with the model of the Islamic Caliphate in its Golden Age, that is, the generations after the Prophet Muhammad (SAW-PBUH).

The four Caliphs mentioned above had established the first Islamic State, undertook the major conquests beyond its borders and laid the economic and administrative foundations for the Muslim Empire. For these reasons the first four Caliphs have been greatly admired in Islam throughout the ages, and many Sunni Muslim movements perceive them as their spiritual fathers. The collective term for the first four Caliphs is Rashidun, that is, those who follow the straight path as instructed by the Prophet Muhammad (SAW-PBUH). Caliphs from the Quraysh tribe (Prophet Muhammad's tribe) ruled it in practice until the time of the Ottoman Turks (1517). They were replaced by Ottoman-Turkish Caliphs, who gave themselves the director title of Sultan. They ruled until 1924, when Turkey, which became a republic under the leadership of Kemal Atatürk, abolished the Caliphate.

Islamic Revivalism

Islamic revivalism refers to those individuals and movements that want to strengthen and restore Islamic influence in political, economic and social life. This movement, according to Lawrence G Potter, Professor at Columbia University, in his paper "Islam and Politics: Egypt, Algeria and Tunisia", appears to be a part of a broader worldwide movement in which people disaffected from their respective governments and feeling 'threatened' by the erosion of traditional values turn to religion as a source of identity. This feeling of insecurity is directly fuelled by the inferiority complex which they have developed with respect to the material and military progress made by the Western world which has left them behind and relegated to a secondary position in the global order. Islamic revivalism is therefore viewed as a revolutionary force whose aim is to topple the established order in the Muslim world, be that authoritarian or democratic.

Revivalist desires have had been given vocal expression at different periods in different places of the world. There has been a whole battery of revivalists in the history of Islam including Ahmad Sirhindi, Ibn Taymiyyah, Shah Waliullah, Muhammad ibn Abd-Al-Wahab, Hassan Al-Banna, Saiyyid Abul Ala Maududi, Ruhollah Khomeini, Jamal-ud-din-Afghani, Muhammad Abduh, and Rashid Rida, to name a few. In India too, we had a Wahabi revolt against the British in the 19th century led by Saiyyid Ahmed of Raibareli who had sought to establish a Caliphate. Since the 1979 Iranian Islamic revolution, the Middle East has witnessed a rising involvement and influence of Islamic movements or Islamic revivalism in regional and domestic politics.

Brutalities of the ISIS and their Pseudo-Religious Arguments

The infamous brutalities of the ISIS, as evident in the executions of prisoners and religious minorities carried out by them, are actually calculated acts. They result from two things: perversity in the minds of the perpetrators; and a deliberate tactic of terrorizing people. Perversity in the minds of those who happen to be placed in complete control of the lives of some people is quite common. That's why we have so many cases of custodial torture and rapes by the police. The famous Austrian neurologist and psychiatrist Dr Viktor Frankl was a Holocaust survivor of the notorious Auschwitz Concentration Camp. In his book *Man's Search for Meaning* he has spoken of many SS Gestapo guards who committed atrocities on the prisoners, having been clearly sadists. Secondly, they know that the West abhors brutality and hence seek to shock them into stupefaction by acts of brutality.

Accepting these explanations would, however, amount to admitting their weakness. That's why the pseudo-religious explanation of the concept of *'takfir'* (discussed later in detail) is advanced at times. In a contrived (and wrong) explanation, prisoners of war are described as spoils of war. Spoils of war are known as *'maal-e-ghaneemat'*. An ISIS operative spoke to the Egyptian terrorist organization Ansar Bayt Al-Maqdis on the ISIS forum on November 4, 2014. In this, one of ISIS's suggestions was for the jihadi fighters in Egypt to attack Christians and Shi'ites. The reason cited was,

> "because they are sectarian groups that cannot be trusted and with whom no agreement can be reached. They are nothing more than the spoils of war given to you by Allah."

The interpretation of the ISIS, even if intended to be taken seriously, is wrong. Dr Noorhan Abbas and Dr Eric Atwell in "The University of Leeds: The Qurany Concepts Tool" elaborate on Surah Al-Anfal Verse No 41 (008:041) [*Qurany* means 'my Quran' in Arabic]. There is a clear injunction regarding spoils of war or *'maal-e-ghaneemat'*. Nowhere has it said that the captives were to be executed or their women raped. Dr Noorhan Abbas and Dr Eric Atwell have cited as many as eight variant English translations of the Quran as well as the Arabic original. This particular Surah is about the Battle of Badr. The Muslims were outnumbered heavily and yet they won. Allah (SWT), in this Surah, delineates many of the etiquettes pertaining to war and Allah's help in its outcome:

> "And know that whatever of war-booty that you may gain, verily one-fifth (1/5th) of it is assigned to Allah (SWT), and to the Messenger, and to the near relatives [of the Messenger (Muhammad SAW)], (and also) the orphans, *Al-Masakin* (the poor) and the wayfarer, if you have believed in Allah (SWT) and in that which We sent down to Our slave (Muhammad SAW) on the Day of criterion (between right and wrong), the Day when the two forces met (the battle of Badr) – And Allah (SWT) is Able to do all things."

Thus there is a prescribed etiquette of the distribution of the spoils of war and wanton, perverse behaviour was not even hinted at.

ISIS and the Jabhat Al-Nusra operatives in Syria and Iraq have desecrated graves and shattered Muslim and non-Muslim statues. There is nothing new in it, however. As readers can recall, the Buddhas of Bamiyan (4th- and 5th-century monumental statues of standing Buddha carved into the side of a cliff in the Bamiyan valley in the Hazarajat region of central Afghanistan) were destroyed in March 2001 by the Taliban in Islamic religious iconoclasm, because Mullah Muhammad Omar, declared them to be idols.

THE ISIS FLAG AND ITS SIGNIFICANCE

The flag of the ISIS is one of the most prominently seen objects on the TV – whenever there is some news regarding the ISIS, the flag is seen. However, few people know its significance. The flag of the ISIS is black with a white inscription of the Testimony (*Shahada*), the heart of the Islamic faith: *La Ilah Illallah* ["There is no god but the God, Allah"]. Below the inscription there is a white circle, the seal of the Prophet Muhammad (SAW-PBUH), and with an inscription in black reading *Muhammadur Rasulullah* ["Muhammad the Messenger of Allah"]. The point to be noted is that the inscription has to be read from the bottom up. According to Muslim tradition, the Prophet Muhammad (SAW-PBUH) adopted a silver seal containing three lines, with one word on each line: Muhammad, Messenger [of] Allah. In most traditions, the words, "Muhammad the Messenger of Allah" were written in the usual order, that is from top to bottom; according to some traditions, however, the lines are read from the bottom up, as in a seal. The inscriptions are purposefully handwritten, instead of a computer print so as to give them an earthy, rustic look; and perhaps make it reminiscent of the medieval era the appeal of which it seeks to evoke.

The flag used by ISIS is known by various names, among them "the oneness flag" (*Rayat Al-tawhid*) because it contains the word of oneness (*Kalimat Al-tawheed*): "There is no god but Allah; Muhammad [is] the Messenger of Allah", "the flag of the Caliphate", and is sometimes mistakenly called "the Flag of the Prophet". It must be kept in mind that the flags of the Salafist-jihadi organizations, including ISIS, are not identical to the flag of the Prophet Muhammad (SAW-PBUH). According to tradition, the flag of the Prophet Muhammad (SAW-PBUH) is called "the banner of the eagle" (*Rayat Al-uqab*) and looks different: the *Shahada* on it appears in full on a horizontal line.

Terrorists across the world have been using the ISIS flag as a symbol of defiance and/or support of the ISIS. The flag has been seen displayed by secessionists even in a far off place like Kashmir. The ISIS may not be directly involved in Kashmir but it is not just a fashionable or 'in' thing or mischief to display the ISIS flags. It is an attempt by such people to identify them and their activities with larger transnational Islamic issues. The flag of the ISIS has been made into a brand. How it came to this pass, we have discussed in the section pertaining to the appeal of the ISIS.

ORGANIZATION OF THE ISIS

Composition of the Leadership

The ISIS is headed by Ibrahim Awad Ibrahim Ali Al-Baghdadi, aka Abu Bakr Al-Baghdadi. Since June 29, 2014, he has held the self-awarded titles of Caliph and Imam – he is also the *Emir Al-Dawla Al-Islamiyya fi Al-Iraq wa-Al-Sham*. In true medieval style, he also holds the lofty title of *Emir Al-Mu'minin* ("our master, the commander of the faithful"). It was originally the title of the Muslim Caliphs who ruled the Islamic state during the first centuries of Islam. Abu Bakr Al-Baghdadi has two deputies responsible for running the various provinces in Iraq and Syria. Officers who served in the Iraqi army during the Saddam Hussein era and Ba'ath activists are found to be prominent within the leadership of the ISIS – their association with the 'professional' terrorists (or Salafist-jihadi operatives, if you like to call them so) dates from the days they had spent together in Camp Bucca, the American detention camp. However, as The Meir Amit Intelligence and Terrorism Information Center at the Israeli Intelligence and Heritage Communication Center believes and I concur with them, this is a marriage of convenience. The 'professional' terrorists are Salafists whereas the Ba'ath activists are secular, socialist guys. The association of the ideologically dissimilar serves for mutual benefit as the ISIS makes use of the military and bureaucratic skills of the army and party members, in which it is severely lacking; on the other hand, the Ba'athists and former Iraqi army personnel found a safe and convenient framework from which to fight the central Shi'ite-affiliated administration in Baghdad, the United States and the West in general.

Administrative Structure of the ISIS

The three highest institutions in the ISIS are:

- The Shura Council or Majlis Al-Shura
- The Military Council or Al-Majlis Al-Askari
- The Sharia Council or Majlis Al-Sharia

The Shura Council is the highest institution of ISIS. It has between nine to 11 members, all appointed by Abu Bakr Al-Baghdadi. It is headed by Abu Arkan Al-A'miri. Theoretically, the Shura Council is supposed to confirm Abu Bakr Al-Baghdadi's nominations. It also has the authority to depose the Caliph if he fails to carry out his duties in accordance with Islamic religious law. According to a comprehensive study of the Islamic State by Richard Barrett of the Soufan Group, an American international strategic consultancy firm, all the members of the Shura Council happen to be Iraqis.

The Military Council deals with planning military moves and supervising local commanders operating in territories under the control of the ISIS. At different times, it has been reported to be headed by different people – may be they got killed or replaced. They include Tarkhan Batirashvili, aka Omar Al-Shishani, a Chechen who had served in Georgia's armed forces; and Waleed Jassem Al-Alwani, aka Abu Ahmed Al-Alwani, a Ba'athist and former officer in the Iraqi army.

The Sharia Council consists of six members and, as the name indicates, is responsible for ensuring the compliance of all other parts of the administration with the Sharia law, or what the ISIS interprets of the Sharia. It also supervises the Sharia police and courts.

Main Support Centres of the ISIS and Training

The ISIS depends to a considerable extent for support and solidarity from other Arab States and entities. Support in Jordan for the Salafist worldview is not new; it had begun in the 1990s itself. Most of Jordan's support for ISIS comes from the outlying regions. Most prominent is the southern Jordanian city of Ma'an, a site of traditional unrest and anti-Hashemite sentiment, but there are other cities as well, among them Al-Salt, Irbid, Al-Rusaifa and Al-Zarqa'. The House of Hashim, better known as the Hashemites, are the royal family of the Hejaz (1916-1925), Iraq (1921-1958), and Jordan (1921-present). Arab nationalists have viewed the Hashemite monarchy as subservient to British and Western interests.

Many Arab foreign fighters who joined the ranks of ISIS came from Libya, especially from the coastal city of Darnah. There are many Tunisians among the foreign fighters joining ISIS and other organizations in Syria. One of the main organizations dispatching fighters to Syria has been a Salafist organization called Ansar Al-Sharia of Tunisia. There is some support for ISIS in the Gaza Strip also from Salafists who were apparently influenced by its achievements. Hamas, however, considers Salafist activity as potentially dangerous and a practical and ideological challenge to its control of the Gaza Strip.

ISIS recruited local operatives in various provinces of Iraq. ISIS has 11 identified training camps in Iraq out of their total of 25 or so. They are located in the provinces of Al-Anbar, Salah Al-Din and Nineveh, and in the Kirkuk and Mosul areas

(Longwarjournal.org, October 24 and November 22, 2014). The remaining 14 in Syria are located in the provinces of Aleppo, Al-Raqqa and Dir Al-Zor. In addition, perhaps there are several training camps in the provinces of Al-Hasakah, Latakia and Damascus also. All of them present identifiable targets which, the day the USAF, takes it upon itself, can be flattened out in one day!

PROPAGANDA MACHINERY OF THE ISIS

Clever propaganda is one of the major strengths of the ISIS. In the battle for hearts and minds, ISIS has been very successful in a relatively short period of time. ISIS's dazzling military achievements and the declaration of the ambitious, albeit unrealistic, Islamic Caliphate, were accompanied by such an effective propaganda campaign which turned ISIS into an international brand. No other terrorist organization before them had used propaganda, psyops or psywar so successfully – so much so that, a sensation-seeking media has inadvertently turned them into a popular brand. It used psychological warfare to frighten its rivals and enemies and horrify world public opinion (by beheading Western captives, for example). The media coverage, in fact, becomes a de facto pulpit for propagating their ideology. The ISIS propaganda machinery is run by skilled professionals from Iraq and Syria, as well as media personnel from other Arab-Muslim countries and the West.

ISIS has media outlets which disseminate the organization's propaganda to its designated media branches. The Al-Furqan Institute for Media Production is ISIS's oldest media branch and the official media bureau for producing propaganda. The Al-I'tisam Media Foundation is a production institution that has made and distributed propaganda videos for ISIS. The Al-Hayat Media targets mainly Western audiences. The Ajnad Media Foundation specializes in broadcasting jihad songs and Islamic vocal music. ISIS has several Internet magazines, the most famous of them being Dabiq, published by the Al-Hayat Media. The Islamic State News is also an online magazine targeting audiences outside Syria and Iraq. ISIS also posts the Islamic State Report (ISR), which has articles about events and the organization's agenda.

It is believed that the ISIS forums, chat rooms and websites etc subtly influence the gullible and thus act as recruiting platforms. Many of them run under various covers but the ISIS has an official Arabic-language forum called Al-Minbar Al-'Ilami Al-Jihadi which posts notices, videos, pictures, audio messages and information about ISIS. As a result of publicizing ISIS's violence and atrocities, its Facebook and Twitter accounts were closed. That forced it to turn to less popular social networks. I am not aware of their presence and activities on the Dark Web.

HOW THE ISIS ATTRACTED FOREIGN FIGHTERS AND 'JIHADI BRIDES'?

Foreign Fighters

Having foreign fighters amidst one's ranks adds a certain 'value' to the group. Abu Muhammad Al-Julani, the leader of the Al-Nusra Front, described (*'Al-Manara Al-Baydhaa'*, November 4, 2014) the ideological importance of foreign fighters, "We are of the opinion that a jihadi group has to have an 'emigrant' that is, foreign fighter". It demonstrates that the ideology and the prowess of the group are regarded so highly that 'volunteers' have given up lives of comfort in their respective homes; have travelled across thousands of miles to join their ranks; and are so devoted to the 'cause' that they are prepared to even lay down their lives for it. It was believed that the number of foreign fighters in the ranks of the ISIS could well be half their total strength. The number of fighters who joined the ISIS in five years had already exceeded the number of foreign fighters who had joined the Mujahideen in the Afghan war in 10 years. Al-Qaida, on the other hand, too has had foreign fighters in its ranks but its operations not being a territorial affair, could not impart that sort of aura to their participation.

It is believed that the increase in its revenues after it took over the infrastructure, especially the oil fields, made it easier to recruit new operatives by promising them high salaries. However, it is highly likely that the lure of unlimited, uninhibited sexual pleasures obtained through a harem of sex slaves out of the captured women was a main driving force in drawing the sexually deprived (or so inclined) to the battle zone.

In September 2014, the CIA had estimated that more than 15,000 foreign fighters from 80 countries had gone to Syria to join the ranks of ISIS. In March 2016, *The Telegraph*, citing the Soufan Group, estimated the number to be around 27,000 to 31,000 from 86 countries. While around 6,500 Tunisians are reported to be fighting in Iraq and Syria, a further 5,000 have been stopped from leaving the country before they could join the fighting. There are approximately 6,000 people from Europe, most of them coming from France, Germany and the UK. The Asian continent has seen the most citizens travel to Syria and Iraq, with over 14,000 people estimated to be in the conflict zone. The report added that about 20-30% of the foreign fighters had finally returned home. In Britain, men, women and even school children, all from a wide range of social backgrounds, have been drawn into the Syrian Civil War and other battles of the ISIS. Many others have provided support from the UK itself. According to a report in the BBC News in late February 2017, the British authorities had determined that hitherto approximately 850 people from UK had managed to go out of the country to fight for the ISIS in Syria and Iraq. Helen Barnett for the Express.co.uk put the figure at 1,600. She cited intelligence officials who claimed that the number of Britons who have gone abroad to join extremists might have been kept at a more modest figure to reduce public fear and panic. Amongst them was the notorious executioner Jihadi John (Muhammad Emwazi), a BSc (Hons) graduate in Information Systems and Business Management from the University of Westminster. According to the former Foreign Secretary Philip Hammond, a further 600 British citizens have been caught trying to enter Syria to join the ISIS or other groups.

From the international perspective of combating terrorism, foreign fighters are deemed to be potentially dangerous to their countries of origin as 'carriers' of terrorism and subversion. If they survive the fighting in Syria and Iraq, they return with military experience and greater jihadi indoctrination. At least some of them can be expected to aspire to continue jihad against their countries of origin, whether for ideological reasons or to support other terrorist organizations.

Jihadi Brides

The women who went to the ISIS included the so-called 'jihadi brides'. They make for a very perplexing phenomenon which was not witnessed at the time of the Mujahideen war in Afghanistan. To some extent, this phenomenon testifies to the strange appeal of the ISIS. Nabeelah Jaffer, reviewer and editor for *The Guardian*, spent months talking to British and American 'sisters', before and after they had travelled to Syria and how were they convinced by promises of a 'perfect' society and life as a martyr's widow. Dr Katherine Brown of King's College London also analysed the phenomenon. They compare the women who have travelled to Syria to join ISIS to –

> "individuals who went out to join the Soviet Union in the 1950s and 60s, who weren't looking to fight, but were looking to become new citizens of the Soviet state. What's interesting is that they believe it's possible.... Islamic State is saying: 'You can have this perfect world – you just need to try a little bit harder.'"

There is a totalitarian impulse behind this. By joining the state, these women think they will become 'perfect people'. Melanie Smith of the Institute for Strategic Dialogue calls the "Caliphate utopian ideal" as one of the common "key pull factors" that drew women over. They imagine a world in which there is little poverty and inequality, governed with perfect fairness under clear-cut, divine laws that work to the advantage of all.

I must add that more importantly, the 'jihadi brides' feel that, even if they cannot wield weapons and fight on the fronts for the 'cause', they too are contributing their bit towards it by marrying the fighters and thus providing them vital support. This idea has had appealed to women in the past too. In Nazi Germany, Goebbels had very unambiguously stated:

> "At the risk of sounding reactionary and outdated, let me say this clearly: The first, best, and most suitable place for the women is in the family, and her most glorious duty is to give children to her people and nation, children who can continue the line of generations and who guarantee the immortality of the nation."

Hitler had made it clearer further:

> "The woman has her own battlefield. With every child that she brings into the world, she fights her battle for the nation."

Then there is, of course, the romantic thrill of doing something unconventional, daring and 'forbidden'.

Indians 'Emigrating' to Join ISIS and How to Control Them?

Even some Indians have not been immune to the appeal of the ISIS. Zee News had reported in December 2015 itself that there could be 23 Indians fighting for the ISIS, including 17 from the southern states. In January 2017, *India Today* reported that the National Investigation Agency (NIA) suspected that the 22

Kerala youths, who had disappeared a few months ago, might have joined the ISIS training camp in Afghanistan. They had all messaged their families to tell that they were safe and had joined the ISIS. *The Huffington Post* reported that they had been regular upper middle class folks, indistinguishable from colleagues and neighbours, going about their lives like millions of Malayalis every day. How exactly they got 'indoctrinated' to such an extent over Internet or otherwise that it made them leave their families and life to join a dangerous 'mission' thousands of miles away where an almost certain brutal death awaited them; even taking along pregnant wives? This question can indeed be answered but that would necessarily involve our coming face-to-face with some deeply unsettling incongruities and problems inherent in the Indian society. That would touch upon some very sensitive chords; some very raw nerves; unleashing a bout of recriminations from those who lack the moral courage to face uncomfortable realities – it is better that the establishment itself answers the question.

As such, keeping a tab on potential volunteers in any country, men or women, without turning the nation into a police state, is admittedly a very difficult task. The Soufan Group had pointed out that the efforts to contain the flow of foreign recruits have had 'limited impact'. Moreover, aware of the Western efforts to counter the 'emigration of foreign fighters'; the ISIS too has instituted security measures in the matter of the recruitment of foreign fighters. These include the demand of a recommendation from at least one sheikh known to the ISIS leadership (Aawsat.net, November 9, 2014).

A country concerned about its citizens going out to join the ISIS will have to decide for itself how it strikes a balance between individual liberties, and measures deemed necessary for national security. One possible legal measure is to provide for stringent punishment to those who go over to the ISIS but eventually come back. Some people have suggested that they must be tried for treason.

WHAT EXPLAINS THE APPEAL OF THE ISIS?

Security forces, intelligence agencies and media all over the world jump to give credit to the ISIS for almost every attack that takes place on their soil. Anybody who happens to get arrested for some terrorist strike somewhere and if the browsing history of his laptop shows his having visited any website related to the ISIS is promptly branded an ISIS sympathizer or member! I am afraid; such an attitude actually goes to help build a larger-than-life image of the ISIS. In reality, the ISIS does not have such an extensive organizational network that they could strike anywhere in the world at will.

Fact is, ISIS, like Al-Qaida in its heydays, is often just a brand name used by both its supporters as well as opponents in their quest of a readily available and well-known object to latch on for the sake of simplicity. The West is using the brand name to typecast anything that opposes it; the terrorists are using it to resolve their identity crisis. Many terrorist groups and even 'lone wolf' terrorists try to make a name for themselves by drawing on the power and aura that has been built around the ISIS trademark. Some are using it as symbol of all things Islamic that are opposed to all things American/Western. With a condescending attitude so typical of the West, you may call it a 'manufactured symbolism' if you like.

But there is a danger hidden in it. Baghdadi, like Osama bin Laden might come to an ignominious end but that would not really solve the problem. For many susceptible Muslims (and I lay special emphasis on the word 'susceptible'), the name ISIS has acquired a life of its own as a rallying point, symbol, brand, philosophy or attitude, and is likely to continue to serve as a potent symbol of their opposition to the West in general and America in particular. Baghdadi the man is no longer important; the sentiments espoused and aroused by him are. He could well be a product of the circumstances peculiar to him; but even if he had not been there, someone else would have come up. The respective personas of Baghdadi or Osama bin Laden are not important; the anti-West/anti-America sentiments that they espoused and with which many Muslims across the world were able to identify, are important. Killing such characters, given the massive resources of sophisticated weapon systems at the disposal of the West, is no big deal. The sentiments would, however, live on unmolested. The West has so far done nothing to address this fundamental issue.

The net effect of all such follies has been that the ISIS has been rather unwittingly imbued with an aura, a halo, a myth which it does not deserve. The Western propaganda machine has made the ISIS larger-than-life. Andy Beckett, author and feature writer for *The Guardian*, cites Adam Curtis, the acclaimed maker of the documentary "The Power of Nightmares: The Rise of the Politics of Fear":

> "The way in which official briefings about terrorism, often unverified or unverifiable by journalists, have become dramatic press stories which, in a jittery media-driven democracy, have prompted further briefings and further stories. Few of these ominous announcements are retracted if they turn out to be baseless."

There is little fact-checking before a news is splashed. The media has been most cavalierly sticking the label of ISIS on every fool who commits a terrorist act anywhere in the world – privately Baghdadi must be laughing up his sleeves! Hardly anyone questions the myths because so many people have got an interest in keeping it alive. Curtis frankly says that the perceived threat of the 'inevitability' of a catastrophic attack is a politically driven fantasy. As the myth of the Al-Qaida had been fading away from public memory, it was quietly replaced by the myth of the ISIS.

At the root of many problems in the world lies American arrogance: the way they treat the world; the way they violate the sovereignty of the nations; the way they make them feel that the US Marines could land anytime anywhere; the way they make you feel that their cruise missiles or GPS-guided bombs could hit any place in the world; the way they throw the weight of being the mightiest nation on earth; the way they make you feel that what they say is right; the way they make you feel that any opposition to the American way of life would be treated a punishable act; the way they make you feel that only that thing is correct which is endorsed by them; the way they look down upon the value system of others if not despising them outright; the way they have declared that "if you are not with me, you are against me"; the way they make the whole world feel that the world is a district of their police station and they can police it anytime anywhere; the way they make you feel that they are superior to others even if their superiority is derived from their military might; the total disregard they have for the sentiments of people of other nations; and the haughty manner in which even lowly employees of the US armed forces and other government departments (such as immigration officials) conduct themselves with people of other nations. This is what drives and fuels the anti-American sentiments of the Muslims in particular.

OPERATIONAL METHODOLOGY OF THE ISIS

Some Significant Terrorist-Style Attacks

The highlight of the ISIS attacks on the institutions of the Iraqi regime in 2013 was breaking into the Abu Ghraib prison, near Baghdad, which was notorious for the torture and humiliation of Iraqi prisoners during American occupation. After the American withdrawal, it was used by the Iraqi government to imprison hundreds of Al-Qaida operatives. Abu Ghraib was broken into on July 21, 2013. It began with artillery fire to soften resistance, after which the walls were breached by two car bombs.

Fifty ISIS operatives entered the prison armed with machine guns and grenades, opened the cells and released about 500 Al-Qaida operatives. The operation, which lasted about an hour, met with no significant resistance from the Iraqi prison guards, most of whom fled when ISIS began firing artillery. The released operatives had extensive experience of terrorism and provided significant reinforcements for ISIS. During a 12-month period, ISIS conducted 24 complex attacks using car bombs. Its operatives broke into eight Iraqi prisons in addition to Abu Ghraib.

ISIS's Early Military Successes

In June 2014, ISIS launched a broad military campaign in northern and western Iraq. ISIS's achievements included the takeover (with the help of Sunni tribes) of most of Al-Anbar province in western Iraq, the important Sunni city of Fallujah, and part of the city of Ramadi, the Al-Anbar provincial capital. The battlefield victories were nothing short of miraculous, the most important of which was the occupation of the oil city of Mosul, Iraq's second largest city with 1.8 million inhabitants, most of them Sunni; and the takeover of the Mosul hydroelectric dam, the largest in the country, located to its north. Forces belonging to the Peshmerga, the autonomous Kurdish Iraqi army, which were defending the dam, retreated after a battle lasting 24 hours. After the takeover of Mosul, ISIS occupied the city of Tel Afar, once again a Sunni majority town.

About the same time, the ISIS attacked and captured Baiji, Tikrit and Samara, all north of Baghdad. Baiji had the largest oil refinery in the country. Tikrit, as we know, is the capital of the Salah Al-Din province and the birthplace of Saddam Hussein. By the end of July-beginning of August 2014, ISIS forces had taken control of Sinjar, a city west of Mosul, the traditional stronghold of the Yazidi community.

An Analysis of their Military Ventures

The operational methodology which the ISIS had adopted is a curious mix of 'territorial conquest' through conventional warfare coupled with acts of terrorism committed against ordinary people also. The ISIS is found committing acts of terrorism (such as the brutal execution of prisoners or random terrorist strikes) both on the people in areas under their control as well as outside their control. There are reasons to believe that the acts of terrorism are actually a form of deliberate psychological warfare for keeping the people in areas under their control in a state of fear and for 'intimidating' the people whom they have yet to 'conquer', that is, mainly the West.

The dazzling victories of the ISIS need analysis because they created a wrong impression in the minds of many analysts regarding the actual military capability of the ISIS and the generalship of its commanders. It needs to be kept in mind that the arsenal of the Peshmerga forces was limited by restrictions because the Kurdish Region is not an independent state. Due to disputes between the KRG (Kurdistan Regional Government) and the Iraqi government, arms flow from Baghdad to Iraqi Kurdistan has been almost non-existent, as Baghdad fears Kurdish aspirations for independence. Peshmerga forces depended mainly on old arms captured from the old Iraqi Army during the 2003 US invasion of Iraq, in which Peshmerga forces were active. Before that, some weapons were also captured during the 1991 Iraqi uprisings. As such, a very serious resistance could not be expected from the Peshmerga forces.

The fall of Mosul with the Iraqi forces literally melting away before the ISIS remains a mystery. They were certainly capable of giving them a tough fight. The truth remains buried. What the ISIS is claimed to have achieved militarily, has been in violation of all sound military principles. Light weaponry alone does not help you keep territory. Light weaponry and ferocity of attack might be of help in isolated engagements – but to keep a large territory under control and protect it from regular forces, one needs a massive support system of a regular kind. In contrast, all that the ISIS has had is ad hoc sources of irregular supply.

Something is seriously amiss in the whole narrative of the collapse of the Iraqi forces and their retreat. It defies logic. Such lucky victories are to be attributed more to the lack of a proper opposition than to any intrinsic military merit in the ISIS. In Mosul, the Iraqi army had collapsed almost without firing a shot – not only that, they abandoned their weapons, armoured vehicles and other military hardware as they fled! Most of the weapons seized by ISIS were taken from the Al-Qayara base in Mosul, the fourth largest in the country. The haul included armoured Humvees, rockets, tonnes of ammunition and assault weapons. Evidence of the large-scale desertion remained littered across the streets of the central city, with flak jackets, camouflage uniforms and ammunition clips being held up by insurgents as they celebrated their victory. It would require a detailed analysis with eyewitness accounts as to what really had happened there. But it stands to reason that the Iraqi army did not put up a serious fight – whatever be the reason: collusion, incompetence or whatever.

A report in *The Guardian* (dated June 12, 2014, by Martin Chulov in Beirut, Fazel Hawramy in Irbil and Spencer Ackerman in New York) claimed that Iraqi officials had told *The Guardian* that two divisions of Iraqi soldiers – roughly 30,000 men – simply turned and ran in the face of the assault by an insurgent force of just 800 fighters! I must point out that even if we allow for sheer impetuosity and some daredevilry to the ISIS attacks, they could not help prevail against two fully equipped divisions replete with their full firepower – no way! Impetuosity of charge is an essentially medieval concept that had been characteristic of the light cavalry of the Islamic armies of the medieval era. It has no relevance in modern warfare. ISIS has thus been a great military misadventure – a very medieval attempt to cross swords with the modern.

The popular notions of some novel tactics of the ISIS are rooted in technical ignorance. Tim Lister, executive producer of CNN, for example, reports that Kurdish commanders near Mosul had told CNN how ISIS had sent more than a dozen fuel tankers converted into massive vehicle-borne suicide bombs against their positions. A similar tactic was used to break the resistance of Iraqi security forces in Ramadi; 28 suicide car bombs in three days, including at least six massive 15-tonne armoured truck bombs in a single attack. These are pure myths. Fuel tankers (as against the highly advanced 'fuel-air-explosives') can, at best, lead to massive fires – they cannot produce explosive force of the kind produced by regular high explosives like TNT and RDX. (Interested readers may refer to my treatise *The Ultimate Book of Explosives, Bombs and IEDs* for more knowledge on the subject.) Serious military analysts should not be carried away by the limited knowledge of reporters.

The Iraqi soldiers were professionals; this melting away could not have been an act of cowardice. Moreover, it cannot be believed that the US claims of having established a competent Iraqi military after more than a decade of training were entirely farcical. Some sort of complicity or subversion amongst their ranks must therefore be strongly suspected. *The Guardian* report had added that senior government officials in Baghdad were equally shocked, accusing the army of betrayal. Maliki too accused some senior military figures of 'negligence' and 'betrayal'. "I know the reasons why the army collapsed," Maliki said.

> "But now is not the time to point the blame to whoever ordered the army to fall back. Even if it's a ploy, the generals who are responsible must be held accountable. A conspiracy has led ISIS to occupy Mosul. Whoever is responsible will not get away with that they did."

Hamad Al-Mutlaq, a member of the Iraqi parliament's defence committee, was forthright:

> "I'm convinced that what happened in Mosul is deliberate negligence or there is an agreement between the parties because it's impossible for an army to be unable to stand up to a group made up of hundreds of men."

I must point out another fact: how could they manage to flee unmolested? It is difficult to believe that they fled in vehicles – even if they did, what prevented the ISIS from giving a chase as they were themselves very well motorized? That they were allowed to flee unmolested also hints at collusion.

The ISIS does not seem to have any military strategy worth its name. In fact, there is no dovetailing of their overall resources, their objectives and their approach to 'war'. One of their senior-most military commanders, Abu Omar Al-Shishani was but a sergeant in the Georgian army. He might have been a good fighter and veteran of the 2008 Russo-Georgian War; still, that did not and could not imbue him with the knowledge and capabilities of a general. In other words, he and others like him might have been good tacticians, but certainly not good strategists. Valour, age or experience is no substitute for professional knowledge that forms the basis of generalship. Generalship entails professional military knowledge; deciding the objective; organizing forces; marshalling various resources; directing large formations; drawing on experience; planning battles; planning campaigns; anticipating enemy strategy and tactics; and making logistics arrangements of all sorts (from food and shelter to weapons) for the armies, among other things. Good generalship has always meant the ability to ensure that what is strategically desirable should be rendered tactically feasible with the resources at one's disposal. ISIS has no one with such capabilities. ISIS occasionally posts pictures of trainees and graduation exercises held in the training camps. The photos betray how rudimentary the training is. They do not have any institutionalized knowledge, no manuals, nothing.

Their Lucky Run is Coming to an End

The ISIS success run was soon contained and halted. During the second half of August and September 2014 itself, ISIS forces were forced out from the dam. The significance of this should have been understood early. But a sensation-seeking media continued to revel in the image of the 'invincibility' of the ISIS they had helped built up. By the time of writing this book in September 2017, as it was expected, the ISIS, a non-conventional fighting force was all set to lose the battle on the ground against conventional armies with much greater overall firepower. As announced by the Iraqi Prime Minister Haider al-Abadi, Mosul had been 'liberated' from the hands of the ISIS by July 10, 2017 after over nine months of fighting and Raqqa, their last urban stronghold, was tottering under a US-backed Arab-Kurdish forces assault. Mosul's Grand al-Nuri mosque and al-Hadba minaret on which flew the ISIS flag was destroyed by the ISIS as they fell back. By September 2017, ISIS was holding on to just nine per cent of the territory it controlled at the height of its powers in 2015.

ISIS's Innate Military Weaknesses

The reverses which the ISIS has been suffering are quite understandable. There is a large gap between ISIS's actual power and its pretensions. There is no historical or scientific reason to believe that an irregular army or an 'army of terrorists' could beat a regular army in conventional battles if the latter had even a modicum of professionalism. At its peak, the LTTE had cadre strength of 18,000 but a regular army of even a small nation like Sri Lanka destroyed them utterly. Sri Lankan army was no match for the rather good Iraqi army that is fighting today.

An army needs much more than just rifles, machineguns, Toyota trucks and a couple of old tanks. There has to be a whole establishment for everything – ranging from food, medicine, provisioning and training to armament. The ISIS has no establishment, no infrastructure to support it. All they have is their fighters and their guns. Moreover, the ISIS has had nothing significant by way of air defence to counter nearly 50 American air strikes a day – a fatal weakness. They tried desperately some elementary things – such as, strictly enforcing security rules, making their military forces less visible, reducing the movement of its forces in open areas (moving in small groups using motorcycles and SUVs) and assimilating within the civilian population. All this is childish at best and ridiculous at worst. You cannot survive the JSOW (Joint Stand Off Weapon), JDAM (Joint Direct Attack Munition) and other smart missiles by such childish measures.

In urban combat, particularly where it is difficult to deploy and use armour effectively due to limited mounted manoeuvre space, the fighting on ground is essentially by light weapons. It is only in such situations that regulars do not enjoy much of an advantage over irregulars because both sides use similar weaponry and defenders can shoot first with both cover and concealment going in their favour.

Hence the fight to take back urban areas where irregulars are well-entrenched may be difficult and get prolonged. The stalemate is often broken by air or artillery support only. The Russians had faced a similar situation in the Battle of Grozny in Chechnya. Thus the time it will take for the ISIS to be completely routed from urban areas depends how effectively the US air strikes act. (For appreciating the nuances of combat in urban areas, interested readers may refer to my treatise *The Ultimate Handbook of Urban Warfare*.)

By the end of February 2017, as Mark Hanrahan, journalist and writer of the NBC News, had reported, Iraqi forces had continued their advance into the ISIS-held western area of the country's second-largest city, closing in on Mosul's strategic airport. Since November 2016, they have already driven ISIS fighters from the eastern half of the city. Given the 7,50,000 civilians in the western section of the city, the risk of collateral damage is a serious consideration slowing the advance. Already shelling and airstrikes are causing heavy casualties among families sheltering in cellars or beneath the stairs in their houses. As reported by Patrick Cockburn, journalist and an award-winning author of eight books, in *The Independent* on March 3, 2017, the last road out of the city to the west was cut by Iraqi government forces on March 1, and they have also captured one of the half-ruined bridges over the Tigris River that bisects Mosul, which they are planning to repair using US-supplied pontoons. By the time of writing this book in September 2017, I reckon that while the battle might probably continue for some time amidst close-packed buildings and narrow, twisting alleyways, and casualties will also take place; but the fall of Raqqa too looks inevitable and will be a calamitous defeat for the ISIS.

Scenario after a Possible Defeat of the ISIS

The ISIS, in my considered opinion as a military analyst, will therefore eventually lose. From a purely military point of view, it's only a matter of time. However, the story does not end there. As ISIS weakens and becomes less of a threat, the edgy détente between different anti-ISIS forces, such as the Iraqi government and the Iraqi Kurds, may begin to fray. People in Baghdad recall that the Kurds had taken advantage of the defeat of the Iraqi army in 2014 to grab extensive lands long disputed between themselves and the Arabs. Once freed of the menace of ISIS, non-Kurdish Iraqis will want these territories back.

As Patrick Cockburn said in *The Independent*, in Syria, there is an even more complicated three-cornered fight between the

Syrian President Bashar Al-Assad, the Syrian Kurds and Turkey for the areas from where the ISIS is retreating. As ISIS is driven out, the YPG and Turkish-backed forces are left facing each other in what might be the beginning of a new Kurdish-Turkish war waged across northern Syria. Even those familiar with the complexities and shifting alliances of the Syrian Civil War are baffled by the likely outcome as the different players in Syria position themselves to take advantage of a likely attack on Raqqa, the de facto Syrian capital of ISIS. Will the US continue to use the devastating firepower of its air force to support a YPG-led ground offensive? Or could the US administration under Trump take a more pro-Turkish stance and, if it did so, would the Syrian Kurds look for an alternative military alliance with Assad and his Russian backers? Only time can tell.

A SWOT ANALYSIS OF THE ISIS AND THEIR FUNDAMENTAL MISTAKES

Ignoring Fundamentals at Their Own Peril

At one time, the self-styled Caliphate ruled territory with a population of five or six million people. That precisely was their undoing – terrorists should not have been doing this. Terrorists must remain terrorists. They should never ever try to become an army, much less a state. The four stages in the classical progression of insurgency are: organization or subversive stage; terrorism stage; guerrilla warfare stage; and mobile warfare stage. In practice, insurgencies may often be obliged to fall back to the terrorism stage whenever the government response becomes effective. Many insurgencies may never even get past this stage. However, in a modern society, it is relatively easy to maintain a certain level of terrorism and thus to continue the terrorism stage almost indefinitely. The LTTE which had progressed almost to the mobile warfare stage frequently fell back to the terrorism phase. The ISIS, as we saw above, after a couple of brilliantly executed terrorist strikes, went on to mount conventional military-style offensives and started capturing huge swathes of territory replete with infrastructure like oil refineries, dams and power plants.

A good insurgent or guerrilla, if he knows his business, must never attempt to hold territory or defend a position. Yes, it indeed gives a primitive high to capture places, rule them and commit atrocities upon captives – the sense of having total power over some people works like an aphrodisiac. But, from a professional angle, it would amount to a military *hara-kiri* if they try to hold and administer an area permanently. I must emphasize the word permanently. Temporary occupation for tactical reasons is permissible. However, the real strength of irregular forces lies in their mobility and fluidity. They should never waste their precious resources in fighting to defend a place even if they have been spending some time there. Ideally they must be mobile. At all times, they should never let it slip out of their minds that their total military potential can never match that of the regular forces. However, even if they have, for tactical reasons, stayed in some place for some time, they should not expose themselves to the superior firepower of the enemy (including his air force and missiles, both of which the insurgent is not likely to possess) by presenting a clearly identifiable target which the enemy may pound at will. If, by any chance, decide to hold ground or defend a position, their write their epitaph.

Guerrillas or irregular soldiers must never commit another fundamental mistake. They must know that they can never match the vast military resources of a regular army. They should therefore never slug it out with a regular army. The moment you decide to slug it out, you are fighting on the terms of the enemy and your intrinsic advantages are lost. The enemy has heavy artillery, air force and what not – the guerrilla has essentially only light weaponry. This is the cardinal mistake which the ISIS committed. Their victories were fortuitous at best; and their military resources were simply not enough to resist the onslaught of regular forces armed with superior weaponry when the latter started turning the tide.

Historical Examples of Follies of Other Terrorists

LTTE and Terrorism/Insurgency in Sri Lanka

The LTTE (Liberation Tigers of Tamil Eelam) was excellent as a terrorist organization with some of the most spectacular, most efficiently executed terrorist strikes in the world attributed to them. The Sri Lankan security machinery was absolutely at a loss to figure out how to deal with them. Had they remained terrorists, they could have survived indefinitely. Yet, the moment they decided to hold and administer territory in northern Sri Lanka (in other words, tried to become a state), they provided a tangible target for the conventional forces of Sri Lanka and were all killed to the last man. They were utterly destroyed because then they had to fight on the terms of the adversary, that is, the regular armed forces which had an overwhelming superiority in firepower.

Bhindaranwale and Terrorism in Punjab, India

Back home in India, terrorism in Punjab could have gone on for quite some more time had Bhindaranwale not committed the blunder of taking up shelter in the Golden Temple. By hiding there and mistakenly thinking that the religious place was inviolable, he presented a tangible target to the Indian security forces and was destroyed. Slugging it out was the cardinal mistake which Bhindaranwale had committed. The security forces took heavy losses, but when push came to shove, howitzers and tanks were thrown in and each one of them was killed.

Taliban After 9/11

By taking over the government, they had presented a clear target to the US when it turned against them. They had never understood that they would not last a day in front of the massive US firepower. Eventually, they were thrown out of power.

Taliban at Present

Having been thrown out of power, they realized their mistake and once again became an amorphous, ubiquitous and invisible entity – sometimes hiding in the hills or other remote, inaccessible areas; sometimes mingling with the villagers. In other words, they once again become the copybook terrorists/insurgents/guerrilla. The US tried everything they could for 16 years – boots on the ground; drone strikes; bombardment; you name it; they tried it. According to "War on Terror Facts, Costs and Timeline" of the authoritative *The Balance*, the 'War on Terror' has, till March 23, 2017, consumed as much as a whopping $2,016.5 billion or over $2 trillion!

In the end, however, the Americans completely failed to destroy the Taliban and were forced to hold secret parleys with them in Gulf countries. Eventually, they departed rather ignominiously leaving a token presence of 8,400 troops in 4 garrisons (Kabul, Kandahar, Bagram and Jalalabad) indefinitely due to Taliban resurgence attempt after the Battle of Kunduz. To add insult to injury, in September 2016, they pardoned Gulbuddin Hekmatyar, better known as 'the Butcher of Kabul', one of the country's most notorious warlords for all past offences including terrorist attacks and alleged war crimes, as part of a peace deal with his militant group, Hizb-i-Islami. The Americans, in spite of all their sophisticated weaponry, could not destroy Taliban.

But since September 2015, the Taliban were found repeating their earlier mistake of holding territory. They attacked and captured the city of Kunduz, albeit for a while. During 2016, they pressured the capitals of the provinces of Kunduz, Faryab, Farah, Helmand, and Uruzgan. While they managed to temporarily enter Kunduz and Tirin Kot, the capital of Uruzgan, fighting was limited to the outskirts of the other cities. By the end of February 2017, as reported by *The Diplomat*, the Taliban had already launched an attack on Mehtar Lam, the capital of the eastern Afghan province of Laghman. The BBC News reported on March 23, 2017 that the Taliban had captured the south Afghan district of Sangin after a year-long battle. They already control large chunks of Helmand. Once again, while the capture of cities could give a 'high' to those with a medieval mind-set, they have forgotten that then they are again presenting an identifiable target. The Taliban could capture more cities also but then the American air force would return, and there is nothing easier for the US than to bomb them out of existence there or any other place. The whole cycle might get repeated.

Al-Qaida

The Al-Qaida has never committed this mistake and that's how it survives till date, despite the US dropping bombs on every hillock and field in Afghanistan for 16 years. They are not holding any territory anywhere in the world and are found literally everywhere.

Portents for the ISIS

They replicated the mistakes of the LTTE in administering territory. Their involvement in non-combat roles ranged from ISIS operatives cleaning and renovating streets, and doing maintenance work on electric lines and irrigation ditches (*Al-Minbar Al-'Alami Al-Jihadi*, October 26, 2014); running their own alternative educational system; judicial and law enforcement networks; to morality police; and managing and operating the oil wells and subsequent commerce in oil, etc – this wasted valuable human resources who could be frontline fighters.

If the ISIS ever comes to understand their follies, they can respond to defeats on the battlefield by carrying out terrorist attacks in the region, Europe, Turkey or other parts of the world. Some spectacular atrocities would enable it once again to dominate the news agenda and show that it is not finished off as yet. The world must be prepared for this. Intelligent terrorists fight the minds of their adversaries; not their military hardware! One who understands this will be successful; others will be decimated. This is what is ordained for the ISIS too.

WHY THE TALIBAN COULD BUILD A STATE AND WHY THE ISIS CANNOT

The Taliban could succeed in their venture for a number of reasons. What we witnessed in Afghanistan during the days of the Soviet occupation/support to a puppet regime was an insurgency which had metamorphosed much beyond insurgency. Courtesy the massive help in arms and armament rendered by the CIA through its great covert operation called Operation Cyclone, the weaponry of the Taliban provided a perfect foil to the weaponry of the Soviets that was more suited for conventional combat. The Soviets were an army of occupation. All that the Taliban had to do was to make continued occupation untenable for them in terms of the expenditure involved and casualties incurred – sheer harassment, the proverbial "death by a thousand cuts" at its best. The Soviets had the option of withdrawing and returning back to their homeland when it became expedient or imperative to do so.

The position and role of the ISIS, on the other hand, is almost reversed. When they sought to 'conquer' and administer territory, they became the de facto army of occupation. Those who are obliged to resist them do not have the option of going back somewhere. Quite like the Taliban, they too have foreign assistance. Hence they have no option but to resist with might and main, and eventually make it untenable for the ISIS to continue occupation – simple! The Soviets had a country to return to; the ISIS has no place to return to. They will be destroyed where they are.

The Taliban could eventually beat the Soviets for a variety of reasons, the most important being their mobility and their being a part of the population – both in keeping with the fundamental principles of insurgency. Since the Taliban operated both in rural and urban areas, there was no easily identifiable small military target which the Soviets could attack with their heavy weaponry. It was extremely wise on the part of the CIA not to give them any such weapon system that would have adversely affected their greatest source of strength, namely, their mobility. Had the CIA given them armoured vehicles and helicopters, they could have been easily chewed up by the Soviets because then they would have been fighting on the terms of the Soviets and then they would have been no match for the great Red Army.

2

Formation and Evolution of the ISIS

THE MESS CALLED THE SYRIAN CIVIL WAR

How the Human Catastrophe unfolded?

Way back in June 1972, Associated Press photographer Nick Ut had taken a Pulitzer Prize-winning photo which shook the conscience of people across the world and brought them face-to-face with the horrors of the Vietnam War. It showed, then a nine-year old girl Phan Thi Kim Phúc, running naked on a road amidst other fleeing villagers after being severely burned on her back by a South Vietnamese air force napalm attack. Kim Phúc was badly burned and had torn off her burning clothes to save herself.

In September 2015, history repeated itself when Turkish journalist Nilüfer Demir took the haunting photo of the lifeless body of a cute three-year old Syrian boy Alan Kurdi washed ashore after he had drowned in the Mediterranean Sea – the rubber inflatable boat in which his family was travelling had capsized. They were trying to reach the Greek island of Kos just 4 km across the sea, and it was their third attempt to cross. The photograph of Kurdi's body caused a dramatic upturn in international concern over the refugee crisis arising out of the

Syrian Civil War. The Syrian Civil War has already taken the toll of over a quarter million people killed, roughly the same number wounded or missing, and half of Syria's 22 million population displaced from their homes.

The trouble had started as protests against the government in 2011 that had begun in part as a response to the arrest and mistreatment of a group of young people accused of writing anti-Assad graffiti in the southern city of Deraa. It quickly progressed to a confused, no-holds-barred military conflict that has drawn in numerous other countries in a free-for-all where, besides tanks and heavy artillery on the ground and air strikes, even chemical agents are reportedly being used. It needs no explanation that however harsh the treatment might have been, was that enough to lead to a Civil War of this magnitude? The answer is a categorical no. There is no historical precedent. It has been said that the protests in Syria had taken place after the dictators in Tunisia and Egypt had already stepped down amidst pro-democracy demonstrations in their respective countries. But those instances could have only acted as beacons of hope to the protesters – hope does not translate into deadly military weapons to lead to a Civil War, does it? From where did they get all those weapons? Obviously, they were supplied by foreign powers. And that's how we got a proper Civil War raging. Even if we accept, for the sake of argument, the accusation of Dominic Tierney, correspondent for *The Atlantic*, that Assad had purposefully radicalized the opposition to delegitimize the rebellion, by releasing terrorists from prisons and avoiding fighting ISIS, it still does not explain how did all that heavy weaponry by the hundreds of thousands reach there?

In the end, it has become a proxy war featuring Russia and Iran supporting one side against the United States and its allies supporting the other side – as if the Cold War era had reinvented itself in a new avatar! Broadly speaking, Russia has intervened on behalf of the regime loyalists against all rebels and the United

States has intervened on behalf of what they claim to be certain 'vetted' rebels against the regime. No one knows what is the 'vetting' about whatever that means – and therein lies the source of most of their machinations. Russia and Iran aim to keep Assad in power; the US-led coalition says that Assad must go eventually while they claim to be focusing on the ISIS at the moment, incidentally one of the strongest anti-Assad forces in Syria!

While the morality and legality of the interventions of the foreign powers are both questionable, the fact that the Americans have 'chosen' certain rebels for support, and the ISIS for attacks, shows that their intentions are far from being innocuous not to speak of being noble. Russia opposes all the rebels. As reported by Don Melvin, Susannah Cullinane and Mohammed Tawfeeq for the CNN, Russian Foreign Minister Sergey Lavrov summed it up nicely at the United Nations:

> "If it looks like a terrorist, acts like a terrorist, and fights like a terrorist, it's a terrorist, right?"

Combatants Galore

An accurate mapping of the Syrian Civil War prepared by Thomas van Linge, a Dutch activist, cartographer and student of political science, has been used by numerous reputed media groups and analysts, including *The New York Times*, CNN, Spiegel and *The Atlantic* and I too will use that. Linge groups the combatants into four broad categories: rebels (from 'moderate' to Islamist and jihadist hardliners including the ISIS); loyalists (Assad regime forces and their supporters); Kurdish groups (who aren't currently seeking to overthrow Assad, but have won autonomy in north-eastern Syria, which they have fought ISIS to protect); and finally, foreign powers such as the USA and Russia carrying out their independent air strikes against the ISIS. Russian air strikes are in coordination with ground operations by Iranian and Hezbollah fighters. Citizens of dozens of countries have travelled there to join ISIS and other armed groups – the US Defense Intelligence Agency puts the total number of all small and large groups at 1,200!

As for their position on the ground, in Syria's more diverse west, President Assad's minority Alawite sect, aligned with a mosaic of Shia militias trained and funded by the Iranian Revolutionary Guard Corp (IRGC), and Hezbollah in Lebanon hold sway. In the centre, they have Sunni moderate, Islamist, and jihadist 'rebel' groups, such as ISIS and the Al-Qaida affiliate Jabhat Al-Nusra, which share control. And in the northeast, the Kurdish-based People's Protection Units (YPG) have united two of three cantons in a bid to expand 'Rojava', a de facto autonomous region consisting of three self-governing cantons in northern Syria, namely Afrin Canton, Jazira Canton and Kobanî Canton, as well as adjacent areas of northern Syria like Shahba region. Turkey, Jordan, Saudi Arabia, Qatar and the UAE are supporting the Sunni-dominated opposition; and the Kurdistan Workers' Party (PKK) is supporting the YPG.

HOW DID THE ISIS BURST ON THE SCENE?

Fall of the Ottoman Empire and the Poisoned Legacy of the Sykes-Picot Agreement

As David Ignatius, journalist, author and associate editor of *The Washington Post*, has pointed out in his article "How ISIS Spread in the Middle-East and How to Stop It" in *The Atlantic*, what is ravaging the Middle East right now is obviously much deeper than ISIS. A bunch of some thousands of terrorists, however well-armed and fanatical, could not have created this terrible mess on their own. There are much larger forces at work and they are being driven by some of the 'sins of history'. What we are witnessing is the collapse of the post-Ottoman order. In other words, the "lines in the sand" conjured in 1916 by the British and

French diplomats Mark Sykes and François Georges-Picot are being blown to dust. However, before we discuss the Sykes-Picot Agreement and its historical consequences; we must understand the Ottoman Empire in retrospect.

The Ottoman Empire was a great power, founded at the end of the 13th century by the Oghuz Turkish tribal leader Osman. The word Ottoman is an old Anglicisation of the name of Osman I, the founder of the Empire and of the ruling House of Osman. After 1354, the Ottomans crossed into Europe, and with the conquest of the Balkans it was transformed into a transcontinental empire. The Ottomans ended the Byzantine Empire with their 1453 conquest of Constantinople by Mehmed the Conqueror. During the 16th and 17th centuries, at the height of its power under the reign of Suleiman the Magnificent, the Ottoman Empire was a multinational, multilingual empire controlling much of Southeast Europe, parts of Central Europe, Western Asia, the Caucasus, North Africa, and the Horn of Africa.

However, during a long period of peace from 1740 to 1768, the Ottoman military system could not keep pace with that of their European rivals, the Habsburg and Russian Empires. Strengthened by the Peace of Westphalia and the Industrial Revolution, European powers regrouped and challenged Ottoman dominance. The Ottomans were to suffer severe military defeats in the late 18th and early 19th centuries. The Ottoman Empire, in the last few decades before its collapse, lost control over many of its territories to the growing colonial powers. France took control of Algeria (1830) and Tunisia (1881); Italy took over Libya (1911); and Britain gained control of the Aden protectorate (1939), Oman (1861), Arabian Gulf chiefdoms (1820) and Kuwait (1899). Egypt fell into British custody in 1882 and Sudan in 1899. According to the Iraqi historian Sayyar al Jamil, the Ottomans' strongholds in the Levant and Iraq, during the Empire's latter years, included the provinces of Damascus, Aleppo, Raqqa, Basra and Baghdad.

As World War I erupted in July 1914, the weakening Ottoman Empire (called "The Sick Man of Europe") allied with Germany and the Austro-Hungarian Empire to confront Britain and France in a hope to escape from the diplomatic isolation which had contributed to its recent territorial losses. Even as the World War I was drawing to a close, Britain and France decided to gobble up the Ottoman Empire, particularly its Middle Eastern territories. Sykes and Picot were the instruments of this devious plot. Much like what Cyril Radcliffe was to do in India decades later, these two guys divided the map of one of the most volatile regions in the world into states that cut through ethnic and religious communities. Later dubbed the Sykes-Picot treaty, the secret agreement was signed by Paris and London (and approved by the Russian Foreign Minister Sergey Sazonov) on May 16, 1916.

Meanwhile, back home, Mustafa Kemal Ataturk led the Turkish National Movement and the Turkish War of Independence. He subsequently proceeded to abolish the Ottoman Empire/Caliphate and proclaimed the foundation of the Turkish Republic in its place.

The Sykes-Picot Agreement, officially known as the Asia Minor Agreement created five entities in the Levant:

1. The first entity extended from Baghdad to the south to include Kuwait, reaching to the Gulf coast. This entity was under the direct control of the British.
2. The second entity combined what is today northern Iraq, Jordan and the Negev desert, reaching all the way to Sinai. This part was under British influence.
3. The third entity included a coastal area that extended from southern Lebanon to the north towards the provinces of Mersin, Iskenderun and Adana. It extended anteriorly to the inside of Anatolia. This part was under direct French control.

4. The fourth entity comprised the Syrian Desert. This part was under French influence.
5. The fifth entity included the Ottoman Jerusalem Sanjak (also called Mutasarrifate of Jerusalem), which was the northern part of historic Palestine. This part was to be an international zone due to its religious significance. Britain was, however, allocated control of Acre and Haifa.

The Bolsheviks were not even aware of the Agreement till they found a copy of it in the archives. Leon Trotsky published a copy of the agreement in *Izvestia* newspaper on November 24, 1917. Lenin called the treaty "the agreement of the colonial thieves". British paper *The Guardian* also published it on November 26, 1917. The exposure of the agreement caused a political scandal in Britain and France.

A Poisoned Tree Starts Bearing Fruits

What were the motives of the British and the French in dividing the region the way they did without any application of mind? Prominent Lebanese historian Kamal Salibi believes that the main considerations taken at that time were related to oil and transportation tracks. The British had faced many difficulties during the War as they tried to occupy Iraq. At that time, Britain was controlling oil resources in Iran. Its main concern was to prevent the Germans, key contributors to the Turkish Petroleum Company, from reaching oil fields that were known to exist in Iraq's Kirkuk region.

In any case, the Agreement is seen by many as a turning point in Western and Arab relations. It very conveniently, very treacherously negated Britain's promises to Arabs made through Colonel TE Lawrence for a national Arab homeland in the area of Greater Syria, in exchange for supporting the British militarily against the Ottoman Empire. No one should forget, how, advised by the legendary "Lawrence of Arabia", the Arab Revolt had played a vital role in the Allied victory over the Ottoman Empire in World War I.

The Arab Revolt

Not one of the modern nation states in the Middle East existed till this post-WWI division. They were all part of the Ottoman Empire and had people of diverse races inhabiting it. Things in this multiracial, multicultural set up had proceeded smoothly till the Empire let people live their way. Problems arose when, during the years of decline, the Empire started the process of 'Turkification' of the Empire by imposing Turkish language, among other things. The Arabs, who made up about 60% of the Empire's 25 million subjects, resented this. This was to become the seed of Arab nationalism and a demand for independence.

Sherif Hussein bin Ali, the Emir of Mecca assumed the leadership of the Revolt and contacted the British in Cairo for help. Henry McMahon, as the classical representative of the Perfidious Albion, made rather vague promises to Hussein bin Ali in return for military support. The promises pertained to creation of independent Arab States in the so-called Fertile Crescent (present-day Syria, Lebanon, Israel, Jordan and Palestine). Hussein was sceptical of the British but when Ahmed Djemal Pasha, the last Ottoman military leader, executed 21 Arab nationalists, he decided that the support of the Allies was the only viable option for the Arab Revolt.

The British were not acting out of any altruistic motives. An Arab Revolt suited them too. They had suffered reverses in Gallipoli in Turkey in 1915, and a British-Indian army was forced to surrender in Mesopotamia in 1916. Even the Suez Canal was threatened, albeit unsuccessfully. Meanwhile, things on the Western Front in Europe were also not looking very bright with a bloody stalemate in trench warfare. A rebellion in the rear of the Ottoman Empire would, therefore, have been, militarily a very sound idea.

The Arab Revolt is the stuff of legends. It began in 1916 with about 30,000 Bedouins and other tribesmen, capricious and untrustworthy fighters, interested basically in plunder. In the end, how the Arabs, assisted by British artillery and seaplanes operating from seaplane carriers got the better of the Ottomans, is a fascinating story. Col TE Lawrence who was formally assigned as the liaison officer to Faisal, son of Hussein, rendered yeoman service and was to earn eternal fame as an intrepid guerrilla fighter, demolition expert, operational tactician and strategic visionary.

Post-World War I British and French Machinations

As the Sykes-Picot Agreement became public, Arab distrust increased and Hussein bin Ali announced that he intended to establish an Arab state that would extend from Aleppo, in Syria, to Aden in the south, as mentioned in his correspondences with Henry McMahon. The British had no intention of honouring that. Not only that Britain and France carved up the Middle East in total disregard of ethnic, linguistic and religious affiliations, they had the temerity to call the newly created states 'mandates', instead of what they actually were: colonies. A proper mess was created in this process – a Hashemite solution rewarding Faisal and Abdullah with kingdoms fabricated from "lines drawn on an empty map", as historian David Fromkin describes it. Churchill and his staff rechristened Mesopotamia as Iraq, apparently from what some Arab tribes had called it, Uruk, the name of an ancient Sumerian city. Christian, Jewish, Muslim, Arab and Kurdish groups were crammed into Iraq's artificial borders. Moreover, its tip was snipped off creating Kuwait and the tribe most beholden to the British found itself elevated to kings.

Palestine: Another Sore that Refuses to Heal

In 1897, when the First Zionist Congress was held to discuss the establishment of a national homeland for the Jewish people,

Palestine had about 6,00,000 inhabitants, about 95% of whom were Arabs, the remaining 5% being Jews. Palestine was then part of the Ottoman Empire. In November 1917, the Arabs found another cause for concern. This came in the form of a letter written on November 2, 1917 by the then British foreign secretary, Arthur Balfour, to Baron Walter Rothschild, a close friend of Zionist movement leader Chaim Weizmann. The British commitment was endorsed in 1920 – the League of Nations granted Great Britain 'mandatory power' over Palestine. This was done with the proviso that Britain was to aid in the establishment in Palestine of a national homeland for the Jews, who had suffered from a long history of European anti-Semitism. Thus, the Palestinian Arabs were slated to pay for the anti-Semitic crimes of the Europeans – there could not have been a bigger travesty of justice! How the rights of the 95% inhabitants were to be protected, was left undefined!

Jewish immigration into Palestine, which started before World War I, continued unabated in the years leading up to World War II. But it reached peak levels after the end of World War II, in the backdrop of the Holocaust. By the year 1947, on the eve on UN decision to partition Palestine between Jews and Palestinian Arabs, there were around 1.35 million Palestinian Arabs and about 6,50,000 Jews, who had acquired roughly 6% of the 'mandated area' of Palestine. Yet the General Assembly deemed it fit to give the Jews around 56% of the territory of Palestine for a Jewish State!

The Palestinians and their Arab brethren in the neighbouring Arab countries refused to accept the UN partition resolution. They waged war on the new state of Israel and lost. In the aftermath of 1948 defeat (which witnessed the birth of the State of Israel), close to half the Palestinian population (around 7,50,000) became refugees, inside and outside what remained of their own country. They number more than 3 million now, with no hope of returning to their former homes, and with little chance of being integrated in the neighbouring Arab countries where most of them live as refugees without any self-respect.

The Ghost of the Sykes-Picot Agreement Still Haunts the Middle-East

The Agreement is frequently cited as having created 'artificial' borders in the Middle East, "without any regard to ethnic or sectarian characteristics, which has resulted in endless conflict." When Saddam invaded Kuwait, by trying to alter the status quo borders, he also sought to portray himself as a leader of the Arab world who was 'rectifying' the "mistakes of the imperial past" – the story about his supporting a local uprising against the Sabah ruling family was essentially a pretext. Since then, the Sykes-Picot Agreement has been invoked by all those who have risen against the West. Osama bin Laden too blamed it for breaking "the Islamic world into fragments".

The ISIS claims that one of its goals is to reverse the effects of the Sykes-Picot Agreement. Abu Bakr Al-Baghdadi, in a July 2014 speech at the Great Mosque of Al-Nuri in Mosul, vowed that "this blessed advance will not stop until we hit the last nail in the coffin of the Sykes-Picot conspiracy". Dr Timothy McGrath, editor at Public Radio International and GlobalPost, in his article in the *Los Angeles Daily News*, has furnished the video of an English-speaking ISIS fighter who slams the 'imaginary borders' established by Western powers in the early 20th century. The ISIS man might be pretending, boasting or simply bluffing but the fact remains that they are trying to give it the colour of an anti-colonial movement that takes Islam's pre-colonial conception of power, namely, an Islamic State or a Sunni Caliphate, as its reference point. Even if ISIS is crushed, this idea of 'our Caliphate' is likely to persist, and return.

BIRTH OF THE ISIS: THE 'OFFICIAL' NARRATIVE

After their complete victory in 2003, the Americans encouraged the establishment of what was supposed to be a democratic, national Shi'ite regime headed by Nouri Al-Maliki. However, the regime alienated the Sunni population, which had traditionally controlled the country, even though they were in minority (about 22% of the Iraqi population is Sunni Arabs, alongside the Kurds, who are also Sunnis – while about 60% of Iraqis are Shi'ites).

The Meir Amit Intelligence and Terrorism Information Center (ITIC) at the Israeli Intelligence and Heritage Communication Center in its publication "ISIS: Portrait of a Jihadi Terrorist Organization", argues that historically speaking, there are similarities between the results of the American invasion of Iraq, the Soviet invasion of Afghanistan and the Israeli invasion of Lebanon. In all three instances the invading country failed to establish a new political order or to stabilize an effective, supportive regime. In effect, all three invasions had a deleterious effect on the existing delicate socio-political fabric. A security and governmental vacuum was created and the country's fragile social fabric (in the middle of which was the volatile Sunni-Shi'ite schism) was severely damaged.

In Afghanistan and Iraq they caused changes that contributed to the establishment of radical Sunni jihadi terrorist organizations. It was Al-Qaida in Afghanistan. In Lebanon a radical Shi'ite terrorist organization Hezbollah following Iranian ideology and receiving Iranian support was born. In Iraq, a branch called Al-Qaida in Iraq (AQI), established in 2004, entered the security vacuum and took advantage of the increasing political-societal Sunni alienation. It became an important actor in the insurgent organizations fighting the American army, and became stronger after the withdrawal of the American troops at the end of 2011. It spread to Syria after the

Civil War began in March 2011. The establishment of Al-Qaida and ISIS in Iraq and Syria occurred in four stages:

Stage One (2004-2006)

The establishment of the branch of "Al-Qaida in Iraq" (AQI) or "Al-Qaida in Mesopotamia", led by Abu Musab Al-Zarqawi, a Jordanian and an associate of Abdullah Azzam in Afghanistan. He was killed in June 2006 in an American targeted attack.

Stage Two (2006-2011)

On October 15, 2006, about four months after the death of Al-Zarqawi, an umbrella network called the "Islamic State in Iraq" (ISI) was established at the behest of Abu Hamza Al-Muhajir and Abu Omar Al-Baghdadi, an Iraqi jihadi. The purpose of joining forces with other organizations with a similar ideology was to re-establish the power of AQI which had suffered following the death of Al-Zarqawi. The ISI took roots mainly in western Iraq, which had a tribal Sunni society, especially in Al-Anbar province, which extends to the Syrian border. Both these characters were killed in April 2010. The mantle then passed on to the man whom we know as Abu Bakr Al-Baghdadi, the current leader of the ISIS.

Stage Three (2012-June 2014)

After the American army withdrew from Iraq, ISI became stronger again. They had established a covert operational infrastructure in Syria. Its objective was to provide logistic support for the armed campaign in Iraq by serving as a way-station for thousands of foreign Arab-Muslim jihadists en route to the fighting in Iraq. Following the outbreak of the Syrian Civil War, the direction of the jihadi operations was reversed and fighters went from Iraq to Syria.

Eventually, dissension broke out between ISI and its associate, the Jabhat Al-Nusra, also called Al-Qaida in Syria.

(Jabhat means a Front; Nusrat means support or help – hence literally, the 'Support Front'. In English, many people call it the Al-Nusra Front also.) In an attempt to halt the process, Abu Bakr Al-Baghdadi declared the unification of the two organizations under his leadership, changing the name of ISI to a new name that would express the unification. This led to the establishment of the Islamic State in Iraq and Greater Syria (ISIS). However, Abu Muhammad Al-Julani of the Jabhat Al-Nusra refused to subordinate himself to Al-Baghdadi. The Al-Qaida leader Ayman Al-Zawahiri sided with him. Both Al-Baghdadi and Al-Qaida accused each other of "straying from the correct path." Currently, they are believed to be operating independently.

Stage Four (after June 2014)

This was the period of dramatic military achievements of the ISIS discussed earlier.

HOW THE US INTERVENTION HELPED THE ISIS?

Presidents Assad's and Putin's Allegations

In April 2015, CNSNews reported Syrian President Bashar Al-Assad having told French television 'France 2 TV' in an interview that the Islamic State of Iraq and Syria (ISIS) was created in Iraq in 2006 under the supervision of the Americans. Assad said,

> "I wasn't controlling Iraq. The Americans controlled Iraq, and ISIS came from Iraq to Syria, because chaos is contagious.... When there is chaos in Syria, ISIS came to Syria.... Before ISIS came Al-Nusra Front, which is Al-Qaida, and before that you had the Muslim Brotherhood. They all represent the same grassroots for ISIS to come later."

Going back to the origins of the Civil War in Syria, which began in March 2011 with citizens demanding more political freedom,

Assad said that from the early weeks of the conflict "the terrorists infiltrated the situation in Syria with the support of Western countries and regional countries." He accused the French government and others of "supporting those jihadists that they called moderate opposition." "The people who are supported now, who have Western armaments, they became ISIS, they were supported by your state [France], and by other Western states," he said (sic). Assad reiterated his view that there is no 'moderate' opposition to his rule.

> "They said they're going to arm the moderate opposition. Can you tell me what is it, where it is? We don't see it."

He may be accused of being an interested party. One may also feel somewhat dismissive about Putin's version of Syrian history, as laid out in his United Nations speech, that the ISIS was "forged as a tool against undesirable secular regimes" and propelled by foreign military support for Syrian rebels. In other words, Western nations helped create the ISIS by rejecting Assad and knowingly supporting other rebel groups whose existence actually boosts the Islamic State. Putin called this an 'enormous mistake'. But there is a whole battery of highly respected analysts, academicians and investigative reporters also who do think so and their views do deserve a closer inspection. These are not conspiracy theories or urban legends.

ISIS Didn't Happen and Could Not Have Happened Overnight

Tony Cartalucci, noted geopolitical analyst and author, in his article "How the US Supports the Islamic State (ISIS): One 'Accidental Airdrop' vs Billions in Covert Military Aid" published in *Global Research*, and the world-famous Pulitzer Prize-winning journalist Seymour Hersh in his report "The Redirection: Is the Administration's New Policy Benefiting Our Enemies in the War on Terrorism?" published in *The New Yorker*, claim that far from springing from the dunes of northern Iraq or eastern Syria, the rise of ISIS is the verbatim fulfilment of long-established documented US conspiracy.

They say that to undermine Iran, which is predominantly Shi'ite, the Bush administration bolstered Sunni extremist groups that espouse a militant vision of Islam. The rise of extremist groups in the wake of the US-engineered 'Arab Spring' is the story of how these clandestine operations reached their pinnacle in the creation of ISIS. Patrick Cockburn, journalist and award-winning author of eight books, has also concluded in his article in *The Independent* in June 2014,

> "It was the war in Syria that destabilized Iraq and, in turn, made ISIS a regional power."

He cited Prince Bandar bin Sultan, once the powerful Saudi ambassador in Washington and head of Saudi Intelligence having told the head of the MI6 Richard Dearlove, that substantial and sustained funding from private donors in Saudi Arabia and Qatar (both US allies), to which the authorities might have turned a blind eye, had played a central role in the ISIS surge into Sunni areas of Iraq.

Geopolitical analyst and journalist Steven Chovanec has alleged in his exhaustive paper in the *MintPress News* that since at least as far back as 2005, the US has been financing and training anti-government opposition in Syria with a view toward regime-change. The ostensible justification for this funding is 'democracy promotion'; however, we should remember what noted international relations scholar John J Mearsheimer had said about Washington's 'democracy promotion' activities abroad in his paper "Why the Ukraine Crisis is the West's Fault", in *Foreign Affairs*. Referring to the crisis in Ukraine, he has stated,

> "and when you talk about promoting democracy, what you're really talking about is putting in power leaders who are pro-

> Western and anti-Russian ... promoting democracy, which was all about putting in power pro-Western leaders."

In a 2007 speech (https://www.youtube.com/watch?v=TY2DKzastu8&feature=player_embedded), Gen Wesley Clark of the USA recounts a conversation he had with then Under Secretary of Defense, Paul Wolfowitz in 1991 regarding Operation Desert Storm. He quotes Wolfowitz as saying,

> "One thing that we learned is that we can use our military in the Middle East and the Soviets won't stop us, and we got about 5 or 10 years to clean up those old Soviet client regimes, Syria, Iran, Iraq, before the next great superpower comes on to challenge us."

American journalist, author and political campaigner David Mizner says in his article in *Jacobin:*

> "The United States supported the uprising against the Syrian government even as ISIS became a fixture. US policy was one of malign neglect at best. We can be certain that American officials were well aware of ISIS's rise. They accepted it in Iraq (a country they wanted to quit and whose president they no longer supported) and approved of it in Syria (a country they wanted to damage and whose president they wanted to remove or at least weaken). With ISIS now public enemy number one, it may be easy to forget that for months – until ISIS became big enough to threaten American interests – US weapons, both rhetorical and actual, were pointed only at the Syrian government. US officials gave major speeches on Syria that didn't even mention ISIS."

Jay Syrmopoulos, author and journalist, in his article "Media Blacks Out Pentagon Report Exposing US Role in ISIS Creation" in the *MintPress News* in June 2015, cited award winning journalist and scholar Dr Nafeez Ahmed having exposed startling information about US complicity in the creation and rise of ISIS, as contained in a declassified Defense Intelligence Agency (DIA) report dated August 2012:

> "The US had three years ago welcomed the emergence of an extremist 'Salafist Principality' in the region as a way to undermine Assad."

Ben Swann, guest writer for *Wake Up World*, in his article "Reality Check: Proof US Government Wanted ISIS to Emerge in Syria", also made a reference to this secret Pentagon document. The document is available at https://wakeup-world.com/wp-content/uploads/2015/11/Reality-Check-Proof-U.S.-Government-Wanted-ISIS-to-Emerge-in-Syria-Seven-pages-of-a-secret-Pentagon-document-.pdf. The document identifies Al-Qaida in Iraq (which became ISIS) and fellow Salafists as the "major forces driving the insurgency in Syria", and states that "western countries, the Gulf states and Turkey" were supporting the opposition's efforts to take control of eastern Syria.

Erica Wenig, expert at The Washington Institute for Near East Policy, has reported in *The Daily Caller News Foundation* that US military officials are training what they call "carefully-vetted Syrian rebels", the initial stages of a $500 million programme to combat the Islamic State in Syria. The programme is intended to train 5,000 fighters. The Pentagon's programme is not affiliated with the Central Intelligence Agency's strikingly similar and largely unsuccessful plan. The CIA has been training Syrian rebels since mid-2013, initially fighting the Assad regime and later focusing on defeating the ISIS. The Hazzm movement, one of the groups trained by the CIA, collapsed after assaults by Jabhat Al-Nusra, a group affiliated with Al-Qaida. Fighters, who went through the agency's training either slipped into Islamist ranks, quit or went missing. "All sides now agree that the US's effort to aid moderate fighters battling the Assad regime has gone badly," *The Wall Street Journal* had concluded earlier in 2015. Sibel Edmonds, the founder of the National

Security Whistleblowers Coalition, had broken the story that US and NATO, accompanied by hundreds of soldiers, were operating a secret training camp in Turkey to "organize and expand the dissident base in Syria," since April-May of 2011. A WikiLeaks cable also speaks of a December 2011 meeting at the Pentagon between Stratfor (a global intelligence company) personnel and United States Air Force (USAF) officers, who would detail how Special Operations Forces, presumably from the US, UK, France, Jordan, and Turkey, were "already on the ground focused on recce missions and training opposition forces." The CIA programme was reported prominently by a twice Pulitzer Prize-winning American journalist Eric P Schmitt in *The New York Times* in June 2012 and again by CJ Chivers and Eric Schmitt in *The New York Times* in March 2013. In fact, Senator Tom Udall (Democrat-New Mexico) told Secretary of State John Kerry, who was testifying in front of the foreign relations committee,

> "Everybody's well aware there's been a covert operation, operating in the region to train forces, moderate forces, to go into Syria and to be out there, that we've been doing this for the last two years."

In a detailed interview to democracynow.org in March 2015, world-famous American academician Noam Chomsky says that the ISIS didn't come from nowhere. It's one of the results of the US hitting a very vulnerable society – Iraq – with a sledgehammer, which elicited sectarian conflicts that had not existed. As reported by the CNN in January 2015 in context with the Paris attacks, Noam Chomsky has called President Obama's drone killings –

> "the most extreme terrorist campaign of modern times – Barack Obama's global assassination campaign targeting people suspected of perhaps intending to harm us some day, and any unfortunates who happen to be nearby."

How the Rebels Got Their Weapons?

On August 1, 2011 Israel's DEBKAfile intelligence news source, awarded Forbe's 'Best of the Web' award, reported [http://www.debka.com/article/21169/] that –

> "Syrian forces are now running into heavy resistance. Awaiting them are anti-tank traps and fortified barriers manned by protesters armed with heavy machine guns.... Syrian troops encountered armed resistance ... there is no shortage of arms."

These were no typical protests, armed with anti-tank machinery and heavy machine guns! How did they accomplish this without significant foreign assistance?

DEBKAfile reported on August 15,

> "NATO headquarters in Brussels and the Turkish high command are meanwhile drawing up plans for their first military step in Syria, which is to arm the rebels with weapons for combating the tanks and helicopters spearheading the Assad regime's crackdown on dissent. Instead of repeating the Libyan model of air strikes, NATO strategists are thinking more in terms of pouring large quantities of anti-tank and anti-air rockets, mortars and heavy machine guns into the protest centres for beating back the government armoured forces ... the arms would be trucked into Syria under Turkish military guard and transferred to rebel leaders at pre-arranged rendezvous."

This report would go on to state,

> "Also discussed in Brussels and Ankara, our sources report, is a campaign to enlist thousands of Muslim volunteers in Middle East countries and the Muslim world to fight alongside the Syrian rebels. The Turkish army would house these volunteers, train them and secure their passage into Syria."

Turkish Intelligence Agency (MIT) veteran Önder Siğircikoğlu also stated that all weapons supplies and militant incursions into Syria from Turkey were organized by MIT. In other words, by August 2011, the protests and the protesters bore the resemblance of a full-on insurgency supported by trained extremist elements – how could this be possible without foreign sponsorship?

Regarding the involvement of Turkey, Washington's Blog has disclosed that CHP (Turkish acronym for the Republican People's Party) deputies Eren Erdem and Ali Seker, members of the Turkish parliament held a press conference in October 2015 claiming that they had wiretapped recordings and other evidence showing that Turkey had supplied the nerve agent Sarin used in Syria (August 2013, Ghouta, casualties 1,300) for which Assad was blamed.

Diplomatic correspondent Barak Ravid has disclosed in the Israeli paper *Haaretz* that the Israeli Defence Forces (IDF) maintained regular contact with members of ISIS since May 2013. *The 21st Century Wire* informed in December 2014 and again in January 2015, as to how the State of Israel had consistently provided both material, medical relief and IDF airstrike support to various terrorist and 'rebel' insurgents fighting in Syria. As reported by *Foreign Policy* in June 2014, UN observers have also identified direct contact between IDF forces and ISIS soldiers, including giving medical care to ISIS fighters.

America's Alleged Creation of ISIS

World-famous journalist Seymour Hersh has categorically maintained in his report "The Redirection: Is the Administration's New Policy Benefitting Our Enemies in the War on Terrorism?" that the US State Department through its global network of foreign subversion funded and directed by the National Endowment for Democracy (NED) and a myriad of faux-NGOs, triggered a coordinated uprising across the Middle East. Protesters served as a smoke screen behind which heavily armed militants began campaigns of violence against the security forces of the respective nations targeted for destabilization. Violence in Egypt went largely unreported because of the speed of which the government collapsed and confrontations ceased. However in nations like Libya and Syria where governments remained resolute, the violence continued to escalate.

In fact, Pete Papaherakles, author, political commentator and writer for the *American Free Press*, disclosed in his article "Is 'IS' a CIA-Mossad Creation?" in August 2014 that a photograph (available at https://socioecohistory.wordpress.com/2014/08/13/senator-john-mccains-whoops-moment-photographed-chilling-with-ISIS-chief-Al-baghdadi-and-terrorist-muahmmad-noor/) actually shows Al-Baghdadi along with half a dozen others, including Syrian rebel Gen Salim Idris, attending a secret meeting with neocon Senator John McCain (R-Ariz) in Syria in June 2013. A second photo shows Al-Baghdadi posing with McCain and another 'rebel'. McCain was instrumental in supporting terrorist forces fighting the Syrian government.

These fighters, it would turn out, were not 'pro-democracy rebels', but rather seasoned militants of the Libyan Islamic Fighting Group (LIFG), an official Al-Qaida franchise in North Africa. One of their leaders, Abdelhakim Belhadj would eventually find himself in power in Tripoli after the collapse of the Libyan government, and have his photograph taken with Senator McCain. After the fall of Libya, Al-Qaida and its affiliates would take their fighters and their NATO-supplied weapons and travel to fight in Syria. They would enter the country through NATO-member Turkey. While the US has repeatedly referred to the militants fighting the government and people of Syria as 'moderates', the vast majority of these fighters are sectarian extremists, many of whom are not even Syrian.

Tony Cartalucci concludes:

> "ISIS is the purposeful creation of the United States in its pursuit of regional hegemony in the Middle East, and ISIS's atrocities were predicted long before the first shots were fired in 2011 in the Syrian conflict, long before the term 'Islamic State' went mainstream."

David Grudge of the California Network says that by the time of the Obama administration, the agenda had developed into one of perpetual war and the need to maintain an American presence in the region. This of course, could not happen if peace broke out, so constant terrorism and factional strife were actually promoted. ISIS was originally a minor player. They really were "Al-Qaida's JV (junior varsity) team", although by the time Obama uttered this infamous quote, they had already made a liar out of him. He says that many of the people who lead ISIS today were once in American custody in Iraq. Many of the soldiers in ISIS were recruited from Saudi Arabian prisons, escaped from massive jailbreaks in Iraq, or were recruited from overseas.

Terrence McCoy, investigative reporter and winner of the Heywood Broun Award, has revealed in his article "How the Islamic State Evolved in an American Prison" in *The Washington Post*,

> "The sprawling Camp Bucca detention centre represents an opening chapter in the history of the Islamic State – many of its leaders, including Abu Bakr Al-Baghdadi, were incarcerated and probably met there. According to former prison commanders, analysts and soldiers, Camp Bucca provided a unique setting for both prisoner radicalization and inmate collaboration, and was formative in the development of today's most potent jihadist force."

According to the terrorism research firm Soufan Group, in all, nine members of the Islamic State's top command did time at

Bucca. Military veteran Andrew Thompson and academic Jeremi Suri wrote in *The New York Times*,

> "The prisons became virtual terrorist universities: The hardened radicals were the professors, the other detainees were the students, and the prison authorities played the role of absent custodian."

Former prison commander James Skylar Gerrond also wrote,

> "Many of us at Camp Bucca were concerned that instead of just holding detainees, we had created a pressure cooker for extremism."

The American intervention in Syria, like many others in the past, is sought to be passed off as humanitarian intervention. Does anyone really believe in it? Noted Islamic scholar and winner of the Martin Luther King Award for services in peace building Ibrahim Kazerooni and theologian Rob Prince have called the bluff of the so-called humanitarian intervention in their paper "Humanitarian Intervention: Destroying Nations to Save Them". They say that humanitarian intervention is part and parcel of a backdoor attempt to re-colonize the rest of the world by strong nations, in an effort to justify imposing their will on weaker ones. It is little more than liberal racism, that is, 'we' (meaning one neo-colonial power or another), magnanimously no less, are invading a country for its own good because those poor dumb folks don't have the wherewithal to protect themselves and need our kind assistance to prevent disasters. They maintain that the doctrine of humanitarian intervention was and is not being revived to combat genocide, but to take advantage of post-Cold War global realities where naked 'Vietnam type' intervention and aggression is more difficult to justify. That's how humanitarian intervention and pre-emptive military strikes go together like a horse and carriage. Humanitarian intervention, in the end, is nothing more than a pretext for imperial military intervention –

a pretext that permits the post-Cold War imperial order and its allies to ravage the world with impunity.

They have cited some very strong words of Gwynne Dyer published in the *Colorado Progressive Jewish News:*

> "The fate of Iraq is a sideshow, the terrorist threat is a red herring, and the radical Islamist's dream of a worldwide jihad against the West is a fantasy, but the attempt to revive Pax Americana is real."

Garikai Chengu, a research scholar at Harvard University, in his article "America Created Al-Qaida and the ISIS Terror Group" in *Global Research* says,

> "America is using ISIS in three ways: to attack its enemies in the Middle East, to serve as a pretext for US military intervention abroad, and at home to foment a manufactured domestic threat, used to justify the unprecedented expansion of invasive domestic surveillance."

Billions in Weapons, Cash, and Equipment Provided to the Rebels

From 2011 onward, terrorists fighting the government of Syria have received billions in cash, weapons, equipment, and vehicles from the United States, United Kingdom, members of the European Union, Turkey, Saudi Arabia, Qatar, and Jordan. The plan, as it was imagined, was to topple Damascus quickly enough so that the general public never found out who was truly fighting in the ranks of America's proxy forces. This, unfortunately, didn't happen. Canadian economist and author and director of the Centre for Research on Globalization Prof Michael Chossudovsky, says in his article "America's 'Global War on Terror', Al-Qaida and the Islamic State (ISIS): A Review" that John Kerry himself admitted,

> "Financial aid to Syria's Al-Nusra, an affiliate of Al-Qaida is part of an R2P (responsibility to protect) mandate."

Chossudovsky says that there are now 'good guy terrorists' and 'bad guy terrorists'. Financial aid is channelled to Al-Qaida 'good guy terrorists' to protect Syrians against the terrorists.

In March 2013, noted journalists CJ Chivers and Eric P Schmitt, in their article "Arms Airlift to Syria Rebels Expands, With Aid From CIA", in *The New York Times* revealed that:

> "With help from the CIA, Arab governments and Turkey have sharply increased their military aid to Syria's opposition fighters in recent months, expanding a secret airlift of arms and equipment for the uprising against President Bashar Al-Assad, according to air traffic data, interviews with officials in several countries and the accounts of rebel commanders. The airlift, which began on a small scale in early 2012, expanded into a steady and much heavier flow, the data shows. It has grown to include more than 160 military cargo flights by Jordanian, Saudi and Qatari military-style cargo planes landing at Esenboga Airport near Ankara, and, to a lesser degree, at other Turkish and Jordanian airports."

The US State Department had also announced it was sending hundreds of millions of dollars more in aid, equipment and even armoured vehicles to militants operating in Syria, along with demands of its allies to 'match' the funding to reach a goal of over a billion dollars. Colombian journalist and member of *The New York Times* editorial board, Ernesto Londoño and Greg Miller, specialist in intelligence agencies and terrorism, in their article "CIA Begins Weapons Delivery to Syrian Rebels" in *The Washington Post* in September 2013, also confirmed,

> "The CIA has begun delivering weapons to rebels in Syria, ending months of delay in lethal aid that had been promised by the Obama administration, according to US officials and Syrian figures. The shipments began streaming into the country along with separate deliveries by the State Department

> of vehicles and other gear – a flow of material that marks a major escalation of the US role in Syria's Civil War."

In *The Telegraph*'s article titled, "US and Europe in 'Major Airlift of Arms to Syrian Rebels through Zagreb'", it was reported that shipments of weapons from former Yugoslavia were paid for by Saudi Arabia at the bidding of the United States, with assistance on supplying the weapons organised through Turkey and Jordan, Syria's neighbours.

Almost everybody has seen the now famous photographs of the convoys of brand-new Toyota Hilux pick-up trucks of the ISIS replete with armed ISIS fighters waving ISIS flags. Ever wondered how they got those trucks? It has now been disclosed in reports by the PRI (Public Radio International, a global non-profit media company) and that these Toyota trucks formed a part of the so-called 'non-lethal' aid which the US sent for the so-called 'moderate rebels' in Syria. Eventually, they ended up with the ISIS. Well, the chickens came home to roost!

America's History of Military Adventurism and Playing with the Devil

It has been confirmed by the *Afghan Project* (http://nsarchive.chadwyck.com/afintro.htm), which has collected hundreds of CIA and State Department documents, cables and memoranda, that since the late 1970s itself, the CIA had developed ties with a number of Islamic organizations. The objective was to use 'Islamic fundamentalist' doctrine to unseat the secular pro-Soviet People's Democratic Party of Afghanistan (PDPA) government as well as unleash a war with the Soviet Union. As is well-known, US military intervention in Afghanistan in the 1980s was supported by the Wahabi missionaries out of Saudi Arabia, which trained the Mujahideen in the US sponsored madaris (religious schools) in Pakistan and Afghanistan. The Wahabi doctrine would not have spread in the way it did without the support of US intelligence. Saudi Arabia worked closely with Washington in recruiting the Mujahideen to fight against the Soviet Union. Even fatwas were issued urging Saudi and non-Saudi youths to go to Afghanistan and carry out jihad there. And it praised those who sacrificed their lives for the sake of Islamic nation's causes. Osama bin Laden was one of those prominent Mujahideen who fought in Afghanistan. The CIA led war on Afghanistan largely contributed to destroying secular education there. As disclosed by Prof Michael Chossudovsky in his article "9/11 Analysis: From Ronald Reagan and the Soviet-Afghan War to George W Bush and September 11, 2001", in *Global Research*, the number of CIA sponsored madaris increased from 2,500 in 1980 to over 39,000 in 2001!

Darius Shahtahmasebi, human rights activist and journalist from the University of Otago, forcefully argues in *Speakout* that –

> "In the same way that Al-Qaida was initially a US creation in order to lure the Soviets into a crippling war – ISIS did not emerge out of nowhere without a reason, without funding, without weaponry and without a cause."

I cite some excerpts from his article "A Brief History of ISIS and the Problem with the West's War on Terror":

> "Before the group was rebranded as ISIS, Islamic State in Iraq and the Levant (ISIL), or simply Islamic State (IS), the group was known by the US intelligence authorities simply as Al-Qaida in Iraq (AQI)…. The US has known since 2012 that the majority of the weapons it was sending into Syria were being delivered one way or another in the hands of extremists, yet the US did not stop sending weapons to Syria – and is still doing it…. In 2014, the various Al-Qaida affiliates in Iraq and Syria merged and we were left with the basis of ISIS as it stands today…. One could still argue that the US-led coalition is intervening to correct its mistakes and is finally doing the right thing by opposing ISIS. Of course, this

> would still require us to ignore the fact that the US and NATO are still backing rebel groups who they know are defecting and giving their weaponry over to ISIS, and who regularly conduct operations together with Al-Nusra, Al-Qaida's official Syrian branch.... This is not to say that Russian and Iranian involvement is a good thing, or that Russian bombs will help the region create any more peace and stability. However, Russia and Iran are right about one thing: Only the Syrian people can decide the future of Assad's government."

The same strategy of supporting Islamic political movements was used by Washington in the post-Cold War era in the Muslim republics of the former Soviet Union as well in Bosnia and Kosovo.

David Mizner, campaigner for People for the American Way and the Vera Institute of Justice, wrote an article "Don't Blame Islam: Al-Qaida and ISIS are Products of US and Saudi Imperialism" in the *Jacobin* in January 2015. Tracing the historical origins of the support extended by the US to 'right-wing jihadists' since the days of Abdel Gamal Nasser and the Muslim Brotherhood in Egypt, Mizner quotes Hillary Clinton herself in the context of Al-Qaida:

> "The people we are fighting today we funded twenty years ago, and we did it because we were locked in this struggle with the Soviet Union. They invaded Afghanistan, and we did not want to see them control central Asia, and we went to work. And it was President Reagan in partnership with the Congress led by Democrats who said, you know what? Sounds like a pretty good idea. Let's deal with the ISI and the Pakistani military. Let's go recruit these Mujahadeen. That's great let's get some to come from Saudi Arabia and other places importing their Wahabi brand of Islam so that we can go beat the Soviet Union."

As Prof Michael Chossudovsky says, the ISIS brigades were involved in the US-NATO supported insurgency in Syria directed against the government of Bashar Al-Assad. NATO and the Turkish High Command were responsible for the recruitment of ISIL and Al-Nusra mercenaries from the outset of the Syrian insurgency in March 2011. According to Israeli intelligence sources (DEBKAFile, NATO to give rebels anti-tank weapons, August 14, 2011) cited by him, this initiative consisted of a campaign to enlist thousands of Muslim volunteers in Middle East countries and the Muslim world to fight alongside the Syrian rebels. The Turkish army would house these volunteers, train them and secure their passage into Syria.

David Grudge of the California Network says that,

> "The mass executions, genocidal activities, enslavements, the destruction of antiquities and the violent chaos in general is part of the cost of using Islamic extremists to do your bidding. It's a classic problem, seen time and again throughout the American history of covert operations. The agents we recruit don't always cooperate fully and once they feel they have the power to do as they please, they simply do otherwise."

I must clarify that the facts and arguments presented above must not be misconstrued to mean a contrived attempt to justify Assad's violence on his own citizens. Violence of any kind can never be justified. However, the fact remains that violence has taken place from both sides, and from one side it is foreign supported. Surely the protests that began before March 2011 were met with violent repression from the Syrian state, and none of these findings absolve the Assad government from blame for this, however it is also true that these opposition movements were financed, trained, and advised by the US through its 'democracy promotion' endeavours. The goal of supporting these groups has been regime-change and from the very beginning the

US has been arming and training the opposition to attack the state. Without substantial foreign backing the relatively small-scale protests would never have been able to spawn into the armed resistance that they did; the 'Civil War' that resulted was very much a product of foreign intervention for regime-change! In December 2015, RT.com had cited former UK MP George Galloway telling RT that the US and its allies are trapped by their own policy, according to which they will consider their 'anti-ISIS campaign' in Syria a success only if Assad leaves power in the process.

The Real Purpose of the US Airstrikes against the ISIS

The ISIS is but a terrorist organization. At best, it could be called an irregular army of a few thousand men capable of wielding weapons. In comparison, the military might of the US is millions of times greater. Should the US find it difficult to destroy them utterly? By all means, a resounding no – not at all! Their absolutely fabulous air force replete with highly accurate smart missiles/bombs, other guided missiles, cruise missiles, JSOW (Joint Stand Off Weapon), and JDAM (Joint Direct Attack Munition) etc can take out even a regular army in no time; the ISIS does not even count anywhere, particularly when they do not have any modern air defence systems capable of countering these weapons. Like a medieval army, they are out in the open in their Toyota trucks. They could put up a fight on the ground – they are absolutely helpless against attacks from the air. Then how is it that the air strikes of the USA started since September 2014 did not prove to be as effective as expected and, in the end, Mossul was captured in ground battle?

Prof Michael Chossudovsky answers this question consummately in his November 2015 article "America's 'Global War on Terror', Al-Qaida and the Islamic State (ISIS)". He categorically accuses that –

> "from the very outset, this air campaign has NOT been directed against ISIS. The evidence confirms that the Islamic State is not the target. Quite the opposite. The air raids are intended to destroy the economic infrastructure of Iraq and Syria."

He says that there is a longstanding US foreign policy agenda to carve up Iraq and Syria into separate territories: A Sunni Islamist Caliphate; an Arab Shia Republic; and a Republic of Kurdistan.

David Grudge concurs that such a scheme would serve a dual purpose.

> "Whoever controls Syria and Iraq also controls a massive supply of oil, which is a major economic commodity and strategic resource. It can be translated into money and power very easily, so it's a natural target. Control over the region should bring stability. Western troops can be stationed there and the region can provide a buffer between states like Iran and Israel, protecting an important ally. The three states would cater to their religious majorities, and this would create stability since each could have their own territory and govern themselves according to their whims. This would help to correct some of the errors made by the British who established the original boundaries and split otherwise homogeneous populations in two."

As reported by *Global Research* in its article "Global Warfare: 'We're going to take out 7 countries in 5 years: Iraq, Syria, Lebanon, Libya, Somalia, Sudan and Iran…'", on January 30, 2017, these plans are not entirely secret either. In 2007, Gen Wesley Clark had mentioned these plans in an interview to *Democracy Now*, explaining that the US government had a controversial agenda going into motion. The plan was, in five years to overthrow seven states,

> "We're going to take out seven countries in 5 years, starting with Iraq, and then Syria, Lebanon, Libya, Somalia, Sudan and, finishing off, Iran."

Former French Foreign Minister Roland Dumas, stated on television (https://www.youtube.com/watch?v=Kz-s2AAh06I&app=desktop) that the Israeli Prime Minister had told him –

> "We will try to get along with the neighbouring states, and those who don't get along, we will take them down.' It is a policy. It is a conception of history."

Seumas Milne, journalist and the Labour Party's Executive Director of Strategy and Communications under Labour leader Jeremy Corbyn, has shown in *The Guardian* that in reality, US and Western policy in the conflagration that is now the Middle East is in the classic mould of divide et impera. American forces bomb one set of rebels while backing another in Syria, and mount what are effectively joint military operations with Iran against ISIS in Iraq while supporting Saudi Arabia's military campaign against Iranian-backed Houthi forces in Yemen. However confused US policy may often be, a weak, partitioned Iraq and Syria fit such an approach perfectly. Tyler Durden, in his exhaustive article "Officials Admit ISIS, Like Al-Qaida, was a Creation of US Foreign Policy" in finance blog *ZeroHedge* in August 2015 said the same thing.

Prof Chossudovsky continues:

> "If they had wanted to eliminate the Islamic State brigades, they could have 'carpet' bombed their convoys of Toyota pickup trucks when they crossed the desert from Syria into Iraq. The answer is pretty obvious, yet not a single mainstream media has acknowledged it. The Syro-Arabian Desert is open territory. With state of the art jet fighter aircraft (F15, F22 Raptor, F16) it would have been – from a military standpoint – 'a piece of cake', a rapid and expedient

> surgical operation, which would have decimated the Islamic State convoys in a matter of hours."

Well, anyway the cloak is off now – no pretensions anymore – the real target is the regime of Bashar Al-Assad! By the time of writing this book, as reported in the media (eg, NDTV), on April 6, 2017, the US military launched 59 cruise missiles at a Syrian military airfield, in the first direct American assault on the government of President Bashar Al-Assad since that country's Civil War began six years ago. The operation, which the Trump administration authorized in retaliation for the alleged chemical attack killing scores of civilians a couple of days earlier, dramatically expanded US military involvement in Syria and exposed the United States to heightened risk of direct confrontation with Russia and Iran. Donald Trump said the strike was in the "vital national security interest" of the United States and called on "all civilized nations to join us in seeking to end the slaughter and bloodshed in Syria. And also to end terrorism of all kinds and all types." The missiles struck an airbase called Shayrat in Homs province, which is the site from which the planes that conducted the chemical attack in Idlib are believed to have originated.

According to ABC News, Syria called it an 'aggression' whereas the rebels welcomed the attack. Maj Jamil Al-Saleh, a US-backed rebel commander whose Hama district in the country's centre was struck by a suspected chemical weapons attack, said he hoped the US attack on a government air base would be a 'turning point' in the six-year war. Syria maintains it didn't use chemical weapons, blaming opposition fighters for stockpiling the chemicals. Russia's Defence Ministry said the toxic agents were released when a Syrian airstrike hit a rebel chemical weapons arsenal and munitions factory on the eastern outskirts of Khan Sheikhoun. Moscow warned against apportioning blame until an investigation had been carried out.

As reported by 'Investment Watch' and many others like secretsofthefed.com in March 2015, Julian Assange gave an interview to *Pagina/12*, an Argentinean newspaper from his Ecuadorian embassy asylum where he claimed that the 'adventurism' of Western countries has already destroyed the Libyan and Syrian society and now is "destroying Iraq for oil and other geopolitical reasons."

Garikai Chengu of Harvard says that America's Middle East policy revolves around oil and Israel. The invasion of Iraq has partially satisfied Washington's thirst for oil, but ongoing air strikes in Syria and economic sanctions on Iran have everything to do with Israel. The goal is to deprive Israel's neighbouring enemies, Lebanon's Hezbollah and Palestine's Hamas, of crucial Syrian and Iranian support. ISIS is not merely an instrument of terror used by America to topple the Syrian government; it is also used to put pressure on Iran.

David Grudge of the California Network also says:

> "Although the bombs and the beheadings are real and the attacks are authentic and bloody, all this gruesome spectacle is intended to terrify the public, obtain our consent for heavy policing and other government intrusions, and to secure a greater American empire in the Middle East to protect the flow of oil and bring a forced stability to a region that is fraught with division."

What the Establishment or the Pro-Establishment People Concede?

Even those who are not as vocal or vociferous in criticizing the US as the authorities discussed above, do admit that the role of the US in the entire phenomenon of the ISIS was far from innocent. Defence and foreign policy specialist Jonathan Broder, writing for the *Newsweek*, says that while both Bush and Obama deserve some blame, ISIS could not have become such a battle-hardened, well-funded jihadi group without the help of leaders and sympathizers in Iraq, Syria, Turkey and the Sunni monarchies of the Persian Gulf. Their support for ISIS – over Washington's objections – underscores the limits of American power and influence in the region. He quotes Douglas Ollivant, a former director for Iraq on the National Security Council for both Bush and Obama, who put it in the following words: "We Americans are the supporting cast, not the lead actors." And they expect the whole world to believe that while all this was happening, the US, the mighty US, was blissfully unaware of the happenings and that its omnipotent, omnipresent CIA had gone on a sabbatical! That does not happen.

In international politics, there is no place for "I did not know" or "holier-than-thou" attitude – the USA was not the quintessentially innocent little Red Riding Hood likely to be seduced by the Big Wily Wolf; they knew what they were doing. "The ISIS that we know today is a product of Syria," says James Jeffrey, who served as Bush's deputy national security adviser and Obama's ambassador to Iraq. "And that's Obama's fault."

Phil Gordon, who stepped down as Obama's top Middle East adviser on the National Security Council, was obliged to caution in an essay in *Politico Magazine:*

> "The US has no good options. Some of the proposed remedies for the region's woes, such as US military intervention in an effort to 'transform' or 'remake' the region or simply to impress our foes, would likely make things worse. This should be clear from the US effort to do so in Iraq just over a decade ago."

Andrew Bacevich, a former Army colonel and now author of *America's War for the Greater Middle East: A Military History*, concurred in a PBS documentary "Obama at War":

> "When we talk about moral obligations, there's also a moral obligation; it seems to me, to take history seriously, to learn from one's mistakes."

He adds,

> "Even where armed intervention has achieved a semblance of tactical success – the ousting of some unsavoury dictator, for example – it has yielded neither reconciliation nor willing submission nor even sullen compliance. Instead, intervention typically serves to aggravate, inciting further resistance. Rather than putting out the fires of radicalism, we end up feeding them."

The ISIS is not the case of an experiment gone sour; it is not the case of the unwitting creation of a Frankenstein either. We cannot grant the benefit of such Victorian maiden-like 'innocence' to a superpower like the USA. Whatever they have done, they have done it knowingly, and with the full knowledge of what had resulted from such machinations in the past. The world and history shall hold them accountable for their misdeeds.

3

Pakistan's State-Sponsoring of Terrorism

THE FUNDAMENTAL REASON OF PAK SKULDUGGERY

Pakistan's support of Islamic terrorists in general and Kashmiri terrorists in particular makes for a rather interesting case study. When Pakistan had aided and abetted pro-Khalistani Sikh insurgents, they did not create the insurgents – they merely provided them material assistance and sanctuary. They knew that the very idea of Khalistan as an insurgency or as a secessionist demand was a non-starter, and hence investing heavily in it would not yield sufficient dividends. For obvious reasons, there was never any popular support worth its name for the idea of secession in Punjab. Precisely for this reason, it never got beyond the phase of pure terrorism. Terrorist acts they could commit at will; they could not invoke popular support to become an insurgency. Moreover, as terrorists, they started committing atrocities upon the very people whom they had forced to give shelter on gun point. That's how intelligence against them started flowing.

In contrast, the involvement of Pakistan in Kashmir has been much deeper and pro-active. Pakistan, from the beginning of its existence, has created, nurtured, supported, trained, financed, and deployed Islamist proxies in Kashmir. While there are several irritants between India and Pakistan, Kashmir is like a festering wound that has refused to heal in nearly seven decades. So crucial is the issue of Kashmir to Pakistan that, in mid-2015, the then Pakistani Army Chief Raheel Sharif described it on two occasions as the "unfinished agenda of the Partition in the subcontinent". Pakistan does know that, in view of the overwhelming military might of India, they cannot wrest Kashmir by force, by insurgency, by terrorism or whatever – and hence their reliance on this expedient technique of 'exporting terror'; waging sub-conventional warfare, proxy war, or subterranean war.

Since the late 1980s, the Pakistani military has financed, trained, armed, and launched the terrorist cadres on their murderous missions into Kashmir and elsewhere inside the Indian union. This is not just a popular notion. A veritable battery of scholars including Bill Roggio, noted American commentator on military affairs and managing editor of *The Long War Journal,* has concluded that, among other terrorist groups, the LeT does receive support from Pakistan's military and its intelligence service. According to Stephen Tankel, visiting scholar at the Carnegie Endowment for International Peace and assistant professor in the School of International Service at American University, in two of his papers, Pakistan began to fund the LeT during the early 1990s itself. By around 1995 the funding had grown considerably. During this time the army and the ISI helped establish the LeT's military structure with the specific intent to use the terrorist group against India. Dean Nelson reported in December 2010 citing a 'WikiLeaks expose' that in a review of Washington's strategy on Pakistan and Afghanistan, its ambassador to Islamabad, Anne Patterson, had said that Pakistan was supporting four terrorist groups, including the Taliban's Haqqani Network and the Lashkar-e-Taiba (LeT) terror group, and could not be persuaded to abandon them. In a cable to Washington in September 2009, the ambassador had said "no amount of money" could persuade Islamabad to turn its back on these terrorist groups.

Incidentally, David Headley had also disclosed that ISI provided financial support to LeT. He disclosed his close association with the ISI. Headley said that ISI provided financial, moral as well as military support to LeT. During the deposition, David Headley admitted that he was working for ISI and also named the officers who instructed him to carry out attack in India. When asked whom he knew in the ISI, David Headley named Brigadier Riyaz, Colonel Shah, Lt Colonel Hamza and Maj Samar Ali. Brigadier Riyaz was handler of Zaki-ur-Rehman Lakhvi, mastermind of 26/11 Mumbai attacks.

Given the unique situation in Kashmir, as far as Pakistan is concerned, their 'adventure' has succeeded in imposing a heavy financial burden on India; losses on the security forces and, of course, the pain of public unrest. In fact, Pakistan has now fine-tuned methodologies to use terror as a tool of coercive diplomacy within and around its border. Since the 'returns' in this business of supporting terrorism from outside are perceived to be quite attractive, Pakistan continues to do so relentlessly.

IS IT A NATIONAL STRATEGY OR A ROGUE OPERATION?

The Pak Army's Existential Crisis

Now the question is whether this is a part of a 'national strategy' of Pakistan or is it a rogue operation – or is it some curious combination of both? To understand this, we will have to examine the issue in the historical context of Pakistani society and its avowed position on its disputes with India, including Kashmir.

A permanent peace or 'normalization' with India would deprive the army of its status as the single institution capable of protecting Pakistan from India's destructive designs and consequently its claims to political and financial resources and to the right to take control of the government when it deems necessary. There is no evidence to suggest that this is likely to occur anytime soon. Given the degree to which the army's understanding of India as an existential threat permeates government institutions and the popular imagination, it is difficult to imagine what endogenous events could bring about such changes.

The Inveterate Obsession to Wrest Kashmir through Non-State Actors

Pakistan has been obsessed with the idea of using non-state actors to snatch Kashmir, so as to be able to invoke the plea of 'plausible deniability' should the need arise on international forums. In 1947, they devised 'Operation Gulmarg', the brainchild of Maj Gen Muhammad Akbar Khan, better known by his nom de guerre, Gen Tariq. While the idea of tribal raiders as a covert intelligence operation was brilliant, the execution fell short of the desideratum. In concept, it was as brilliant an idea as one could think of and should rank alongside the 'Post Quit Plan' of the MI6 in terms of its ingenuity. Still, if the objective was to capture territory, the attack by the tribal raiders with covert support of the Pakistani army regulars was deficient in many aspects. In the first place, from a purely Pakistani or professional perspective, the raiders should have been more numerous and better armed. Further, they should have been better disciplined so as to keep focused on the military objectives and not waste time in rape and rapine. That way the advance could have been faster. The raiders' having wasted precious time in their plunder and rape has been described by numerous sources including Margaret Parton of the *Herald-Tribune*. From a purely military perspective also, some out-of-the-box thinking was required. Paratroopers, for example, could have been dropped in Srinagar to capture the ruler alive even as the raiders were advancing towards Srinagar. Not involving the aircrafts in any way in the entire operation was a terrible mistake. If they could raise a raider army, they could have hired some transport planes as well.

The same mistake was repeated in 1965. The Pak Army HQ believed that the Kashmiri people were dissatisfied with Indian rule and that there was widespread popular support for Pakistani rule – and hence a rebellion could be instigated. This was the 'Operation Gibraltar'. This must be regarded as a massive failure of Pakistani intelligence. Obviously, they could not read the ground situation correctly and imposed their own pre-conceived notions on the reports received from the field. Apparently, the aim was that a specially trained irregular force of some 40,000 men would mingle with the local populace and incite them to rebellion. Meanwhile, sabotage operations would be conducted. It was assumed that India would neither counter-attack, nor involve itself in another full-scale war, and the liberation of Kashmir would rapidly follow. The very conception of the plan was absurd with too many assumptions about people who were not under your control. In any case, India swiftly launched counter attacks across the cease fire line, attacking the Pakistan divisions in POK that had provided cover for the infiltrators, and foiled the plan.

They were to repeat the fundamental mistake once again in 1999 in Kargil. Pakistan failed in all its strategic objectives in Kargil in spite of having conceived a tactically brilliant plan. Once again, they had hoped that the operation would give new stimulus to the decade-long insurgency in Kashmir and will also raise the military costs for India in Kashmir. What they did not understand was that while irregulars could climb mountains and make bunkers alright, there was little to be gained by the irregulars by doing so. They had also hoped to be able to cut the strategic highway link between Srinagar and Leh. They never realized that disrupting movement and transportation on a highway by sporadic shelling is one thing; cutting it off for good and denying its use completely to the enemy was quite another. They could achieve neither of the strategic objectives in spite of flawless tactical execution of the plan. Poor strategy can never be compensated by tactics, however good that be. (For details, interested readers may refer to my treatises, *Indian Defence: Crisis and Challenges* and *India's Wars and Warfare: A Perceptive Analysis*.)

How Afghanistan Changed Their Perception, Albeit Wrongly?

Pakistan was emboldened in its Kashmir venture by the roaring success of the covert operation in Afghanistan. They thought that the experiment could be easily replicated in Kashmir and Indian forces would be driven out as the Red Army had been driven out of Afghanistan. However, the ISI could not appreciate that there were qualitative differences between Afghanistan and Kashmir. In Afghanistan, the Mujahideen could fight the sort of war they fought because of several reasons unique to them and the situation there.

Firstly, they were in very large numbers – hundreds of thousands and were prepared to incur heavy casualties in conventional actions. According to Alan Taylor, senior editor at *The Atlantic,* in his article "The Soviet War in Afghanistan, 1979-1989", in the brutal nine-year conflict, an estimated one million civilians were killed, as well as 90,000 Mujahideen fighters, 18,000 Afghan troops, and 14,500 Soviet soldiers. Kashmir does not come up to this scale in any way. Secondly, they were heavily armed, possessing almost all the weapon systems of a regular army except the air force, courtesy the billions of dollars spent by the CIA in equipping them through its 'Operation Cyclone'. The Stinger MANPADS and the RPG-7 anti-tank weapon were the main game changers. Thirdly, they were fighting in their own country against the Soviet invaders and enjoyed the same advantage which the Viet Cong had over the Americans in the Vietnam War. The Soviets had an option of going back when the situation became untenable or unviable – India is in its own land and cannot go anywhere. The terrorists in Kashmir which Pakistan sponsored and had them infiltrated, had no chance of scripting the Mujahideen's success story, even if they had scaled the Kargil heights and taken us by surprise.

Pakistan has been making a serious miscalculation in respect of their thinking about the strategic effect of insurgencies. Since 1947, they seem to feel that if they encouraged insurgency in Kashmir, it would grow exponentially and eventually create a 'climate of collapse' – and then it would automatically secede from India without a war. Obviously, they never factored in the sheer size of India and India's ability to absorb both casualties amongst the security forces and also the extremely heavy expenditure on counterinsurgency in spite of a poor handling of the insurgency. The expected 'climate of collapse' could never set in.

The Pakistanis have never properly understood the social dynamics of insurgencies and the peculiar characteristics of the Indian masses. Supporting insurgencies can pay dividends in the short-term – whether it would pay dividends in the long run depends on the nature of the target country. From 1989 to the early 1990s in Kashmir, as the state got gripped by insurgency, it indeed appeared that the collapse was near, with the state government paralyzed due to strikes and subversion, and knee-jerk reactions going by the name of administrative decisions. But the people arc essentially opportunists and when they realized that India was not going to cave in quickly, the support for insurgency waned. In fact, elections could be held as early as 1996. Unfortunately for Pakistan, India is not such a country that would crack under the pressure of an insurgency, however virulent it be. The huge 'moment of inertia' of India allows it to absorb much damage even if they are not responding in a textbook fashion.

Pakistan's support to insurgency in Kashmir has indeed led to the bogging down of huge numbers of Indian security forces in counterinsurgency operations besides a massive expenditure on keeping the forces there as well as in keeping the state economically afloat. But India can afford both and has been doing that for 29 years now. Pakistan had presumed that their support to insurgency would inflict the classical "death by a thousand cuts". Yes, they did inflict the thousand cuts, but India did not die – as simple as that. The Pakistanis failed to take into account the capacity of India to take punishments. Moreover, on a political level also, extending support to insurgency and terrorism did not help the cause of Pakistan in any way – if anything, it weakened it, projecting Pakistan as the exporter of terrorism.

Guiding an insurgency in Kashmir from outside had some inherent flaws:

- The difference in the military potentials of the two sides was great – there was no way the terrorists could have defeated the Indian security forces. They could have harassed them alright but nothing more. As such, the dicta of the progression of a classical insurgency did not apply here.
- Popular support was indeed there but not adequate. In any case, it was more sentimental in character than material. The popular support did not really result in any fifth columnist action or sabotage of vital installations.
- Wherever revolutions have succeeded, the revolutionary forces they had become numerically almost equal to or bigger than the government forces. Also there was no generation gap in technology between the two sides. Such a situation cannot be envisaged in India.

What Pakistan has Gained Through Sponsoring of Terrorism and What Keeps It Going?

As such, complete success, in the sense of anybody being able to wrest Kashmir, was bound to elude them. The Pakistani experiment has had, however, limited successes:

- They have been able to keep India generally harassed and 'off-balance'.
- India is never at peace; and is forced to devote a tremendous amount of time, energy and resources to fight this proxy war.
- India is gripped by an all-pervasive sense of frustration. The people know who is doing all this and yet they know that ending this once and for all does not seem possible.
- They have been able to impose a heavy financial burden on India besides losses on the security forces and, of course, the pain of public unrest.
- The number of terrorists in Jammu and Kashmir might be less than say, 200 in 2017, but they, and the public unrest, have necessitated the deployment of a very large number of soldiers in the state, running into lakhs.
- The 'export of terrorism' allowed Pakistan to use it as an instrument of coercive diplomacy and punch way above its geopolitical weight.

By all accounts, Pakistan should be happy with the returns of this sub-conventional warfare, proxy war, subterranean war or whatever you call it. By now they should have learnt enough to not bother about 'fomenting insurgency' as it would not lead them anywhere; it is not a simple 'fomenting terrorism' either – now they are "fomenting terrorism in such a manner that it acquires an insurrectional focus." If conducted suitably, this is indeed a low-cost operation with very good dividends.

I will elaborate on it. Kashmir has a long history of people protesting during anti-terrorist operations, after them and also during the funerals of the slain terrorists where they are eulogized as martyrs – this is an example of 'subversion' of those who do so. On February 17, 2017, the Indian army chief had warned:

> "Those who obstruct our operations during encounters and are not supportive will be treated as over-ground workers of terrorists.... We are giving them an opportunity, should they want to continue to then, we will continue with relentless operations may be with harsher measures and that is the way to continue."

And yet, to cite but one example, a little over a month later on March 28, 2017, three civilians were killed in Chadoora, Budgam indulging in exactly the same type of activity against which they were specifically warned, showing that they did not bother about the warning and were prepared to die. The clashes erupted after a militant was shot dead in an encounter in the morning. Locals protested at the encounter site and pelted stones at the CRPF and police personnel present on the spot.

The public protests opposing counterinsurgency operations during the operations, after the operations, and during the funerals of the terrorists, braving the bullets of soldiers, show that the ISI is succeeding in its very clever operation. The fact that, at some point of time in the history of Kashmir, people protesting against India and in support of the terrorists were prepared to get killed, as if consumed by a 'collective death wish', must not be ignored. We will be guilty of an Ostrich-like attitude if we ignore the phenomenon. The ISI is very craftily, very consummately acting like a catalyst in a chemical reaction. Now they are "fomenting terrorism in such a manner that it acquires an insurrectional focus."

Yes, they are emboldened somewhat by the nuclear power status of Pakistan, but that is not the only reason of their adventure. There is always a possibility that India could be provoked enough to launch a full-scale war. But the trick for the ISI lies in keeping the level of terrorist violence to a notch below that unacceptable level. (For a detailed discussion on the possibility of a conventional/nuclear war between India and Pakistan, readers may refer to my treatise *Next War: India, Pakistan, China*.)

HOW DID THE ISI BECOME A 'STATE WITHIN A STATE'?

The Unique Position of the ISI in Pakistan Courtesy the Afghan War Legacy

Observers are often perplexed as to how the ISI has come to acquire the functional autonomy, independence or 'unaccountability' within the Pakistani system of governance? After all, Pakistan is also a democratic country and in no other democratic country, intelligence agencies are supposed to be doing things about which the elected leader of the country might not be even aware, not to speak of the agency having obtained proper approval of the government. Yes, intelligence agencies all over the world undertake covert operations in national interest and, strictly speaking, many of them do cross the boundaries of morality as well as legality. However, two things are taken care of in such operations. The first is that they try to maintain 'plausible deniability'. The second is that the operations are undertaken with the approval of the government. (For a detailed discussion on covert operations, readers may refer to my treatise *Intelligence and Security Management*.)

As far as the ISI is concerned, it has frequently been speculated that they do not necessarily take the political leadership into confidence or seek their approval. How they managed this? Once again, the origin of this is traced to the role and functioning of the ISI in the Mujahideen war. This operation, the subject of many a fascinating book, was the first time in the history of covert operations that an intelligence agency 'handled' hundreds of thousands of fighters. The involvement of the ISI ranged from talent spotting to indoctrination and military training of the Mujahideen in the madaris opened and run by them and the CIA, to keeping them continuously stocked with illegal arms and ammunition sourced from all over the world. It was but natural that the ISI operatives would develop very close relations with the Mujahideen.

Moreover, there are reasons to believe that many ISI operatives and officers genuinely believed in the 'cause' of the Mujahideen. As such, the relationship became even deeper. The immense success of the Afghanistan operation meant that the ISI had come to enjoy a prestige in the body politic of Pakistan which, perhaps with the exception of the CIA, no other intelligence agency in the world has ever enjoyed in public perception. A direct consequence of this enhanced prestige was that it diluted the intensity of any criticism which someone could mount on the agency in future for whatever reason, if not rendering them immune to it. The ISI officers did take full advantage of it.

Currently, the most 'problematic' elements within the Pakistani State, however, are believed to be those ISI officers in the field who were tasked with managing liaison with the terrorists over the years. They find themselves in a rather privileged position. As Ashley Tellis, senior fellow at the Carnegie Endowment for International Peace, says in his numerous works on Pakistan, some simply feel loyal to their 'old clients'. In other words, they find themselves in sync with the ideology or 'approach' of the terrorists and are more than eager to help them and, in the process, take such work out of them which will serve the purpose of the organization or the nation. Second, they are acutely aware of the fact that given the strong anti-India sentiments in the minds of the people and the immense popular support for Pakistan's stance on Kashmir, hardly anyone would dare openly criticize something done by the ISI as long as it is against India. In other words, the chances of the agency getting condemned or publicly censured for their doing something immoral or illegal are greatly reduced. This emboldens them into undertaking the so-called 'dirty' operations. Third, many officers and operatives exploit their leadership's own ambivalence about the terrorists. And finally, for either nationalist, ideological, or personal reasons, some are prepared to disregard leadership directives that enjoin interdicting the terrorists, if they believe they can get away with it. In simple words, the integrity of the ISI, in so far as their government's commitment to the War on Terror is concerned, is quite doubtful.

This is both a complex and curious phenomenon – complex for the reasons discussed above and curious for the reason that, prima facie, nothing in the organizational structure of the ISI would seem to suggest that it is either an autonomous or a rogue entity. The reportedly 10,000-strong ISI is staffed primarily by Pakistani military officers who are assigned to the service on deputation for a fixed period of time, and its leadership reports to the chief of army staff. The pay, promotions, and operations of the directorate are also regulated by military rules and procedures, and by all accounts the Pakistan Army is a professional and bureaucratically efficient organization. As such, to anyone familiar with the functioning of governments, the popular notion that ISI officers might be undermining policies pursued by the corporate leadership of the Pakistan Army appears counterintuitive at first sight and cannot be reconciled with the image of the Pakistan Army as a tightly centralized organization.

If the Pak government ever **really** wanted, they could tighten the screws on ISI – the emphasis is on **really**. There is no reason to believe that the ISI is all-powerful or that it could engineer serious trouble in the country. Regarding Gen Musharraf's coup in 1999, Lt Gen Shahid Aziz, the then DG Military Operations and close aide of Musharraf, has revealed in his book *Yeh Khamoshi Kahan Tak* (Urdu), that even as the then ISI chief Lt Gen Ziauddin Butt was appointed army chief, the Joint Staff HQ refused to follow the orders of the new army chief, and the commanders of the army corps decided to defend Gen Musharraf by ordering to arrest the ISI chief Ziauddin Butt so as to pre-empt him from taking the control of the military. The coup went ahead with a remarkable speed – the 111th Brigade had moved at 1700 hrs; Gen Musharraf landed from Sri Lanka at 1947 hrs; and at 2215 hrs as the army resumed television transmission, it was announced that Sharif had been dismissed. Both Sharif and Ziauddin were arrested by the coup-makers and taken to different locations. Ziauddin was kept in solitary confinement for two years. Gen Musharraf had but one brigade, the 111th, with him that had moved to Islamabad – nothing more. Had the ISI been really as powerful as it is made out to be, Lt Gen Ziauddin should have been able to do something to counter it. In fact, he could have presented Musharraf with the frightening prospect of a battle between different units of the Pak Army, if not a vertical split in the army. In the end, he could do nothing and accepted his fate meekly. So much so for the ISI bandied and touted as all-powerful!

The Mechanics of ISI's Autonomy

From this it would follow that the autonomy, independence or 'unaccountability' which the ISI enjoys in its functioning for doing 'immoral and illegal things' is, to some extent 'acquired' by it and, to some extent, 'granted' to it by the government, albeit informally.

There is nothing so unusual about it – this happens everywhere. Back in 1975 in the USA, a Senate Committee headed by Senator Frank Church (Democrat-Idaho) had called CIA Director William Colby to testify on revelations that US intelligence agencies had engaged in controversial covert action against foreign leaders and US citizens – all with government approval. The Committee had investigated the legality of intelligence operations by the CIA, NSA, and FBI, including attempts to assassinate foreign leaders, spying on Martin Luther King, Jr, and monitoring the political activities of other US citizens. The Director CIA put up a vehement defence and claimed that such inquiry had placed American intelligence in danger. The Church Committee was very curious about knowing the budgetary allocation of the CIA. They were astounded when William Colby told them how the budgetary allocation of the CIA was very surreptitiously, and yet 'legitimately', 'concealed' amongst other publicly known allocations and was thus effectively rendered 'off-the-books' – that is, a form of 'granted autonomy'. There was another United States House Permanent Select Committee on Intelligence chaired by Democratic Representative Otis G Pike of New York, generally known as the Pike Committee. It also investigated illegal activities by the CIA, FBI and the NSA. In the hearings of this committee also, Senator John L McClellan (Democrat-Arkansas) argued brilliantly against disclosing the actual budgetary allocation to the intelligence agencies. The point being made is that if a self-proclaimed defender of liberty could take its intelligence agencies off the radar of public scrutiny, what prevents Pakistan and the ISI from doing so? Governments have never been vestal virgins. Quite possibly, as in the case of the CIA, at least part of the budgetary allocation of the ISI also must be carefully camouflaged. In effect, that amounts to, both for the CIA and the ISI, that they have funds for which they are not obliged to submit accounts.

That was an era, as Thomas Young, communications adviser at Brookings, writes in his article "40 Years Ago, Church Committee Investigated Americans Spying on Americans", when liberty was valued in the American society. After the terrorist attacks on 9/11, and the passage of the USA Patriot Act of 2001, however, public attitude toward such shady activities of the government has changed. Stuart Taylor, Jr, writes in his *Brookings Essay*, "The Big Snoop: Life, Liberty, and the Pursuit of Terrorists", the emergence of this new menace to America and its allies brought about an upsurge in political and public support for aggressive surveillance of potential terrorists, and a muting of the concerns that had arisen in the 1970s about the past sins and excessive zeal of the US intelligence agencies. Viewed in this light, we cannot say whether the CIA too has 'acquired autonomy' or not.

The ISI has a greater 'operational latitude' than most other intelligence agency for one more reason: it does not depend entirely on government budget – even the mighty CIA takes all of its funds from the public exchequer only even as there are devious means to conceal their source. (For details of CIA's finances, readers may refer to my treatise *Intelligence and Security Management*.) Since they do not depend so much on government funds for some of their operations, they need not even explain to the government as what they did and how they did it? How the ISI generates the funds required for certain covert operations is a matter for a separate book. However, most observers agree that they are involved into narcotics and gun-running etc.

Once an agency has the liberty to do what it wishes to do, the rest is just a matter of detail. In this book we do not have space to dwell at length on covert operations but I may mention that the main concern in covert operations is to maintain 'plausible deniability'. After that the agency is free to hire outright criminals, retired officials, even serving soldiers or intelligence operatives who have been 'sheep dipped', or even outsource – who cares, as long as you can deny any connection with them?

Further, the independence of the ISI comes partly from the fact that the implementation of many ISI operations is typically regulated by 'directive control' as opposed to 'detailed control' (or micro-management). Their field officers have the flexibility to accomplish strategic goals without having to secure prior approval of every particular from their superiors. Musharraf's management of this organization historically was manifested primarily through the promulgation of broadly defined policies, which were then implemented by a chain of subordinates who acted upon their understanding of his strategic intent.

ISI'S COMPULSIONS AND DILEMMAS

The Compulsions and Complications of Supporting a Multiplicity of Tanzeems

Even after a drastic reduction in the number of *tanzeems* supported, the ISI still controls a multiplicity of organizations. Ever wondered why they should do so when the groups' respective objectives and the ISI's objective are the same? As I mentioned earlier in the chapter, the ISI learnt the ropes of sponsoring and conducting terrorism abroad gradually and after considerable experimentation. In the early days of insurgency in Kashmir, they had hoped, albeit mistakenly, that it would start a chain reaction culminating in a massive upsurge of violence and anti-India sentiments. Hence in the initial phase, they considered it expedient to give arms to anybody who was willing to take up arms. But, at the same time, they were not very sure about the leadership potential of those novices. A logical presumption was that if you had a large number of guys, natural selection would automatically throw up persons from amongst them with qualities of dynamism, charisma and perhaps some professional skills; and who would be fit to become leaders and then make their organizations thrive. Then, in the early days, a large number of terrorist groups also served to create a false impression of the strength of the insurgency.

Later, as the insurgency 'stabilised' somewhat, the ISI realized that a large number of groups was actually creating hurdles in the progress of the movement. Ego hassles of various leaders; inter-group clashes; the increasing possibility of infiltration (you cannot keep a watch on every guy) of intelligence operatives amongst the ranks of the terrorists; the increased possibility of betrayal by someone, somewhere; and the difficulty of maintaining effective command and control from across the border; all made it imperative for the ISI to cut down on the number of groups to manageable level. That's where it stands today.

There are several good and practical reasons for the number of groups they support now. The first is legal: if one group is banned, somebody else will be available to carry on the work till such time that cadres of the banned group are re-structured, brought under a new banner, and the assets redistributed.

The second is pragmatic. The ISI is a professional service organization – they cannot expect a soldier-like proficiency, commitment and dedication to duty amongst the terrorists who suffer from a host of vices, ego problems and perversions. I do not have space here to discuss the psychology of the terrorists here but the fact remains that even though he is a fanatic, prepared to give up his life, there is a difference between him and a soldier. No doubt, a terrorist could display some extraordinary feat of daring but you can count on the reliability of a soldier. As such, the terrorists, even as they are serving the purpose of the ISI for the time being, are not very reliable people whom the ISI could trust implicitly or forever. Anyone of them could waver in his resolve at a critical moment; ditch the main objective and start pursuing some transient objective of his own; commit some silly mistakes in some operation; get captured alive like Ajmal Kasab; or break under sustained interrogation and reveal critical information. The ISI cannot afford to put all their eggs in one basket. Having a multiplicity of organizations ensures that no one knows more than what is strictly necessary for him.

One may recall the rape and rapine in which the tribal raiders had indulged in the 1947 attack on Kashmir in Baramulla – wasting full three days there; their crucial advance to Srinagar was delayed irreparably because of this. Margaret Parton of the *Herald-Tribune* and Tom Cooper/Air Combat Information Group have narrated how there were occasions when the Pak army regulars with them had to literally beg them catching hold of their *'salwars'* pleading to focus on the main objective of advancing. Abdul Qayyum Khan had to send their religious leader Pir Manti to plead with them to advance towards Srinagar. The cupidity of the raiders lost the Kashmir Valley for Pakistan.

It also ensures that no terrorist leader, however good and fiery, grows in popularity and stature beyond a certain level. By ensuring that no one becomes too powerful, it is ensured that they remain under effective control of the ISI. B Raman reports in his article for the *South Asia Analysis Group* that in the famous intercepted telephone conversation between Musharraf, then in Beijing, and Aziz, then Chief of the General Staff in the GHQ in Rawalpindi, released by New Delhi in June 1999, Aziz could be heard reassuring Musharraf: "Sir, the scruff of their (referring to the irregulars/terrorists who had invaded and occupied the heights) neck is in our hands". Still, in this business no one can take it for granted that the terrorists they created would always be under their strict control – no one can. After all, Osama bin Laden, who as a Mujahideen fighter in the Afghan War was in a way, created by the CIA, eventually became one of the staunchest enemies of the USA. Somewhat similar is the case of the ISIS. And that's why the ISI cannot rest in peace.

A multiplicity of groups also ensures that they are not likely to become quite independent in their finances and arms supply. Then, the larger a group grows or more autonomous its cadres become, it finds it increasingly difficult to carry out its internal counter-intelligence operations meticulously and hence more vulnerable to infiltration by hostile intelligence agencies or groups. Muzamil Jameel, for example, reported in *The Indian Express* that –

> "Early 2004, Indian intelligence agencies used a mole deep inside the Jaish to organise a meeting, in Lolab, of the group's entire Kashmir brass, and killed them all. The Jaish struggled for years to get a foothold in Kashmir after that."

Running terrorist organizations is a delicate game demanding great finesse, quite like keeping the nobles during the imperial era of say, the Mughals. The Empire could not afford a very large standing army because, for most of the time, it would remain unproductive and drain the treasury. A practical solution was to let the regional nobles and feudal lords keep their own armies and make them produce the armies for the services of the Empire whenever needed. The system could, however, work fine only as long as the nobles did not grow very ambitious and start eyeing the Empire itself. If the nobles had rather large armies and if they banded together, they could threaten the Empire. The trick, therefore, lay in meeting several mutually conflicting demands simultaneously. To protect the empire from an 'internal' threat of revolt, it lay in not allowing the nobles to have very large armies in the first place, and keeping a standing army which was just large enough to ensure that if, God forbid, the nobles banded together, the standing army would take care of them. Of course, diplomacy demanded that the Empire must keep on playing the nobles/feudal lords against each other and not allow them to conspire together. To protect the Empire from 'external' threats, it was necessary that the garrisons which the nobles/feudal lords maintained at the borders were strong enough. If they were deliberately kept weak out of the fear of an 'internal' uprising, foreign invaders could easily overrun them and threaten the Empire. A calculation mistake either way could cost you your life and Empire. Now you can understand why uneasy lies the head that wears the crown. The same principles apply to running terrorist organizations. Keep them, equip them, and maintain them so as to make use of them – never allow them to grow out of hand, go out of control or turn upon you.

The ISI's Dilemmas and Difficulties in Letting Go of Terrorism

Now you can appreciate how the ISI has struggled to meet the mutually conflicting demands inherent in running terrorist organizations. They cannot afford to pamper them more than necessary; they cannot afford to annoy them more than necessary. They cannot afford to arm and train them too well lest they lead to a situation where Pakistan is forced into a direct military confrontation with India; they cannot afford to keep them armed and trained below a certain level lest they become an impotent force. They cannot afford to control them too much lest they start feeling 'drained' like regular government employees and lose the zeal of whatever they perceive themselves to be ('holy warrior', 'liberator', 'soldier of Islam', 'conqueror' or whatever – who cares?); they cannot afford to grant them too much autonomy lest they deviate from the main objective. They cannot hope to keep them like a ferocious dog which has been permanently de-clawed and muzzled; if the dog has to be ferocious for whatever brief moments at your command, he has to 'know' that he is capable of doing something. They cannot hope to 'redirect' the 'energy' of the terrorists into some innocuous, humane or productive purpose. By God, who could ever imagine 'reformed' terrorists toiling in shifts in some armament factory, or coaching cadets in some defence academy?

Real life is different from fiction. Real life is not the life of the Phantom created by Lee Falk. It is only in the Phantom comics that you find Phantom having defeated the pirate leader Redbeard and his three lieutenants, Big Bart, Salla, and Crusher in single combats with swords after which they became his faithful followers – the 'reformed pirates' eventually becoming the foundation force for the Jungle Patrol, the private army of Phantom which maintained law and order in that vast African jungle. There cannot be any 'reformed terrorists' in real life – that's a contradiction in itself.

De-weaponisation, for example, was once the buzzword of the Musharraf regime immediately after it took over in October 1999. But the process could never take off – it was never seriously intended to! If you had to disarm the terrorists you had created, why you created them in the first place? The ISI can make them extinct, crush them brutally should they so desire; but the temptation to keep them going is so great, so persuasive that they cannot have the heart to do it. Deep down their hearts, they know that if they do it, Pakistan will be effectively 'defanged' in relation to India forever. Their missiles and the nukes will remain in place but they know that, in terms of total military potential, they will be decisively, conclusively reduced to an inferior power, losing the only instrument with which they could bleed and harass India quite out of proportion to their military prowess. We can find an echo of the same logic in an article of Christine Fair, associate professor at the Center for Peace and Security Studies, Georgetown University, "Bringing Back the Dead: Why Pakistan Used the Jaish-e-Muhammad to Attack an Indian Airbase" in *The Huffington Post:*

> "India and the United States must understand the strategic imperatives that motivate Pakistan to keep organizations like the Jaish in its vast stable of terrorists. Pakistan does so not merely to 'disrupt peace' with India; rather, to prosecute the Pakistan army's endless war on India within its borders and across South Asia."

Once you understand the complexities inherent in this business, you will immediately grasp why all the trite lamentation in books on terrorism, media, academic conferences, diplomatic circles and various international forums regarding the Pakistan government not 'taming' the terrorists is pure childish rhetoric. That was not to be; cannot be and is not going to happen sooner or later!

In the light of the above 'irredeemable' factors, it is only logical that India must be both mentally and materially prepared for the long haul. There are reasons to believe (and many scholars like Hein Kiessling, a political scientist and historian from the Maximilian University besides having been awarded with the Order of Merit of the Federal Republic of Germany, who had spent 13 years in Pakistan researching and interacting with its intelligence and military elites, also support it) that the ISI, under any leadership, would continue supporting Kashmiri secessionists and run terror camps in POK to keep the conflict with India alive. The ISI is flexible and could increase or decrease the 'intensity' of the proxy war and even change its strategy in Kashmir to advance its hostile relationship with India – but it will not cease to focus on Kashmir.

4

Lashkar-e-Taiba: Our Bête Noire of Long Years

A QUICK SURVEY OF VARIOUS TERRORIST GROUPS OPERATING IN AND FROM PAKISTAN

Once upon a time, the number of terrorist groups supported by Pakistan and operating in Kashmir used to be very large. In the early 1990s, the total number of terrorist outfits was well over hundred. The Indian army officers of the era, who struggled with even pronouncing their Arabic names, were utterly at a loss to remember their names or distinguish one from another. Hence they abandoned the names altogether and gave them a generic name – ANEs (Anti-National Elements)! Ignorance is bliss, isn't it? Most groups were so small that someone with a total of 12 guys with him used to call himself a division commander! Some of the names of the era which have been all but forgotten now include the Al Jihad Force, Al Barq, Al Umar Mujahideen, Muslim Mujahideen, Jamiat-ul-Mujahideen and Al Badr, etc. Fortunately, for the army officers, the number is small now.

At present several terrorist groups operate in and from Pakistan. The terrorist groups call themselves *'askari tanzeems'* or just *'tanzeems'*. The word *askari* in Arabic means a soldier. The

A Summary of Terrorist Groups Operating in and from Pakistan

Group Name	*Sectarian Background*	*Regional Activities*	*Overlapping Membership*
Al-Qaida (in Pakistan):	Salafist	Facilitated attacks within and without Pakistan and has planned international attacks from safe havens in Pakistan.	TTP, Afghan Taliban, other Deobandi terrorist groups.
Afghan Taliban	Deobandi	Wages insurgency in Afghanistan, enjoys safe havens in Pakistan.	TTP and other Deobandi terrorist groups, Al-Qaida
Jaish-e-Muhammad (Harkat-ul-Jihad-Islam (HuJI), Harkat-ul-Ansar/Harkat-ul-Mujahedeen etc)	Deobandi	Traditionally focused upon Jammu and Kashmir, has operated in Afghanistan and continues to do so, factions have targeted the Pakistani State.	Al Qaida, TTP, Afghan Taliban, Deobandi sectarian terrorist groups as well as JUI.
Sipha-e-Sahaba-Pakistan/ Lashkar-e-Jhangvi	Deobandi	Historically anti-Shia, has operated in Afghanistan for decades, currently targeting the Pakistani State with the TTP and allied groups.	TTP, Afghan Taliban, Al Qaida, other Deobandi terrorist groups and JUI.
Hizbul Mujahedeen and al Badr	Jamaat-e-Islami	Jammu and Kashmir.	Jamaat-e-Islami
Tehreek-e-Taliban-e-Pakistan (TTP, Pakistani Taliban)	Deobandi	Targeting the Pakistani state with some commanders mobilizing fighters in Afghanistan	Afghan Taliban, Deobandi terrorist groups in Pakistan and possibly Al Qaida.
Lashkar-e-Taiba	Ahl-e-Hadis	Fights in Jammu and Kashmir and the Indian hinterland, limited out of theatre operations.	Historical links with Al Qaida. Al-Qaida members have been detained in LeT safe havens. Organizational ties to Al-Qaida remain controversial.

word *tanzeem* in Arabic means a group, community, or organization formed for a specific purpose. They differ in their sectarian orientation, primary theatre of operation, ethnic constitution, and even preferred attack techniques.

Theological Leanings

The sectarian orientation of different terrorist groups ranges from Salafist/Wahabi to Deobandi, Ahl-e-Hadis and Jamaat-e-Islami. In this book, I have discussed the theological aspects of the various sects/schools of Islam separately. The distinctions are fine and must always be kept in mind. The LeT, for example, is not a Deobandi group.

The Deobandi groups in Pakistan are found to target Pakistan's Shia and Ahmadiya community, among other religious minorities. These Deobandi groups have also been attacking Sufi shrines in Pakistan. They are opposed to the Barelvi school of Islam. Barelvi is a movement of Sunni Sufism in South Asia that was founded by Ahmed Raza Khan of Bareilly, India (hence the term Barelvi). The Barelvi doctrine, clearly a very much 'Indianized' version of Islam, provides a space for holy men/saints, use of a special type of devotional music (*Qawwali*), and esoteric practices like shrine-worshipping and grave-worshipping, etc. Barelvis are a sizable portion of the Hanafi Muslim communities in India, Pakistan, Bangladesh, South Africa and the United Kingdom, besides having a presence in other places around the world. In India and Pakistan they are in majority. In practice, many Barelvis do not even know that they are Barelvis though because of family traditions they visit such shrines and a great deal of immensely popular devotional poetry and music has been associated with them which millions do like sincerely.

An extreme orthodox version of Islam would hold going to such shrines and mazaars, as a sin called *'bid'at'* as they maintain that no one can intercede between a man and Allah (SWT).

Deobandi terrorist groups say that anyone who does not espouse their beliefs is a *munafiq*, a group decried in the Qur'an as Muslims who were secretly unsympathetic to the cause of Muslims and actively sought to undermine the Muslim community. Since Pakistan's participation in the so-called Global War on Terror was obviously unacceptable to the terrorists, they started targeting state targets too. JeM and LeJ for instance, have collaborated with the TTP by providing suicide bombers and logistical support, allowing the TTP to conduct attacks throughout Pakistan, far beyond the TTP's area of influence.

Ethnic Composition

The groups cannot afford to be extremely choosy about the ethnicity of their cadres. However, different groups differ in the percentages of Kashmiris, men from the POK, Pakistanis and Afghanis, or other foreigners amongst their ranks. To call certain groups as Kashmiri groups is actually a misnomer. Kashmiris might be in majority in groups like Hizb-ul-Mujahideen but they are not allergic to people of other places joining their ranks. Mast Gul of Charar-e-Sharif fame was from Khwaja town in Peshawar. Bambar Khan of the 1990s (not to be confused with Hamid Gada aka Bambar Khan who was very much a Kashmiri and was killed in 2000) was from Balochistan. I mentioned Bambar Khan specially because after he was killed, his funeral procession was perhaps one of the longest in the history of Kashmir with scores of vehicles and the frenzied people shouting slogans like *'Bambar ki HM zinda hai'*, *'Ye khoon baha kar zinda hai'*, *'Seene par kha kar zinda hai'*, *'Bambar ki HM zindabad'*, etc. In a way, Bambar, a foreigner, was being projected as the face of Hizb-ul-Mujahideen in Kashmir. The foreign component in the terrorist groups has also depended on the state of the 'movement' at a given point of time. At times, foreign fighters were deliberately injected to the ranks to enthuse the locals or train them better; at other times, the idea was to impart a truly jihadic, transnational character to the movement. Expedience rules.

Theatres of Operation

Some groups like Hizb-ul-Mujahideen would like to concentrate exclusively on Kashmir; may be because their cadres would not find it easy to unobtrusively blend elsewhere in the country. The JeM operates in other parts of India also maybe because the Pakistani Punjabi component in it can blend better in other parts of India than the Kashmiris. Some groups like the LeT would like to operate outside India too in pursuance of their global aspirations arising out of their anti-Americanism. On the other hand, some groups are creating trouble in Pakistan itself and have been attacking targets belonging to other sects of Islam which they do not approve of.

Preferred Attack Techniques

Once again, there are no hard and fast rules, nor can they ever be; it is basically a matter of pure expedience. No one has a copyright on a particular technique; nor are terrorist groups like the so-called 'criminal tribes' of colonial India, of whom ignorant police officers loved to speak in terms of their *modus operandi*. The habit of journalists and police officers to claim that if it was a so-called *fidayeen* attack, then it should necessarily be such-and-such terrorist group, because it is their 'signature' technique, is sheer ignorance. Depending on what was expedient at a given point of time; some could go for outright communal attacks, such as the attack on the Raghunath Temple in Jammu; some had preferred attacking camps of security forces or their vehicles; whereas some (the Jaish-e-Muhammad, for example) liked to go for spectacular attacks to rattle the target.

Of all the groups, the Lashkar-e-Taiba and the Jaish-e-Muhammad are the most important from the point of view of India and hence we would be focusing on these two.

LASHKAR-E-TAIBA: THERE IS MUCH IN A NAME

Lashkar-e-Taiba (LeT) is one of the largest and most active terrorist organizations in the Indian sub-continent. The correct phonetic spelling of its name in English would be Lashkar-e-Tayyibah – other spellings generally used in the media and literature, such as Lashkar-e-Toiba, are simply wrong. According to authoritative dictionaries, such as that of Muhammad Mustafa Khan 'Maddah', the word *'Taiyyibah'* (with an aspirated sound at the end) means holy; virtuous; or morally and spiritually perfect woman; it is also used as a prefix before the names of places of great religious significance, especially Medina/Madinah. According to *Mu'jam Al-Buldan* (Dictionary of Countries) of Yaqut Al-Hamawi, the famous 13th century Arab scholar, the adjective comes from the Arabic word *'tib'*, meaning 'perfume'. Madinah is the city of Prophet Muhammad and the second holiest city in Islam (after Mecca). It is from there that Muslim warriors had embarked upon their conquest and had spread out in the world "like the fragrance of perfume". Thus, far from being just a reference to a specific place, the name has connotations of a desire to return to the old-school 'warlike' Islam originating in the Arabian Peninsula. It is in the latter sense that the word is used in their name. Lashkar means an army. You could not possibly imagine a terrorist organization calling itself 'Army of a Holy Woman'! So it means the 'Army of Madinah'. Another proof of the correct meaning of the translation of the organization's name can be found in the 15th issue of the Jamaat-ud-Da'wah periodical, published in Lahore under the name of *Taiba Bulletin* (May 27, 2000). That issue clearly states that the translation of the organization's name into English is 'The Army of Madinah'.

Quite interestingly, the Israelis know this, as is evident from a publication *Lashkar-e-Taiba, A Pakistani Islamic Organization ...* of The Meir Amit Intelligence and Terrorism Information

Center. But such nuances are often lost upon most Western authors – a significant indicator of their general ignorance in matters of Islamic theology. Popular interpretations of the meaning of Lashkar-e-Taiba such as Army of the Good, Army of the Righteous, or Army of the Pure are examples of sheer ignorance. However, I have stuck to the spelling Lashkar-e-Taiba (LeT) in this book because this spelling has gained considerable currency over the years and I do not want the readers to get unnecessarily confused.

FORMATION OF THE JAMAAT-UD-DA'WAH, MARKAZ-UD-DA'WAH-WAL-IRSHAD AND THE LASHKAR-E-TAIBA

In 1985, Hafiz Muhammad Saeed and Zafar Iqbal, both academicians by profession, formed the Jamaat-ud-Da'wah (Organization for Proselytizing, or JuD) as a small missionary group dedicated to promoting the Ahl-e-Hadis version of Islam. Christine Fair, in her Testimony for the US Senate, Foreign Relations Committee, repeatedly mentioned Hafiz Saeed as a professor of engineering. He was never a student of engineering. Some other authors like Bruce Hoffman and Fernando Reinares in *The Evolution of the Global Terrorist Threat – From 9/11 to Osama bin Laden's Death* are also seen committing the same mistake. According to the authoritative *Pakistan Times* biographical note on him, Hafiz Saeed comes from a family of Islamic scholars of repute. He has two Master's degrees (1972 and 1974) from the University of Punjab, and a Specialization in Arabic Language from the Jamia Malik Saud (King Saud University). He joined the University of Engineering and Technology in Lahore as a lecturer, eventually becoming professor and chairman of the Department of Islamic Studies. I mentioned this because Christine Fair had claimed that the MDI's (Markaz-ud Da'wah-wal-Irshad) commitment to technical and other education came from LeT's founding fathers being engineering professors. We should eschew the desires for such simplistic explanations. She is seen to have corrected her mistake in 2015 in her article in the *India Today*. Diego Gambetta and Steffen Hertog (of the Nuffield College and University of Durham respectively), in their book, *Engineers of Jihad: The Curious Connection Between Violent Extremism and Education* mention their educational backgrounds correctly.

In 1986, Zaki-ur-Rehman Lakhvi merged his group of anti-Soviet jihadists with the JuD to form the Markaz-ud-Da'wah-wal-Irshad (Center for Proselytizing and Guidance, abbreviated as MDI). The MDI had 17 founders originally, and notable among them was Abdullah Azzam. Abdullah Azzam, a close associate of Osama bin Laden, was affiliated with the International Islamic University of Islamabad and the *Maktab-ul-Khidmat* (Bureau of Services for Arab Mujahideen, which was the precursor to Al-Qaida), also provided assistance.

The LeT was founded in 1987 by Hafiz Saeed, Abdullah Azzam and Zafar Iqbal in the Kunar province of Afghanistan, with funding from Osama bin Laden. Azzam was killed in Peshawar a year later. Kunar is home to numerous Ahl-e-Hadis adherents in Afghanistan. For this reason, Kunar has had been an attractive safe haven for the Arabs in Afghanistan. The LeT gained prominence in the early 1990s as a military wing of MDI. The MDI, along with numerous other militant groups, was involved in supporting the Mujahideen in Afghanistan from 1986 onwards, and had established militant training camps for this purpose. One camp called Muaskar-e-Aqsa was in the Kunar province of Afghanistan, and the other Muaskar-e-Taiba in Jaji, Paktia province.

PRESENT ACTIVITIES OF THE MDI AND THE JuD

Objectives

In 1993, the MDI divided its activities into two related but separate organizations: the MDI proper continued the mission of proselytizing and education while LeT emerged as the militant wing. Probably, the intention was to provide a cover to the LeT in case some action was contemplated against it. After the Soviets withdrew from Afghanistan, LeT/MDI shifted focus to India and Kashmir. MDI's primary concern was *da'wah* and the LeT focused on jihad even as the members did not bother to distinguish between the functions of the two groups. Hafiz Saeed had himself explained,

> "Islam propounds both da'wah and jihad. Both are equally important and inseparable. Since our life revolves around Islam, therefore both da'wah and jihad are essential; we cannot prefer one over the other."

Its stated objective is to introduce an Islamic State (or *Nizam-e-Mustafa*, as disclosed by David Headley also) in South Asia and to 'liberate' Muslims residing in what they call Indian Kashmir.

The Logos of the MDI and the JuD

The MDI logo features a Kalashnikov rifle positioned on a green-colour Quran and a rising yellow sun. In the upper part is a verse from the Quran calling for jihad to turn Islam into the dominant religion of the entire world with the words Markaz-ud-Da'wah-wal-Irshad in the background.

In the logo of Jamaat-ud-Da'wah, the name appears on the bottom, on a red background, with two swords above. At the centre is an open Quran with the sun rising from its edge (similarly to the logo used by the MDI). The text in the upper part of the logo again reads from the Quran about making Islam the dominant religion but does not mention jihad.

Leadership

The chief is Hafiz Muhammad Saeed. On 25 June 2014, the United States declared JuD an affiliate of LeT to counter Saeed's claim that he had nothing to do with the LeT. The second-in-command is Abdul Rehman Makki. He is the brother-in-law of Hafiz Muhammad Saeed. The US has offered a reward of $2 million for information leading to the location of Makki. Another senior member is Zaki-ur-Rehman Lakhvi, named as one of the masterminds of the 2008 Mumbai attacks. Yusuf Muzammil, another senior member of LeT was also named as a mastermind of the 2008 Mumbai attacks by Ajmal Kasab. Zarrar Shah is believed to be one of LeT's main liaisons with the ISI. Muhammad Ashraf was LeT's top financial officer but Geo TV reported him to have died in 2002 itself. Nasr Javed is a Kashmiri senior operative of LeT. All these characters are based in Pakistan. Mahmoud Mohamed Ahmed Bahaziq is a leader of LeT in Saudi Arabia and is one of its financiers.

Zafar Iqbal, one of the three founders, was, according to the write-up of Amir Rana in *The Fact* magazine of Pakistan, reported to have developed differences with Hafiz Saeed in 2004. When Saeed's brother-in-law Maulana Abdul Rehman Makki, then a teacher at Medina University in Saudi Arabia, was appointed as the foreign affairs head of the party as well as his second-in-command, overlooking Zafar Iqbal in spite of his seniority, Zafar Iqbal accused Saeed of nepotism and of promoting the 'Gujjar baradari' to which he belonged,. They also objected to his marriage with the 28-year-old widow of a fallen comrade Abu Musa, who was killed in Srinagar two years ago. The dispute between Iqbal and Saeed was personal, but spilled over into party affairs.

LeT's Offices, Recruits and Training Camps

LeT's headquarters, now called Markaz-e-Taiba is in Nangal Saday, about 5 km north of Muridke, on east side of the GT Road; and about 30 km from Lahore. It is spread over 200 acres of land and contains a madrisa, hospital, market, residences, a fish farm and agricultural tracts. The organization maintains offices in most of the major cities throughout Pakistan. These offices undertake recruitment as well as funds collection.

Recruits typically come from cities in central and southern Punjab (for example, Faisalabad, Gujranwala, Bahawalpur, Vehari, Khaneval, Kasur), reflecting the dominant Punjabi nature of the group and also the fact that its main infrastructure is in Punjab. In addition, some recruits come from Afghanistan and Pashtun areas in Pakistan. Young Pakistanis with British passports are particularly valued for possible operations in the West. Contrary to popular perceptions, LeT recruits are not predominantly drawn from Pakistan's *madaris* (pl of *madrisa*). The days of the Mujahideen war seem to be over, at least in this regard. Rather, LeT recruits are generally in their late teens or early twenties and, on an average, tend to be better educated than those from other militant groups such as the Deobandi SSP or JeM. A majority of LeT recruits are found to have completed secondary school with good grades and some have even attended college. Reportedly, LeT also actively targets women both to expand their recruitment base of males, and also, to recruit women for militant operations. There is no publically available – much less accurate – accounting of the organization's end-strength, and I do not consider conjecturing advisable.

In addition to offices open to the public, JuD/LeT maintains covert training camps throughout Pakistan. The LeT training camps are presently located at a number of locations in Pakistan including the base camp, Markaz-e-Taiba in Muridke and the one near Manshera. Mariam Abou Zahab and Olivier Roy in their book *Islamist Networks: The Afghan-Pakistan Connection* speak of three training camps in POK. Muhammad Amir Rana in his *A to Z of Jehadi Organizations in Pakistan* lists five training camps. Four of them, the Muaskar-e-Taiba, the Muaskar-e-Aqsa, the Muaskar Umm-Al-Qura and the Muaskar Abdullah bin Masood are in POK and the Markaz Muhammad bin Qasim training camp is in Sanghar district of Sindh. Ten thousand militants are claimed to have been trained in these camps till 2004. Information about camps in Afghanistan is sketchy.

In these camps, the following courses are run:

- 21-day religious course (Daura-e-Sufa)
- 21-day basic combat course (Daura-e-Aam)
- 3-months advanced combat course (Daura-e-Khaas)

A French anti-terrorism expert, Jean-Louis Bruguière, in his work *Some Things that I Wasn't Able to Say* has claimed that the regular Pakistani army officers trained the militants in the LeT training camps until recently. He reached this conclusion after interrogating a French militant, Willy Brigitte, who had been trained by the LeT and was arrested in Australia in 2003. Zabiuddin Ansari alias, Abu Jundal arrested by Indian intelligence agencies is reported to have disclosed that paragliding training was also included in the training curriculum of LeT cadres at is camps in Muzaffarabad. Looks like someone in the LeT is a fan of Bond films or has heard of Ingo and Holger Bethke's escape from East Germany across the Berlin Wall in two ultra-light aircrafts in 1989 – from a military point of view this is just an exotic fantasy.

Current Status and Activities

Both the USA and the UK have banned LeT since 2001. It was banned in Pakistan on 12 January 2002. It is banned in India as a designated terrorist group under the Unlawful Activities (Prevention) Act. On 2 May 2008 it was placed on the Consolidated List established and maintained by the Committee established by the United Nations Security Council Resolution 1267 as an entity associated with Al-Qaida. The report also proscribed Jamaat-ud-Da'wah as a front group of the LeT. Bruce Riedel, a senior fellow in the Saban Center for Middle East

Policy at the Brookings Institution believes that LeT with the support of ISI is more dangerous than Al-Qaida.

While the primary focus for the Lashkar remains Kashmir, it has frequently provided support to other international terrorist groups also. Primary among these is the Al-Qaida Network in Afghanistan. LeT members also have been reported to have engaged in conflicts in the Philippines, Bosnia, the Middle East and Chechnya. Bruce Riedel in his article in the *Brookings*, and Isambard Wilkinson, AFP Asia Pacific desk editor, in *The Telegraph* have disclosed that with increasing American pressure on Al-Qaida following the September 11 attacks, Al-Qaida operatives who escaped from Afghanistan found shelter in the homes of LeT colleagues in Pakistan. Notable amongst them was Abu Zubeida who was arrested in 2002.

Though formally banned by Pakistan, the general view of India and the Western countries, including of experts such as former French investigating magistrate Jean-Louis Bruguière and New America Foundation president Steve Coll is that the ISI continues to give LeT help and protection. When LeT was banned in Pakistan, Jamaat-ud-Da'wah (JuD), was not initially banned despite its recognition by the UN Security Council as a LeT front. JuD continued to remain un-banned until 2015. However, JuD still continues to work openly as LeT's charitable wing.

In February 2017, after the Pakistan government placed Hafiz Saeed and his four accomplices – Abdullah Ubaid, Zafar Iqbal, Abdur Rehman Abid and Qazi Kashif Niaz – under house arrest, the Jamaat-ud-Da'wah renamed itself as 'Tehreek Azadi Jammu and Kashmir' (TAJK). Hafiz Saeed had indicated about a week before his arrest that he might launch Tehreek Azadi Jammu and Kashmir (TAJK) to "expedite the freedom of Kashmir". It shows that Saeed had got a wind of the official plans and already had worked out how to resurface and survive after the clampdown on his ostensible network of Jamaat-ud-

Da'wah (JuD) and Falah-e-Insaniyat Foundation (FIF). Various offices of both JuD and FIF were closed earlier following the house arrest of Saeed. Both organisations were also put on observation under Pakistan's Anti-Terrorism Act, 1997. Official sources confirmed that the two organisations had started activities under the name new of TAJK.

Jamaat-ud-Da'wah operates several websites (in Urdu, Arabic and English); publishes periodicals and books; and distributes tapes of Hafiz Muhammad Saeed for propaganda. It has a monthly in Urdu called *Ud-Da'wah*, distributed in about 80,000 copies. The organization also has other periodicals, such as: a weekly in Urdu called *Ghazwa* (an Arabic term meaning 'raid'); a monthly in English called *Voice of Islam*; another monthly in English (albeit with an Urdu name) called *Idara Khidmat-e-Khalq*; an Arabic-language monthly called *Al-Rabat*; an Arabic-language periodical named *Al-Anfal*; a students' monthly in Urdu; and a weekly in Urdu called *Jihad Times*. There are also various periodicals which can be downloaded from the organization's websites: a magazine named *Zarb-e-Taiba* (Strike of Madinah) in Urdu; a women's magazine called *Taibat* (The Women of Madinah); a monthly called *Bab Al-Islam* (The Gate of Islam); and a monthly named *Rawdat Al-Atfal* (The Kindergarten).

Contrived Means of Financial Support

It was reported in 2013 that the Punjab provincial administration, led by Sharif's Pakistan Muslim League – Nawaz (PML-N), had allocated $6,20,000 to facilities run by the proscribed charity, Jamaat-ud-Da'wah (JuD). The funds were allocated to the JuD/LeT's Markaz-e-Taiba for the fiscal year 2013-14. This was not the first time the Punjab government has allocated funds for the banned but still operational JuD charity. In June 2010, the government had allocated a grant of $8,06,000 for schools, a mosque, hospital and other health facilities inside the Muridke campus and another grant of $30,000 for JuD's Al-Dawa school network across Punjab (AFP, June 17, 2010). To the chagrin of India, the Punjab government came forward with a justification of its new grant to the JuD. The Punjab government said that it had already taken administrative control of the JuD's facility in 2008 following the proscription of the JuD and the budgetary allocations were needed to continue services being provided to people through welfare institutions like the dispensaries, hospitals and schools of the Markaz. JuD spokesman Yahya Mujahid also claimed that the funds were not placed in the JuD's own account and that the Pakistani judiciary had cleared JuD of all past allegations, leaving it free to carry on its work for the Pakistani people. The government takeover and appointment of Khaqan Babar as administrator of the Markaz-e-Taiba was considered to be a face-saving measure for Pakistan. Little changed on the ground, however.

In January 2017, Pakistan had submitted a report to the FATF, scripting down the points through which it plans to bring the country into compliance with the United Nations Security Council Resolution 1267 and order states to impose sanctions against designated terrorist groups. However, no strong measures were taken.

A Specific Utility of the LeT for the ISI

As we know, the Deobandi *tanzeems* in Pakistan have been attacking Shias, and sufi shrines etc. By the time of writing this book in September 2017, the last such attack was on February 16, 2017 at the famous shrine of Lal Shahbaz Qalandar in Sehwan, Sindh in a suicide bombing, killing about 90 and injuring about 300. Such attacks are a great pain in the neck for the Pakistan government because it speaks very poorly of the security environment in the country. Understanding this anti-*Munafiqin* violence perpetrated by the Deobandi groups is critical to understanding the specific utility of the LeT for the ISI and the Government of Pakistan. In contrast to the Deobandi groups, the LeT does not fight in Pakistan and does not target Pakistanis. In its manifesto titled *"Hum Kyon Jihad Kar Rahen Hain?"* (Why Are We Waging Jihad), the author explains why it is that LeT does not wage jihad in Pakistan instead of Kashmir and other venues in the Muslim world where Muslims are oppressed. It clearly says that the LeT is committed to the integrity of Pakistan. The author says that Pakistanis who are Muslim are all brothers irrespective of their sectarian leanings and that Barelvis, Sufis or Shia should not be attacked. He argues that Kafirs outside of Pakistan (Hindus, Jews, Christians, atheists, etc) are at war with Muslims and should be attacked. The author urges all Muslims to fight the Kafirs.

In a way, it is the only organization that actively challenges the Deobandi orthodoxy that has imperilled the state of law and order in the country. While Islam has been beset with sectarian disputes and violence since centuries, this is one line of thought with which many people in Pakistan who are tired of the violence, can easily identify. Identifying a common enemy and exhorting to fight against him, even if it cannot address the fundamental reasons of the intra-Islamic schism, may make some of them put their differences aside for the time being. It needs no explanation that it is music to the ISI's ears even though it complicates Pakistan's external relations with India, the United States and others.

OPERATIONAL LATITUDE GIVEN TO THE LeT AND CLEVER DESIGNS OF THE ISI

Officially, Pakistan denies any connection with LeT activities. However, the fact remains that the ISI allows it to operate with immunity from Pakistan's soil and supports and protects them. Legal actions taken against them are often reduced to farcicalities. Pakistan might be condemning terrorism per se; it does not condemn LeT activities – if questioned, particularly after the 26/11 attack, they start demanding legal proof.

In fact, over the years, as their financial dependence on the ISI has decreased, their functional autonomy has increased proportionately. Today, for example, LeT relies on the ISI primarily for safe haven and political protection for its leadership, intelligence on selected targets and threats, campaign guidance when necessary, and infiltration assistance, particularly in regard to long distance operations involving transits through third countries. Ashley Tellis also confirmed in his *Congressional Testimony* that most LeT operations against India today do not require the other forms of assistance that was needed during the early years.

As long as they are operating within the bounds of the broad strategy of striking India by any means, LeT operations can be undertaken with minimal reference to the ISI provided sufficient care is taken to ensure that these attacks cannot be readily attributed to the ISI, the Pakistani Army, or formally to the Pakistani State. Plausible deniability must never be lost sight of – that's the Cardinal Principle. Thus the ISI control is now more or less, a directive control rather than detailed control. This comes with a clear rider, though – no action must be foolish enough to provoke India into launching a war.

PORTENTS FOR INDO-PAK RELATIONS

To a casual observer, it would appear that LeT activities pose a major hindrance in the normalization of relations between India and Pakistan. However, there is a fallacy in the belief. It would mean that when the LeT was not there, our relations had to be normal. But, as we know, it has not been so. This means that the LeT and its activities are but a current manifestation of all those forces and entities within Pakistan existing and thriving since long, that stand to profit from continued hostility with India for their existence, sustenance and furtherance – be it the Pakistani

Army, the ISI; the politicians; the influential elite and anybody else who think that anti-India sentiments are the leitmotif and lifeblood of Pakistan.

Since sentiments are not amenable to cold reasoning, they would not be effaced by international opprobrium, sanctions, and inducements or even bullying by the USA – on the contrary, there is a chance that they could get even exacerbated in reaction. Ashley Tellis also admitted in his *Congressional Testimony:*

> "Ten years and many billions of dollars in military and economic assistance later, we have to admit – with deep regret – that our efforts to wean Pakistan away from its obsession with India and away from fomenting terrorism to satisfy this obsession have failed."

If the LeT is an existential threat for India, it is an existential asset for Pakistan. From a policy perspective, the sooner we understand this, the better.

All the actions which they take, would ensure that their real operation on India is not harmed – they would target only those terrorist groups that threaten its own security (such as the Tehrik-i-Taliban Pakistan) while a quiet run is allowed to the LeT. They will continue to make a pretence of imposing restrictions, house-arrest etc; but let the 'real' activities continue.

And that's not the end of it. They have to harass India and yet not harass so much that India would go to war. What marvellous equipoise – the most experienced demi-vierge would be put to shame! It is almost like regulating the reaction rate and heat output in a nuclear reactor. The controllers of the terrorist groups have hitherto successfully ensured that there is no meltdown in the reactor of India-Pakistan relationship even as it has been often coming dangerously close to it! The moment they slip on the tightrope, it will be curtains for them. The ISI may not know anything else but they know the Red Line.

WHY THE ISI DOES NOT ARM OR TRAIN THEM VERY WELL?

There is a reason for it. This too relates to the delicate balancing game they are playing. The ISI does not want terrorists who are very proficient in the job. The primary objective is 'modulating' the violence – never, ever let it go beyond a limit – eschew all desire to do something of orgasmic proportions. It is for this reason that the ISI would not give them MANPADS or even 81 mm mortars. The MANPADS would enable them to shoot aircrafts, civil or military. The 81 mm mortar or anything bigger than that like the 107 mm MBRL rocket would enable them to fire at installations from a safe distance and disappear. India would not tolerate such things.

This also explains why, even as the ISI is capable of arming them well and even training them well; the terrorists have been repeatedly found professionally very poor as combatants. Generally, most people are not aware but the fact is that the training of the terrorists leaves much to be desired. In most of the attacks which they have made in India, they have not been able to properly exploit the weaponry at their disposal.

These guys are so dumb that they have been firing RPG-7 on houses where it cannot do anything. They hold PK machineguns in hands as if they were rifles and have never used them in the designated role of a machinegun. The terrorists in Kashmir have yet to learn proper use of IEDs – the self-taught Naxals, on the other hand, are doing much better with a daisy-chain of as many as 179-192 IEDs (May 2011, Lohardaga, Jharkhand), perhaps the longest in the world to their credit. Once upon a time, the ISI used to give them Motorola MC14536B chip-based programmable timers in which the leads were prominently marked A, B, C and D so that no one goofed it up. Not only that, the circuitry was permanently encased in sealing wax so that nobody could fiddle with it. In fact, the terrorists (and the equally ignorant security forces), used to call it ABCD timer! The terrorists in Kashmir have yet to lay a proper ambush – once again the Naxals do it much better.

Usually, they hurriedly open automatic fire on large and vulnerable targets like buses carrying soldiers and then try to run for their lives. Even in the usual urban combat situation, the vast amount of ammunition at their disposal remains often under-utilized and it is not unusual for a dead terrorist to be found with some 100-200 rounds still intact with him. Those who had attacked the Chhatrapati Shivaji Terminus (58 killed), Taj hotel (31 killed) and Oberoi Trident (30 killed) in Mumbai on 26/11, could have inflicted far greater casualties if they had known their job better. The attackers had carried AK rifles with 7 magazines each, 9 mm pistols with two clips of ammunition each, and hand grenades (8 to 10 grenades each, according to one report). Five IEDs were also found. Each device reportedly contained the high explosive RDX, ball bearings to create shrapnel, a digital timer, and a 9-volt battery. Two were left behind in taxis used by the attackers, and three others were left at other locations along their route. The two devices left in the taxis exploded. The others failed or were rendered safe by Indian bomb disposal squads.

The terrorists have actually no idea of urban combat. Most of them fight from their natural reactions, not from acquired responses. It all reflects on poor training. The Naxals who have definitely inferior weaponry, do inflict more casualties on the forces. I have reasons to suspect that their poor capabilities are deliberate. The ISI does not teach them to be good combatants because then they could actually cause so many casualties which would be unacceptably provocative to India. Some idea of the poor state of training can be had from the interrogation of Muhammad Naveed Yakub who was captured alive by villagers he had taken hostage in Jammu's Udhampur during an ambush on a BSF convoy on August 5, 2015. Rajesh Ahuja reported in the *Hindustan Times* that, as told by Yakub, novice jihadis get to fire just 100 rounds from an AK-47, five light machine gun rounds and 10 rounds from a pistol as well as shown how to handle hand grenades. This is ridiculous to say the least, particularly when viewed in the light of the fact that they are made to wake up at 3:30 AM. The emphasis throughout the day, stretching up to 19 hours is on religious indoctrination, prayers and physical fitness, besides GPS and map-reading, etc. There is nothing on the science of combat per se.

USA'S FAILURE TO COMPREHEND PAKISTAN'S TIGHTROPE WALKING

Pakistan has been very deftly playing a very delicate balancing game – walking on razor's edge would actually pale before it. All these years they have been holding out lollypops to the Americans. They have been playing on American expectations that a fundamental shift in their deviously complex strategy is in the offing – obviously, so as to avoid sacrificing the large quantity of US assistance that the Americans are compelled to offer for geopolitical reasons. If the Americans are not able to see through this charade, this speaks volumes about their comprehension and/or their intent. Pakistan might be genuinely scared of India's military might; from this it does not follow that giving more military assistance or some other form of assistance to Pakistan would make it abandon its covert operation against India.

Christine Fair in her 2011 Testimony *Lashkar-e-Taiba beyond Bin Laden: Enduring Challenges for the Region and the International Community* prepared for the US Senate, Foreign Relations Committee says,

> "The widely-held explanation for Pakistan's reliance upon LeT and a raft of other Islamist militants as a response to its enduring rivalry with India over the disputed territory of Kashmir specifically and deep neuralgic fears about Indian intentions towards Pakistan more generally results in policy

> recommendations that stress resolution of the enduring rivalry between India and Pakistan as a necessary if insufficient condition for Pakistan to strategically abandon its Islamist proxies. Inevitably, calls are made for international intervention to encourage both sides to reach some accommodation.... A resolution of the Indo-Pakistan dispute – howsoever improbable in the first instance – will not be sufficient to motivate Pakistan to strategically abandon LeT. Moreover, Pakistan's reliance upon LeT will deepen as Pakistan's internal security situation further deteriorates."

In my view, the concern about Pakistan's internal security situation is exaggerated. If the internal security situation worsens in Pakistan, they can always blame India and its alleged covert operations.

For the simple reason that their covert operation is so cost-effective, it would be foolish for the ISI to abandon it as long as they can walk the tight rope. In comparison to the back-breaking expenditure on conventional military hardware and the possible frightening consequences of a war that could well turn nuclear, the covert business of making India bleed, both economically and psychologically through terrorism is so utterly cheap that few can resist the temptation.

In spite of certain attacks in the world in which the involvement of LeT was suspected (including the 'shoe bomber' Richard Colvin Reid of Britain, trying to take a little amount of explosive in his shoes on a Paris-Miami flight in 2001; attempted attacks in Australia in 2003; and the July 2005 London bombings), I am of the firm opinion that of all the countries in the world, India must worry the most about LeT. They might be capable of doing something somewhere else in the world; in India, they are capable of doing very many things and to deadly effect. It is for us to protect ourselves; the USA will not come here to protect us, nor will their actions taken in Washington will be of much help.

5

Jaish-e-Muhammad: Terror Came Home to Roost

FORMATION OF THE JAISH-E-MUHAMMAD (JeM)

The Jaish-e-Muhammad (literally "The Army of Muhammad" and abbreviated usually as JeM) is active in Kashmir. Its founder Maulana Masood Azhar, originally a native of Bahawalpur, was earlier associated with the Harkat-ul-Ansar. The generally accepted notion is that the ISI took Masood Azhar along to create the JeM.

Ahmed Rashid claims in his book *Descent into Chaos: The US and the Disaster in Pakistan, Afghanistan, and Central Asia* that the JeM was formed in 2000 by ISI and Maulana Masood Azhar in the aftermath of the hijacking of the Air India flight IC-814 to Kandahar. Christine Fair in her article "Bringing back the Dead: Why Pakistan Used the Jaish-e-Muhammad to Attack an Indian Airbase" in *The Huffington Post*, and Bruce Riedel in his article "Blame Pakistani Spy Service for Attack on Indian Air Force Base" also claim that the ISI created Jaish-e-Muhammad by working with several Deobandi terrorists associated with Harkat-ul-Ansar/Harkat-ul-Mujahideen. This is an excellent illustration of the complicated game which the ISI has been playing with such consummate finesse, aplomb and élan for so long. On one hand, they patronize the LeT, an Ahl-e-Hadis group; on the other hand, they patronize JeM, a Deobandi group too and use them for a common objective! Even the CIA has never displayed such masterful adroitness.

After his release, Azhar had reportedly wished to create a conglomerate of all jihadi groups but failed. He had also developed differences with Maulana Fazlur Rehman Khalil, which finally led to the launch of Jaish which was created out of the Harkat cadre loyal to Azhar – reckoned to be almost three-fourth of the total strength. His links with the Taliban were well-established during the hijack drama. In an article, "From Imprisonment to Freedom", soon after his release, Azhar says that he was greeted by Maulvi Muhammad Akhtar Usmani, the Kandahar corps commander of Taliban at the foot of the stairs.

According to Rohit Honawar's paper in the "IPCS Special Report", the JeM was established on February 4, 2000 at a congregation at Masjid Falal in Karachi. It is also said that by 2003, JeM had undergone a split into the so-called Khuddam ul-Islam (KuI), led by Azhar and Jamaat ul-Furqan (JuF), led by Abdul Jabbar. Not much is known about them and whether they are really existing or not. In any case, in practice, we hear of the JeM only. More realistically, I believe, it could be a simple trick to avoid the legal hassles of a banned organization. It is believed that organizations like the Convoy of Mercy, Al Hadid, Muslim Brotherhood, Al Faran Al Jihad, Mujahideen E-Tanzeem, Muhammad's Army, National Movement for the Restoration of Pakistani Sovereignty, Army of the Prophet and Tehrik-ul-Furqaan have had been created to serve the same purpose.

It is also believed that for convenience of obtaining funds and having a medium to deal with the mainstream society, they are aligned with Jamiat Ulema-e-Islam (JUI). The JUI is also known as JUIF faction, the 'F' standing for the initial of its leader Maulana Fazlur Rehman (a politician). The other faction JUIS is led by Samiul Haq. The JUIF is a Sunni Deobandi political party in Pakistan. The party claims that it had carved itself out of the Jamiat Ulema-e-Hind (JUH) in pre-partition India to demand the creation of Pakistan, alongside the Muslim League.

MASOOD AZHAR, THE MAN, AND WHY HE IS VALUED SO MUCH BY THE TERRORISTS?

Born in a family of ten siblings with a dairy and a poultry farm, it would be interesting to know how he became what he became. In *Fazail-e-Jihad* (The Virtues of Jihad), one of the seven books believed to have been written by him, Azhar reveals that his father had Deobandi leanings and was extremely religious. He wrote,

> "One of my father's friends, Mufti Sayeed, was working as a teacher at the Jamia Uloom-ul-Islamia at the Binori/Banuri Mosque in Karachi. He prevailed upon my father to admit me in the Jamia."

Azhar joined the Binori madrisa and this was his first contact with the jihadi movement. He continued his studies in the madrisa, received the degree of 'alim' and was soon given a teaching assignment in the madrisa. Leaders of the Harkat-ul-Ansar enjoyed a great influence on the madrisa and many of the students had even joined the Afghan jihad. Azhar, too, got involved. Azhar recalled,

> "A leader of Harkat-ul-Ansar, Commander Akhtar, had come to invite the principal of the madrisa to visit Afghanistan. The principal, Mufti Ahmadur Rahman, suggested that Maulana Masood Azhar should also participate in the training course of jihad."

However, being physically weak, Azhar is said to have failed in completing his 40-days military training at a Harkat camp at Yavar in Afghanistan. Nevertheless, he joined the war against the Russians and was injured. After he suffered injuries, Azhar was chosen as the head of Harkat's Department of Motivation and became an editor for the Urdu-language *Sad'e Mujahideen* and the Arabic-language *Sawte Kashmir*. He also came close to Maulana Fazlur Rehman Khalil, the man who had co-founded Harkat-ul-Jihad-ul-Islami (HuJI) in 1980 with Irshad Ahmad and Qari Saifullah Akhtar – all the three were graduates of the Jamia Uloom-ul-Islamia. He would later go on to found and lead Harkat-ul-Mujahedeen (HuM). Khalil was a signatory of Osama bin Laden's 1998 fatwa called the International Front Against Jews and Crusaders.

Azhar later became the general secretary of Harkat-ul-Ansar. By this time, he was recognized as the best orator of the group. He visited many international locations to recruit, to raise funds and to spread the message of Pan-Islamism. Among his destinations were Zambia, Abu Dhabi, Saudi Arabia, Mongolia, the United Kingdom and Albania. Azhar confessed that in 1993 he travelled to Nairobi to meet with leaders of Al-Itihaad Al-Islamiya, an Al-Qaida-aligned Somali group, who had requested money and recruits from Harkat-ul-Mujahideen. It is believed that he made at least three trips to Somalia and that he also helped bring Yemeni mercenaries to Somalia.

BBC News had reported in April 2016 that, in August 1993, Azhar had entered the UK for a speaking, fundraising, and recruitment tour. His message of jihad was given at some of Britain's most prestigious Islamic institutions including the Darul Uloom Bury seminary, Zakariya Mosque, Madina Masjid in Blackburn and Burnley, and Jamia Masjid. Azhar made contacts in Britain who helped to provide training and logistical support the terror plots including "7/7, 21/7 and the attempt in

2006 to smuggle liquid bomb-making substances on to transatlantic airlines."

The *Kashmir Herald*, in its article on Masood Azhar, writes that Azhar had reportedly infiltrated into India on a brief trip in early 1994 on a 'mission' to ease tensions between Harkat-ul-Ansar's feuding factions of HuJI and HuM. The Harkat factions did merge subsequently but Azhar was arrested in February along with another top commander, Sajjad Afghani and imprisoned. Incidentally, his entry into India was dramatic – unlike most militants he did not cross the Line of Control in Kashmir, may be because of his health issues. In January 1994, he flew into Delhi from Dhaka as a Gujarat-born Portuguese national, Wali Adam Issa. He checked into Hotel Ashok and later shifted to Janpath Hotel, from where he left for Deoband with two Harkat men from Kashmir. He flew to Srinagar and met Harkat's top commanders, Sajjad Afghani and Amjad Bilal, in the Lal Bazaar area of downtown Srinagar. In those days, south Kashmir used to be the hub of Harkat activities and Azhar, along with Afghani, had left to meet their men in the heights of Anantnag. On February 10, 1994, he was nabbed by the security forces along with Sajjad Afghani at Khanabal.

The notorious kidnapping of the five foreign tourists in Kashmir by a hitherto unknown group called Al-Faran (perhaps a purposefully created front of the Harkat for the job) took place in 1995. One of the demands of the kidnappers was the release of Masood Azhar. The demand was not acceded to. Then there was a jail break attempt which was also foiled. Afghani was, however, killed by the police, allegedly in a jail uprising. The repeated attempts to get Azhar freed made it clear that Azhar was someone special to them, a highly prized asset – why, we do not know for sure – perhaps because he is believed to be a particularly good motivator or there is something such about him for which there is no information in the public domain. For a man who, unlike Hafiz Saeed, makes very few public appearances, if his comrades place so much value; there has to be something about him. Knowing that could indeed help us in dealing with him better or in neutralizing him. Then IC-814 happened and the world changed.

TERROR COMES HOME TO ROOST

Masood was one of the three terrorists released by India in the wake of the hijacking of IC-814, namely, Maulana Masood Azhar, Ahmed Omar Saeed Sheikh and Mushtaq Ahmed Zargar, all imprisoned in India. Ahmed Omar Saeed Sheikh is a British-educated Pakistani. He was arrested in 1994 in Ghaziabad, in connection with the kidnapping of three British and one American tourist from New Delhi. Mushtaq Zargar alias Latrum was a Kashmiri. According to Azhar, they had first met in the Tihar jail. This friendship eventually got Zargar out of jail. Sheikh Omar, a former London School of Economics student, was to later become instrumental in the launch of Azhar's new group Jaish-e-Muhammad.

Yaniv Barzilai says in his book *102 Days of War: How Osama bin Laden, Al-Qaida and the Taliban Survived 2001* that the three above mentioned released terrorists were escorted to Pakistan by the ISI. The ISI is said to have paraded Masood Azhar on a victory tour through Pakistan to raise money for the new organisation. Zahid Hussain reported in abcnews.com that shortly after his release, Azhar made a public address to an estimated 10,000 people in Karachi. He proclaimed, "I have come here because this is my duty to tell you that Muslims should not rest in peace until we have destroyed India," vowing to liberate the Kashmir region from Indian rule.

Azhar, in a write-up in *International Mujahid*, spoke about the strategic benefits of his alliance with the Kashmiri terrorist

Zargar. Zargar also helped Azhar in Pakistan, particularly when the group was facing internecine struggles. Moreover, Zargar's Al-Umar outfit had a very strong network across the Valley, especially in downtown Srinagar, his home. No wonder then that his first suicide bomber, Afaq Ahmad, was a class 12 student from downtown Srinagar. In May 2000, this 17-year-old schoolboy drove an explosive-laden car into the 15 Corps HQ at Badamibagh Cantonment, Srinagar. It was not just the first suicide bombing in Kashmir; it was the beginning of a new phase of terrorism in Kashmir. It launched Jaish-e-Muhammad's activities in India and announced that its founder, Maulana Masood Azhar, who was released in exchange of the crew and passengers of the hijacked IC-814 at Kandahar in the January of that year, was back in business. Later, the same year on Christmas Day, a 24-year-old British cadre of the Jaish blew up another explosive-laden car, again at the 15 Corps HQ gate. The bomber was subsequently profiled in the official Jaish publication *Zarb-e-Momin*. This was followed by the deadly car bombing attack on the Legislative Assembly in Srinagar in 2001 in which 38 people were killed. The Jaish-e-Muhammad claimed responsibility within hours, and in an unusual step, identified the suicide bomber as Wajahat Hussain, a Pakistani national.

OBJECTIVES OF THE JeM

A giant mural over the entrance of the Jaish-e-Muhammad's headquarters at Bahawalpur reads "To Delhi, O Hindus, the army of the Prophet will soon return." Well, that says it all. While the Lashkar could possibly have aspirations outside India too, Jaish is totally Kashmir/India-centric. The objective is to 'liberate' Kashmir and merge it with Pakistan – never mind the cost or the feasibility. In his book *Fath-ul-Jawad* (Victory of the Bountiful/Tremendously Generous), Azhar writes,

> "The life of nations depends on martyrs. The national fields can be irrigated only with the blood of the best hearts and minds."

They are not very clear about what they want to do with the rest of India though Azhar has made occasional references to the Babri Masjid, Delhi and Amritsar and the destruction of India. He has also spoken of the destruction of Israel and America for having violated the rights of the Muslims. Anyway, it only shows that they are not short of pompous words and the education had been indeed good – the question is what they are actually capable of?

CURRENT STATUS

It is reckoned by the US State Department that the Jaish should have several hundred cadres located mainly in Pakistan Occupied Kashmir (POK), Pakistan and India's southern Kashmir and Doda regions. The cadres come mainly from Multan, Bahawalpur and Rahim Yar Khan Districts, and many from Punjab. The JeM is closely associated with the Binori/Banuri Town Mosque and Jamia Uloom-ul-Islamia. It is a Deobandi school with about 12,000 students, founded by Maulana Yusuf Binori soon after independence in 1947. It has been described by the International Crisis Group as the "fountainhead of Deobandi militancy" in Pakistan, due to the madrisa playing a major role in helping establish and sustain a number of jihadi organisations, including HuM, JeM, and Sipah-e-Sahaba Pakistan (SSP). Masood Azhar himself is an alumnus of this school; other notable alumni include Mullah Omar, Fazlur Rehman Khalil of Harkat-ul-Mujahideen, and Abdul Aziz Ghazi of the Lal Masjid.

Their training camps were earlier (that is, till 2001) in Afghanistan but subsequently, they relocated to Balakot, in the

North West Frontier province, Peshawar and in parts of Pakistan Occupied Kashmir (POK), such as Muzaffarabad.

THE FARCE OF ACTION AGAINST JeM IN PAKISTAN

In the wake of the India-Pakistan face-off during Operation Parakram following the Parliament attack, the United States, annoyed with the dilution of the War on Terror as well as the threat of an Indo-Pakistani war, delivered an ultimatum to Musharraf, asking him to make "a clear statement to the world that he intends to crack down on terror". Pushed to a corner, Musharraf announced on 12 January 2002 that no organisation would be allowed to indulge in terrorism in the name of Kashmir. He declared a ban on five extremist groups including the JeM. Hundreds of militants were rounded up, states Ahmed Rashid (the author of *Descent into Chaos*), giving rise to severe hostility and derision from them. However, by March 2002, all the arrested militants were freed and curbs on them were quietly lifted. Financial and intelligence inputs to JeM were resumed. Masood Azhar was detained for a year by the Pakistani authorities but was never formally charged. However, as the BBC News reported in December 2002, the Lahore High Court ordered an end to the house arrest on 14 December 2002, much to the chagrin of India.

Media sources (such as Praveen Swami in *The Indian Express*) claimed that the so-called split within the JeM took place because Maulana Abdul Jabbar had begun pushing for attacks on Western targets. In 2003, it was suspected that some cadres of JeM along with those of Lashkar-e-Jhangvi and some foreigners were involved in two attacks on Gen Musharraf himself as he was perceived to be acting under American pressure against terrorists. JeM cadres were also suspected to be involved in the siege of the Lal Masjid. For some time, therefore, Masood Azhar and JeM went into hibernation.

Another attack on a pro-Western target was the kidnapping and murder of the American journalist Daniel Pearl. Pearl was investigating alleged connections between a radical Pakistani cleric and the 'shoe bomber' Richard Reid. Omar Sheikh, the mastermind of the kidnapping, set the trap which lured Pearl to his captors. He put the reporter in touch with a man who, he pretended, would introduce him to the extremist Muslim leader whom Pearl wished to interview. The MEA website hosts an article by Najam Sethi, a Pakistani journalist, in the *Friday Times*, titled "Why was Daniel Pearl Killed?" Sethi says that following 9/11, the US had been demanding the arrest and extradition of Ahmed Omar Saeed Sheikh. Consequently, Omar went, or was pushed, underground in order to avoid an extradition that might have 'exposed' the ISI, so to say. Sethi claims that the arrest or detention of Masood Azhar had convinced Omar that his erstwhile Pakistani 'handlers' couldn't be trusted in the circumstances and he should distance himself from them. Omar Sheikh was furious that he had to turn himself in because his family was being harassed by the police. The Pakistanis had thought that if he could be persuaded to help free Pearl quickly it would be a feather in Gen Musharraf's cap when he met President Bush in Washington some days later; if he did not cooperate, he would be better kept under wraps. An agitated Omar lectured his 'handlers' about betraying the cause of jihad and becoming American stooges. When all else failed, he decided to put an end to the ordeal by claiming before a judge that Pearl had already been killed. His statement amounted to a death sentence on Pearl, even if he was not killed by that time. Sethi adds that Pearl had stumbled upon hard-core elements of the Jaish in Karachi and Bahawalpur despite news of the 'mass arrests' of its cadres by the government earlier. The Daniel Pearl episode once again demonstrated that even if you have had been 'controlling' a terrorist organization, you could not take it for granted that they would always do your bidding.

On 7 December 2008, it was claimed that Azhar was among several arrested by the Pakistani government after a military raid on a camp located on the outskirts of Muzaffarabad in connection with the 2008 Mumbai attacks. *The Times of India* reported on December 9, 2008 that he continued to live in Bahawalpur. As reported by the BBC News on December 18, 2008, Pakistan's government denied it had arrested Masood Azhar and said it was unaware of his whereabouts. On 26 January 2014, Masood Azhar reappeared after a hibernation of six years. He addressed a rally in Muzaffarabad in which, according to the report of *Newsweek Pakistan*, he called for the resumption of jihad in Kashmir.

As reported by the *Dawn* in January 2016, Pakistani authorities again took him into 'protective custody' after the Pathankot attack in India, which was widely reported by channels like Geo News as an 'arrest'. Praveen Swami reported for *The Indian Express* (January 15, 2016) that Jaish-e-Muhammad had rejected claims that its leader Maulana Masood Azhar had been arrested for his alleged role in the terror strike on the Pathankot airbase. The statement came amidst a series of confusing comments by Pakistani officials on reports of Azhar's arrest. Khalilullah Qazi, spokesperson for Pakistan's Ministry of Foreign Affairs, said he was "not aware of such an arrest". Earlier, Prime Minister Nawaz Sharif's office had issued a statement saying,

> "several individuals belonging to Jaish-e-Muhammad have been apprehended. The offices of the organisation are also being traced and sealed".

The *Hindustan Times* reported in April 2016 that Azhar was seen to be free. And thus the game of pampering in private and chastising in public continues.

As for action on its finances, it is believed that in anticipation of asset seizures by the Pakistani Government, JeM had withdrawn funds from bank accounts and invested in legal businesses, such as commodity trading, real estate, and production of consumer goods.

International Action against the JeM and the Chinese Stonewall

JeM has been designated as a terrorist organisation by Pakistan, Australia, Canada, India, the United Kingdom and the United States. After the attack on the IAF base in Pathankot, India wrote to the UN in February and called for immediate action to list Azhar under the Al-Qaida Sanctions Committee. UN Sanction Committee's listing would force imposition of freezing of assets and travel ban on Azhar by countries including Pakistan.

In April 2016, the Chinese government blocked a UN Security Council Sanctions Committee listing of Azhar as a terrorist, thwarting international efforts to disrupt the activities of his group. China moved to protect Azhar again in October 2016 when it blocked India's appeal to the United Nations to label him as a terrorist. The US and other members of the UN Security Council had sought action against Azhar by including him in the 1267 Sanctions Committee list but the move was first put on a technical hold and later formally blocked by China. China had defended its second technical hold to prevent a UN ban on Pakistan-based JeM chief Masood Azhar saying there were 'different views' on India's application and that Beijing's move will allow more time for the 'relevant parties' to have consultations. When India reacted to this development, the Chinese Foreign Ministry said the listing application member states submitted to the 1267 Committee of UN 'must comply' with specific requirements of relevant resolutions of UN Security Council (UNSC).

As reported by *The Indian Express* on December 30, 2016, much to India's chagrin, China yet again blocked a proposal at the United Nations to list Jaish-e-Muhammad's chief Masood

Azhar as a global designated terrorist. India has accused China of pursuing double standards on terror as it asserted that 14 out of the 15 UNSC members were in support of a ban on Azhar. The latest act in this series, by the time of writing this book, was in February 2017 when China blocked the US move to get Masood Azhar banned by UN. The Chinese action came just before the expiry of the 10-day deadline for a proposal to be adopted, blocked or put on hold. The 'hold' remains for six months and can be further extended by three months. During this period, it can be anytime converted into a 'block', thereby, ending the life of the proposal.

JAISH'S REAL CAPABILITIES: FACT VERSUS FICTION

B Raman, in his paper for the *South Asia Analysis Group*, describes Jaish as the 'deadliest' and "the principal terrorist organisation in Jammu and Kashmir". It is maintained in the media and the circle of the so-called analysts that they are known for 'spectacular attacks', as was very much evident in the Pathankot Airbase attack case. In other words, the Jaish is projected as some sort of particularly bright Special Force in the pantheon of terrorist organizations – capable of doing what others cannot do so.

A professional analysis of their attacks does not support any of these notions or beliefs – they are just over-effusive, unsubstantiated observations of the un-critical. Jaish terrorists are only as good or bad as other terrorists. Spectacular does not necessarily translate into professionally sound. Moreover, that it is a small force, does not mean that it is necessarily a crack force. The point being made is that the terrorists of Jaish or any other group could indeed do better and cause more discomfort to us. Their incompetence, their stupidity should not be any solace to us. Today they are dumb, tomorrow they could be deadlier. We must prepare for the worst-case scenario – one in which the terrorist really know their job.

Analysis of the Parliament Attack Case

The Parliament attack was a daring one, but executed in a most unprofessional manner. As I have shown below, analysts like Bruce Riedel in *Deadly Embrace: Pakistan, America and the Future of the Global Jihad* were unnecessarily alarmist and sensation-seeking when they described it as an 'extraordinary attack'. No, it was not – there was nothing extraordinary in it.

On December 13, 2001, five terrorists infiltrated the Parliament House in a car on the strength of Home Ministry and Parliament labels which managed to befool the security personnel there. Upon entering, they started racing towards one of the gates of the building. The car of the terrorists happened to collide with the rear of a car in the carcade of the Indian Vice-President. That seems to have upset their plans and confound them. Then they got out, and began firing. The Vice-President's guards and a large number of security personnel present in the campus shot back at the terrorists. All of them were killed before they could enter the Parliament building. Five policemen, a Parliament security guard, and a gardener were killed, and 18 others were injured. No MP was hurt.

As reported by S Chakravarty in the *India Today*, the terrorists had four AK rifles with Urdu markings and green stickers thereon, 15 hand grenades, one grenade launcher, three 7.62 mm pistols, 15 kg plastic explosive, 12 spare magazines, two IEDs and 30 detonators made in Pakistan's Wah Nobel factory. They were also claimed to have planned the attack meticulously for eight months.

In my considered opinion, daring though the attack was, a simple analysis shows that the execution of the strike was not all commensurate with the claimed planning and resources. Yes, they managed to gain entry by deception. Once again it shows how an officious appearance can defeat the system. But obviously, they had no idea of what to do afterwards. Their plan went haywire from the moment their car had a small accident with one of the cars inside the Parliament. There was no contingency plan or consideration of various situations that could have arisen. A simple accident upset their plans and confounded them completely. They went by their natural reactions and came out and started firing. Now what it was supposed to accomplish? Were they not aware that there shall be plenty of armed guards to return fire and they had no cover or protection at all – they were as exposed as they could be. Obviously, they were going to get killed before they reached anywhere.

Then the question is, what they could have done even if one or more of them had, by sheer luck, survived the shooting and raced to the main building of the Parliament. Mind it, the Parliament is huge and a complex building. For anyone who is entering there for the first time, it is extremely difficult to find his way in that maze. There was no evidence that they had detailed layout plans of the interiors of the building, even if they had as many as 21 photos of the exterior, as reported by D Kumar in the *Outlook*. One who did not have layout plans of a building such as the Parliament was, could only hope to shoot at anything that came in sight – it would have been extremely difficult to do anything with a larger objective of reaching inside and taking hostages. As we know, both the Rajya Sabha and the Lok Sabha had been adjourned 40 minutes before the incident. If the plan was to take hostages, they should have known as to how many people would be present at a given place at a given point of time through some means. A professional attack is not simply a matter of collecting a bunch of guys willing to lay down their lives and unleashing them.

They should have known that even if their car would have reached as far as it could go without being questioned anywhere, the moment they got out of the car, their appearance and weapons would betray them. They were likely to have been fired at immediately. I mean, they could not have casually, leisurely just climbed the stairs and strolled inside with their weapons. Had they tried to jump out and make a dash for it, it would have made them all the more conspicuous. Gaining entry into the campus by deception was possible given the loopholes in the system; doing anything else by deception was not possible.

They were claimed to be meticulous enough to keep dry fruits worth ₹2,000 to keep them going in a hostage-taking situation. But, given the number of armed security personnel in the premises, how they would have reached that stage, particularly when they had no idea of how to identify the MPs; who was where; and whom to take hostage? If the purpose was just to inflict casualties on anybody who came in sight irrespective of whether he was an MP or not, they should not have bothered about making a dash for the main building. They could have fired from the moving car itself, going round the campus! In fact, they could have done a bit of improvised armouring of the car also beforehand for such a situation. Firing from the open, without any protective cover at all, was nothing but utterly foolish.

6

Financing of Terrorism

TERRORISTS' NEED FOR A RELIABLE CASH STREAM

Terrorism is a cost-intensive affair. Execution of terrorist activities requires a reliable cash stream. In terrorist organizations, the peripheral operational wings need a continuous flow of funds and material resources from the core for their sustenance and execution of plans. Even the synchronized suicide attacks of September 11th, infamous for their crude simplicity, cost between four to five hundred thousand dollars, or about half a million dollars! According to the FBI, the hijackers had to engage in fundraising in order to carry out the attacks.

According to Gil Feiler of the Begin-Sadat Centre for Strategic Studies, Israel, the combined annual budget of Islamic terror groups in the decade 1995-2005 had hovered around the $1 billion mark – or about $100 million per annum. Now, with the advent of the ISIS flush with innovative sources of money including control of oil and gas reservoirs, banks, and robbery of economic assets besides the 'conventional' methods used since long, it must have increased dramatically. According to a US Intelligence report cited by Stephen Tankel in a "National Security Studies Program Policy Paper", the LeT alone had a military budget of more than $5 million by 2009.

From procuring weapons and explosives from the international illicit arms bazaar to training the cadres; housing them safely and often paying them; collecting intelligence on the targets; despatching the cadres to the place of action and retrieving them if it was not a suicidal operation; and taking care of the families of those who get killed in action, everything costs money. Jean-Charles Brisard, a French international consultant and expert on terrorism, has shown in his report on the financing of terrorism prepared for the President of the Security Council of the United Nations, that 90% of terror financing goes toward general maintenance of cells and equipment. Less than 10% actually finances the execution of operations. Most of the above operations took a number of years to plan. Therefore the real total cost of funding the operational cells and the operation should be multiplied by, at the very least, a factor of 20.

To complicate matters, the money needs to be raised on the sly. And that too must come from several sources. Depending on only one source makes the operation potentially vulnerable to action by the law enforcement agencies of the states. Moreover, the sheer scale at which money is required is difficult to come from legitimate businesses unless it is a case of state sponsoring of terrorism. But even in the case of state sponsoring of terrorism, the governments or intelligence agencies concerned would not like the money to be spent in such a manner which could be traced back to the government coffers.

Hence terrorists all over the world tap into different streams of financial resources ranging from something as innocuous as *zakat* to something as heinous as proceeds of organized crime. Since organized crime can easily yield the kind of money which the terrorist need, the worlds of terror financing and international crime are often inextricable. Till such time that a terrorist attack occurs, the practical distinction between terrorists and criminals is rather slight. All this makes keeping track of terror financing a very difficult task. In view of such complexities, it needs no emphasis that only by truly understanding how terrorist and insurgent groups raise money, and how these funds are spent; can states and governments begin to formulate a strategy for countering the financing of terrorism.

COMPLEXITIES INHERENT IN FINANCING OF TERRORISM AND COUNTERING IT

The Fiendish Ways

Islamic terrorism is financed by a global array of individuals, fronts, businesses, banks, criminal enterprises, nominally humanitarian organizations and states. No other form of terrorism or group of terrorists has ever had such global reach and presence. Financial flows take a variety of routes – some complex; some simple; but all are highly evasive. The US Treasury Department's "National Terrorist Financing Risk Assessment" (2015) report provides the details of innovative terror financing and shows that many techniques come with a legal façade.

Terror financing is often an international network drawing on every resource in the global economy and the so-called international global jihad network. Therefore, terror financing is intertwined with money laundering, bogus accounts and skeleton companies stretched across several countries. The bank accounts of the terror financier could be, for example, in a European country; they could be in the name of some American company; he could have transmitted funds to allegedly pay invoices for the services of an Information Technology company with branches in Russia; the invoices could be false; and the money could have been transported to Syria and used for 'other purposes'.

One of the major factors that make financing of terrorism so difficult to crack, is the use of fictitious, shell, and offshore fiduciary companies, which all pose a challenge to those organizations attempting to regulate business transactions and provide terrorists and insurgents with financial safe havens where they can conceal their funds. Companies, funds, entities, or businesses may be got registered in an extraterritorial financial centre, such as International Business Corporations (IBC) which can be used to construct complex financial structures. These entities can be established using bearer shares and do not have to publish accounts. Residents of financial centres can act as fictitious directors or shareholders in order to disguise the genuine directors or owners. These entities are obviously attractive to investors who seek anonymity or wish to carry out their activities beyond the official scrutiny of their national government.

To Starve the Beast

The original idea behind tracking and blocking terrorist funding is, in the words of Lee Hamilton, a former Congressman and vice-chair of the 9/11 Commission, to 'starve the beast', so to say. It is critical to deny money to terrorists and insurgents. Without money, terrorists can neither function as cohesive organizations nor conduct attacks in a concerted manner. This denial can be done by disrupting and destabilizing their financial operations. Employing 'smart financial power' in combating financing of terrorism, means being able to 'follow the money' and conduct sound financial network analysis.

The most direct consequence of such disruption is to force them to expend more effort devoted to financing per se. This, in turn, leaves them with lesser time to train and recruit or to plot, plan, and execute attacks thereby directly affecting their combat power and operational efficiency adversely. As Jacob N Shapiro and David A Siegel (associate professor at the Princeton University, and a businessman respectively) also note in their paper in the *International Studies Quarterly*,

> "Seizing funds and thereby tightening terrorists' budget constraints can increase friction within an organization to

> the point where leaders choose to spend on activities other than attacks."

If the disruptive operations render the funding flow between the core and the periphery stagnant, with no substantial money moving to the periphery, local peripheral cells would be forced to finance their own activities thereby hampering their operations and affecting their operations.

Without belittling the purely combat part of counterterrorist operations in any way, it needs to be kept in mind that while the ability to kill, capture, arrest and prosecute terrorists depends on actionable intelligence and a capable 'kinetic force', terrorist and insurgent groups are not comprised solely of 'shooters'. A well-knit, 'devoted-to-its-cause' terrorist organization is much more than a bunch of fanatics armed with AK-47 rifles and suicide bomb vests ever-ready to kill and get killed. While having a loyal and devoted cadre is critical, the absolute necessity of maintaining functional, operational and existential secrecy – ranging from safe shelter and training; and arranging weapons and explosives; to travel to various destinations – it places severe demands on the organization's finances. Therefore, even as combat is the obviously glamorous part, a purely kinetic approach in counterterrorism will yield only short-term, tactical gains, without any effect on the vital entrails of the beast.

MULTIFARIOUS METHODS OF FUNDING OF ISLAMIC TERRORISM

Islamic Charity

Intrinsic Advantages

Islamic charity (*zakat*) continues to be one of the 'safest' methods of financing of terrorism. It is one of the fundamental duties of the pious. While the amount that can be raised this way is not as high as could come from say, organized crime; there are certain advantages of this method. The first is that it is almost impossible to ban it or control it without raising a furore with serious consequences in the body politic of the country concerned. Second, it is extremely difficult to follow the money trail and determine exactly how it had been spent or how much of it was diverted for 'unholy' purposes. Third, since the funds are raised through a front organization of the terrorists in the name of helping the people of the region where they would be operating (such as Kashmir) or for a purely religious cause, the donors feel rather 'good' about donating. This makes for an indirect 'involvement' of the donors in the 'cause' of the terrorists and, at least in the perception of the donors, the subsequent activities of the terrorists are 'de-criminalized' to some extent. In other words, those who have donated to the front organization of a terrorist group for Islamic charity, subsequently find it difficult to openly criticize the terrorist group for fear of contradicting themselves. Many individuals not directly connected to charities are found collecting funds through their personal bank accounts and transferring funds to terrorist organisations under proper 'cover'.

Charities and the LeT

The JuD and the MDI raise funds throughout Pakistan and the Middle East (especially Saudi Arabia), and even Maldives and Sri Lanka, in the name of Islamic charity. This is one source of funds which is never going to dry up. The gradually resulting measure of financial independence has released the LeT from a purely client-patron relationship with the ISI. This means that if, sometime in the future, the ISI or the Pakistan government try to tighten the screws on them under international or American pressure, the LeT would be able to weather it. The portents for India should be clear.

As for the ostensible utilization of funds thus received, the JuD runs many Islamic centres, schools and religious seminaries, a network of hospitals, orphanages, and charity centres. Their network of schools serves more than 18,000 students. Over 2,000 doctors volunteer their services for the group. In many areas, the services the JuD provides are not available or affordable by other means. These services target impoverished communities whom state services are not able to reach, fostering support for LeT among those Pakistanis. As is well-known, they were especially successful in rendering humanitarian aid, for instance, in the wake of the 2005 earthquake in Muzaffarabad. It is believed that, in effect, they seek to create a parallel system to the civil society by replacing NGOs, human rights groups and humanitarian organizations in Pakistan. To evade government proscription and international scrutiny, JuD established many charity fronts, namely, Idara Khidmat-e-Khalq (IKK) and Falah-e-Insaniyat Foundation (FIF). In the past they have had used umbrella conglomerates like the Tehrik-e-Hurmat-e-Rasool (THR-Movement for Defending the Honour of the Prophet), Tehrik-e-Tahafuz Qibla Awal (TTQA) and Al-Anfal Trust also.

Charity and the JeM

They receive funds through charitable foundations such as Al-Rashid Trust/Al-Rahmat Trust (ART), a trust fund recognized by the US as a financial facilitator of terrorists for raising funds for Al-Qaida and the Taliban in 2001. The Al-Rashid Trust is known to fund JeM and other jihadi groups too. However, the organizational ties between ART and JeM are believed to extend beyond simple funding. The ART might well be a front organization for JeM and other jihadi activities. It is known that the ART had founded the newspaper *Zarb-e-Momin* in the 1990s. *Zarb-e-Momin* is now published as JeM's official newspaper.

Funding by Foreign States

Role of Saudi Arabia and Kuwait

Declan Walsh, journalist and the Cairo bureau chief of *The New York Times*, writing for *The Guardian* has reported that according to a secret December 2009 paper signed by the US Secretary of State (as revealed from the August 2009 cables of the US Embassy in Saudi Arabia), "Saudi Arabia remains a critical financial support base for Al-Qaida, the Taliban, LeT and other terrorist groups." According to Jonathan Fighel, a retired colonel of the IDF and senior Researcher at the International Institute for Counter-Terrorism (ICT), Israel, Saudi Arabia covertly supports and promotes the "Saudi-Wahabi political and religious influence in the Sunni Muslim world" through its worldwide network of charities. LeT is one of the beneficiaries. Bruce Riedel says the Afghan Taliban is also "still getting an awful lot of money from private sources" in the Persian Gulf, as evidenced by the multiple trips former Taliban leader Mullah Akhtar Mansour took to Dubai before he was killed by a US drone strike in Pakistan. In Kuwait, the 'Revival of Islamic Society' has also provided direct support to Al-Qaida and LeT.

Gulf Connection of the LeT

LeT is known to have used a Saudi-based front company to fund its activities in 2005. It is believed that the Gulf link to terror in India is thriving and there are LeT cells operating in the Gulf that have financed and facilitated terrorist operations in India. It may be recalled that following the serial local train blasts in Mumbai, the Anti-Terrorist Squad had seized approximately 37,000 Saudi Riyals from the residences of the LeT's Mumbai cell chief, Faizal Ataur Rehman Sheikh (*The Indian Express*, August 2, 2006). The money reportedly came in two instalments from Saudi Arabia via the hawala network operated by Faizal's London-based brother Rahil Sheikh and another Lashkar operative identified as Rizwan

Ahmed Davre, an IT professional based in Riyadh. Rizwan acted as a conduit between the unidentified Saudi financier, Pakistan-based LeT commander Azam Cheema and Faizal Sheikh. Cheema reportedly designated Davre the *Amir-e-Baitulmaal* (chief exchequer) for his able handling of monetary transactions (*The Indian Express*, October 1, 2006).

Investigations following the 2008 urban terrorist attacks had also uncovered ties to many Gulf hotspots, especially the financial networks in Muscat (Oman). At least four LeT operatives handled India operations from Gulf cities like Muscat and Sharjah. They were identified as Wali (aka Shameem), Muslim Basheer, Sarfaraz Nawaz (aka Hakeem Sarfoor) and Abu Haroon. These four are believed to be of Pakistani origin and to have been deputed in the Gulf to raise funds and monitor operations planned for India. Three other terrorists involved in the July 2008 Bangalore serial blasts and other incidents have been identified as Saleem and Jaheed from Bangladesh (hawala operators) and Ali Abdul Azeez Hooti of Oman, the chief terrorist financier.

Gulf Connection of the JeM

Masood Azhar is on record having toured abroad and collected funds. He was, in fact, caught carrying fake dollars at Jeddah airport during one of these trips. Both Masood Azhar and Fazlur Rehman Khalil were close to Osama bin Laden – Osama was learnt to have been upset when they fell out and separated. Bin Laden helped financially in this split, compensating both. As disclosed by Adnan Rasheed, an air force officer-turned-terrorist sprung by the Taliban from a Bannu jail, the Mansehra training camp near Abbottabad, was set up by Azhar. No wonder, bin Laden was living in Abbottabad for five years so as to be close to the camp he was allegedly funding.

Money Laundering, Hawala and Black Money

Money Laundering

Money laundering is a fundamentally simple concept. It is the process by which proceeds from a criminal activity (such as drugs, arms trafficking, extortion, and black money) are disguised to conceal their illicit origins and the money is then invested in legitimate activities. Money launderers send illicit funds through legal channels in order to conceal their criminal origins. On the other hand, those who finance terrorism transfer funds that may be legal or illicit in origin in such a way as to conceal both their source and ultimate use, which is the support of terrorism. Disguising the source of terrorist financing is important to the extent that it remains available for future terrorist financing activities also.

With regard to money laundering, the International Monetary Fund has estimated that the aggregate amount of funds laundered in the world could range between 2 and 5% of the world's gross domestic product. Even if we do not know how much of it is devoted to financing terrorism, it gives an idea of the enormity of the problem.

The techniques employed for money laundering by terrorist organizations are often the same as those employed by other money launderers. This means that they are liable to be detected and disrupted by the same application of intelligence and investigative techniques which are employed for other money launderers. Havens for money laundering and terrorist financing are found have:

- A weak AML (Anti-Money Laundering)/CFT (Combating Financing of Terrorism) regime;
- Some or many types of financial institutions that are not covered by an AML/CFT framework;

- Little, weak or selective enforcement of AML/CFT provisions;
- Ineffective penalties, including difficult confiscation provisions; and
- A limited number of predicate crimes for money laundering.

From this it follows that a comprehensive and effective AML/CFT framework, together with timely implementation and effective enforcement, on the other hand, can significantly reduce the profitable aspects of this criminal activity and, in fact, discourage criminals and terrorists from 'utilizing a country' for their nefarious activities. This is especially true when the proceeds from criminal activities are aggressively confiscated and forfeited as part of a country's overall AML/CFT legal framework.

The Basics of Hawala

In simple terms, hawala has been defined as "money transfer without money movement". The person wishing to transfer money to some part of the world gives it to a hawaladar at his location. The hawaladar informs his associate or a member of his network at the desired location and he delivers the money there immediately – he charges a little commission for his services. The hawala system functions like promissory notes and is run in parallel to the conventional banking system. Unlike traditional banking, hawala makes little use of negotiable instruments. One could compare it to an international courier service for cash where cash does not move physically. The general technical terms for hawala are IFTS/IVTS/ARS (Informal Funds Transfer Systems/Informal Value Transfer Systems/Alternative Remittance Systems). Gil Feiler maintains that the hawala system laid the foundation for the genesis of the Islamic banking system.

In India, Arabic peninsula, Pakistan and Afghanistan it is known as hawala; it is also known as hundi in India, Pakistan and

Bangladesh. In China, it is known as Fei chien, Hui k'uan, Ch'iao hui, and Nging sing kek; it goes by the names of Phoe kuan in Thailand, padala in the Philippines and Bangelap in Indonesia. The Black Market Peso Exchange (BMPE), well-known in connection with Colombian money laundering schemes is also a variant of hawala. The word *hawala* (pronunciation hawalah – with an aspirated sound at the end) in Arabic, according to the dictionary of Maddah, means, among others, 'the act of entrusting'; and transfer. The Arabic word *hawaalaat* for police lock-up (now in use in Hindi/Urdu also) comes from the 'act of entrusting' – the person being entrusted to the police. The word for the military rank of *hawaladar* (usually mis-spelt as hawaldar or havildar) which is equivalent to a sergeant in Western armies also comes from this – he is the man to whom a certain number of soldiers are entrusted.

The origins of hawala are disputed, but it has developed into the standard remittance system throughout cash-based economies with undeveloped or underdeveloped banking systems, especially in the Asian subcontinent, the Middle East and parts of Africa. Hawala constitutes a traditional and ethnic fund and value transfer operations and businesses. It is frequently used by guest workers attempting to transfer small amounts of remittances home. Workers trying to avoid taxes and foreign exchange regulations, or not wishing to draw attention to expired visas also use it liberally. For illegal workers in the US who do not have a social security number or adequate identification, opening a bank account can be problematic. But the hawaladar requires only the customer's cash and some link for trust, usually one based on a cultural or ethnic relationship.

Hawala and Financing of Terrorism

Terrorists find hawala a very expedient method of funds transfer. First, a hawala transaction is often completed more rapidly than international wire transfers that involve corresponding banks.

Second, it leaves practically no trace. Third, because hawala depends on a network of trustworthy workers and is incredibly fast, it suits the terrorists who need both trustworthy people as well as speed in their business. Fourth, it is cost-effective because the overheads are very low.

Suppose a terrorist, who has somehow infiltrated the US; or a sympathizer of terrorists living in the US, wishes to transfer $20,000 to his comrades in Lahore. He could find a Pakistani expatriate (or a regular hawaladar) based in US who has business both in US and in Lahore. Now the terrorist could give the expat $20,000 in the US and he could arrange with his business contact in Lahore to give $20,000 or its equivalent to the comrade of the terrorist right away. Money never leaves the US; yet the funds are delivered to the intended person and the process is totally untraceable. The sheer discreetness of the system is awesome.

Hawala is not necessarily an independent or separate business. Some people run such operations on the side or as a free or extra service to clients (for example, of a travel agency or even a grocery store). The transfer of clients' money may be combined with gold, diamond or other commodity deals. Hawala and criminal activities can be concealed in the mass of other ordinary and non-suspicious transactions. If the remittance amounts are not excessive, they can easily 'disappear' in otherwise legal trade. For example, an exporter could deliberately under-invoice some item by, say a few thousand dollars. If the overall trade is in the range of millions of dollars or has high turnover rates, a few thousand dollars would not draw attention. The importer would then be making an 'extra' profit by the under-invoiced amount. That money could be given to the real intended recipient, the terrorist at the other end.

In view of the fact that the amounts thus involved cannot be large, scholars like Thomas J Biersteker and Sue J Eckert (the former an American political scientist, a notable constructivism scholar, and Curt Gasteyger Professor of International Security at the Graduate Institute of International and Development Studies in Geneva; and the latter an Adjunct Senior Fellow at the Center for a New American Security, respectively) have categorically concluded in their work *Countering the Financing of Terrorism* that hawala is neither the only nor the most important financial vehicle used by international terrorists nor the most vulnerable to abuse. Policy-makers and enforcement agencies must keep this in mind as an ounce of facts means more than a tonne of popular notions. They also points out that, despite some claims made in the press about the methods used by the 9/11 hijackers to transfer their funds, all available evidence points to their use of banks, wire services, credit card accounts and other regulated remitters. So, while the funding of terrorism may well occur through IFTS, there is little empirical ground to support the belief that terrorists generally prefer to use this method. In any case, to deal with the problem, a IMF study titled "Informal Fund Transfer Systems: An Analysis of the Informal Hawala System" has recommended that in countries where an informal hawala system exists alongside a well-functioning conventional banking sector, hawala dealers be registered and must keep adequate records in line with the FATF recommendations.

Hawala in the Indian Context of Terrorism

Hawala assumes significance in the Indian context, because in India, the trans-border sponsors or 'handlers' of terrorists have only to pay the terrorists for a particular job, and which does not involve a big amount. The Lashkar-e-Taiba might require hundreds of thousands of dollars for running its terrorist training camps and procuring weapons from the international black market. But their operatives in India need to be paid only for their 'services'. The *Kashmir Herald*, for example, claims that the monthly remuneration to local terrorists in Kashmir ranges from ₹3,000-10,000. The reward for some spectacular terrorist attack is in the range of ₹1,00,000-2,00,000. While the actual amounts could vary a little, I am inclined to agree with this estimate because the figures are generally similar to the rate of contract killing (*supari*) by regular criminals elsewhere in the country. In January 2017, the Chief Minister of Jammu and Kashmir, Mehbooba Mufti had said that hawala money was used to fund terror and unrest and since 2001, there have been 173 such cases. She cited the report of the Criminal Investigation Department while submitting a written reply in the J&K assembly. Readers can draw their own conclusions regarding the magnitude and dimensions of the problem from this.

Fake Indian Currency Notes (FICN)

Historical Example of Operation Bernhard

Counterfeiting the currency of the enemy country to damage its economy has been an old trick. During World War II, the Nazis had devised a secret plan called Operation Bernhard, to destabilise the British economy by flooding the country with forged Bank of England £5, £10, £20, and £50 notes of such high quality as to make them almost undetectable. The Bank of England first detected the existence of the notes in 1943, and found them "the most dangerous ever seen". To avoid panic in the public, the circulation of the counterfeit currency was, however, never admitted officially. Still, as a countermeasure, in April 1943 the Bank of England was forced to quietly stop releasing all notes of £10 and above. Operation Bernhard produced nearly nine million banknotes with a total value of £13,46,10,810 (nearly £134 million in that era, or over £4 billion in today's value). The counterfeit currency continued to turn up in circulation in Britain for many years, which forced the Bank of England to eventually withdraw all notes larger than £5 from circulation, and not reintroduce the denominations until the early 1960s (£10), 1970 (£20), and 1980 (£50).

Since FICN has the direct effect of adding to the finances of the terrorists and making availability of cash to them easier, and because it has the indirect effect of subverting Indian economy, it has been dubbed 'money jihad' or 'economic terrorism' also. Transactions in counterfeit currency are fairly profitable too. The Directorate of Revenue Intelligence (DRI) notes in its Annual Report (2005-06),

> "The rate (per ₹100) on the India-Pakistan border is around ₹35, which goes up to around ₹40 in Delhi and ₹45-50 in the district and mofussil areas, where chances of detection are perhaps lower. These rates are however flexible and depend upon quality, availability and negotiating strengths at particular points of time."

Printing really good quality FICN would demand technical resources that are likely to be unavailable to non-state actors or terrorists. For the Operation Bernhard, even in that era, the Nazis had to assemble a team of as many as 142 counterfeiters, develop the appropriate rag-based paper with the correct watermarks, engrave the complex printing plates, and break the code to generate valid serial numbers – they had to establish a whole factory! A Jewish Slovak printer-turned-counterfeiter Adolf Burger, in his memoirs, has provided a firsthand account of the how things were done. Since then, the technology of printing the currency notes has become enormously more complex and many more security features have been incorporated. This means that counterfeiting currency is now much more difficult than it was in the World War II. There is no way a terrorist group anywhere in the world can print FICN in a backyard.

This means that, as far as terrorism in India is concerned, FICN has to be a state-sponsored effort. Pakistan is the most likely candidate. It has been speculated in the media that the currency notes printed at the Malir Cantonment security printing press, Karachi are rather high quality FICN. There could be several ways of injecting them in India. One speculation is that the notes are first planted in banks at Dubai, Kathmandu, Bangkok, Dhaka and Singapore, from where they are physically smuggled through Qatar Airways, Royal Nepal Airlines and Pakistan International Airlines. Counterfeit currency is also believed to be sent by couriers through India's porous borders with Nepal and Bangladesh, or over air and sea routes via West Asian and Southeast Asian countries.

Narcotics and Drug-Trafficking

Militia and terrorist commanders, criminal organizations, and corrupt officials have exploited narcotics as a reliable source of revenue since long for the simple reason that the returns in this business are very high. In some cases, drugs have even been used as 'currency' in the commission of terrorist attacks; for example, in the Madrid bombings. The narcotics trade through Pakistan has been used for funding terrorism in a big way. Gen Muhammad Zia-ul-Haq, during his tenure (1978 to 1988), encouraged the cultivation of poppy and cannabis to finance terrorist activities in India.

According to the United Nations Office on Drugs and Crime (UNODC) 2015 Report, Pakistan has been mentioned 3,216 times as transit point in individual seizures. Afghanistan is the world's largest producer of illicit opium and heroin. For the past decade, the country has accounted for an estimated 80% of global illicit opiates and it has fuelled instability, insurgency and terrorist groups. The opiates derived from the 3,300 tonnes of opium produced are valued at $1.49 billion, which is 7.1% of the GDP of Afghanistan. Senior Terrorism Prevention Officer Irka Kuleshnyk of the UNODC says that the magnitude of the numbers involved make the relationship of terrorism and the illicit drug trade worrisome. Even a small percentage of this huge income would be more than sufficient for some individuals or groups to plan, finance and carry out terrorist acts.

Organized Crime

Organized crime thrives with the connivance of corrupt police officials and other government agencies. Their being in connivance means that the perpetrators are simultaneously 'secured' from the law. Dawood Ibrahim has been included in the US Treasury Department's list of 'Globally Designated Terrorists' since 2003. And yet, as *India Today* reported in its article "Pakistan Deploys Special Army Commandos to Secure Dawood Ibrahim", special army commandos have been deployed at Dawood's residences in Islamabad and Karachi. An earlier article in *India Today* titled "ISI Promised Dawood Ibrahim Protection, Shelter if he invested 30% of his Earnings to Fund Terror: Sources" had claimed that according to their sources, the ISI had promised Dawood protection and sanctuary if he invested at least 30% of his earnings to fund terror activities. Abdul Karim Tunda, arrested terrorist of the LeT had reportedly told in his interrogation that Dawood had also been provided a 'shelter' in the national capital's Margalla Road area, besides his two other residences. With police patronage, it is easy to raise enormous funds through all sorts of criminal activities including kidnapping for ransom, contract killings (at times even for sectarian reasons – such as killing of Shias), extortion/*hafta*/*bhatta* (protection money) and bank robberies, etc. Karachi is believed to be in the grip of as many as 25 militant groups with several areas claimed to have been reduced to 'no-go' zones for the police.

Donations from Pakistani Diaspora and Public Donations in Pakistan

Pakistani Diaspora, both in North America and UK, is known to be funding several terrorist organizations in the name of Islamic charity. The Wikipedia article on Lashkar-e-Taiba claims that more than half of the £5 million mobilized by the Pakistani expatriate community for the Muzaffarabad earthquake was diverted for the LeT. In July 2016, video footage was obtained by *The Indian Express* that showed members of JeM shouting "Help the Mujahideen of the Jaish-e-Muhammad, the Mujahideen of Islam, fight jihad in Kashmir against the Indian Army, and in Afghanistan against the Americans" and openly collecting funds outside a mosque in Karachi's Jacob Lines area in the presence of police officials, despite being formally banned in Pakistan.

Clever Exploitation of Internet Advertising

Some of the world's biggest brands (including Mercedes-Benz, Waitrose, Marie Curie, Jaguar F-Pace, Sandals Resorts, Dropbox, Victoria and Albert Museum, and Thomson Reuters) were found to be unwittingly funding Islamic extremists, white supremacists and pornographers by advertising on their websites by automated technology programmed to track users around the Internet. An advert appearing alongside a YouTube video, for example, typically earns whoever posts the video $7.60 for every 1,000 views. Some of the most popular extremist videos have more than one million hits.

Legitimate Businesses in Pakistan

Both LeT and JeM control many legitimate businesses that include fish farms, commodity trading, real estate, and even production of consumer goods. A fundraising method unique to LeT is collecting animal skins (up to 1.2 million hides) from religious sacrifices on Eid Al-Adha and selling them to tanneries.

Cross-LoC Barter Trade: Over-Invoicing and Under-Invoicing

According to the cross-LoC trade agreement between India and Pakistan, 21 items including clothes, *'badam giri'*, *'dupatta'* (stole) and herbs etc may be exchanged under barter system. Terrorists are also reported to be using the cross-Line of Control barter trade to fund its operations in J&K. Goods from Pakistan Occupied Kashmir are under-invoiced and the excess money generated is collected by the fighters in India (*Economic Times*, August 27, 2016). Under-invoicing also occurs when certain Kashmiri carpet dealers reduce the value of their exports to Gulf countries, and the difference in the true value of the merchandise and the value shown on the invoice returns to India through the hawala channel.

THE RELATIVELY UNIQUE SITUATION OF THE FINANCES OF THE ISIS

The Claimed Size of the Coffers

In his work *The Islamic State*, Richard Barrett, a former British diplomat, intelligence officer, and a globally recognized expert on terrorism, reckoned the total assets of the ISIS at about $1.3-2 billion in 2014. ISIS is one terrorist organization which has its own sources of money. According to the daily *Al-Quds Al-Arabi* on September 25, 2014 and the *Financial Times* on September 21, 2014, ISIS had taken control of six out of 10 oilfields in Syria including the Al-Omar facility, and seven oilfields including those at Ajeel and Hamreen in Iraq, besides two refineries. Each of the two refineries in Mosul alone produced 16,000 barrels of oil a day. According to David S Cohen, the US Treasury Under Secretary for Terrorism and Financial Intelligence, ISIS sells its oil "at substantially discounted prices" to a variety of middlemen, including some from Turkey, who resell it to other customers. Some of it is sold to Kurds in Iraq and from there it is transported to Turkey. The Syrian government has also made arrangements with ISIS to purchase oil. Richard Barrett quotes estimates according to which oil production from facilities under ISIS control is between 30,000 and 80,000 barrels a day. He notes that even selling the oil at the heavily discounted price of $25-$50 per barrel would provide daily revenues of $2-$4 million. It must be kept in mind that the ISIS did not create the oil smuggling network. It has existed since long. The network in northern Iraq, north-eastern Syria, southern Turkey and parts of Iran, began in the 1990s when the Iraqi regime tried to circumvent the energy sanctions imposed on it by the UN.

Other sources of revenue of the ISIS include various criminal activities like smuggling, selling of antiques, bank robberies and the takeover of banks in Mosul; confiscating the properties of their opponents; collection of taxes/protection money from local residents and businessmen; demanding head taxes from non-Muslims; donations from the rich; and ransom from captives. The ransom amount is said to be typically $2 million for Western captives. According to Daniel S Cohen, in 2014 alone, ISIS had received at least $20 million in ransom. *The Guardian* put the figure at $45 million (Theguardian.com, October 30, 2014). As reported by Barbara Slavin, American journalist and foreign policy expert, writing in the *Al-Monitor*, according to Daniel Glaser, the Assistant Secretary for Terrorist Financing in the Office of Terrorism and Financial Intelligence, ISIS had access to an estimated $1 billion in 2015, half of it from oil and gas, about $360 million from "taxation and extortion" of local populations under its control, and the remainder as reserve cash pilfered from banks in Mosul.

Estimated Expenses of the ISIS

As reported by Paul Rivlin, author and Sandra Glass, Senior Fellow at the Moshe Dayan Center for Middle East and African Studies at Tel Aviv University, ISIS is believed to be paying monthly salaries to an estimated 25,000 operatives, at the rate of about $200 to $600 per operative per month – the salary depends on the operative's nationality and family size also. Administration personnel get from $300 to $2,000 for senior positions. A hypothetical average rate of $500 per month would require about $12.5 million a month for salaries alone. Then, ISIS also has to maintain the logistics of its military forces – arms, ammunition, fuel, vehicles – the whole enchilada. In effect, the ISIS is maintaining something like two divisions of army and the expenditure on logistics would be on the same scale, even if they save some money in salaries.

Gradually Drying Up?

Following the aerial attacks by the Americans and their allies which targeted ISIS's oil refineries and the entire supply chain, its oil profits are claimed to have declined to about $1 million a day (Theguardian.com, October 30, 2014). In support of this, Daniel Glaser of the US government has pointed to what he calls "signs of financial distress" as ISIS was learnt to have cut back salaries to fighters by 50% and increased arbitrary fees, fines and taxation. He also referred to the Iraqi government having had blocked money from several exchange houses in ISIS-held areas. However, in the assessment of the Meir Amit Intelligence and Terrorism Information Center (ITIC), Israel, its revenues, even after the American attacks reduced it, far exceed its expenses.

I must point out that the claimed finances of the ISIS are not really commensurate with their repertoire of weaponry and military accomplishments on ground. If they really have had that kind of money, they should have been able to procure much better weaponry and perhaps a larger number of fighters too. If the estimates of their income are correct, some of the money must be getting siphoned off somewhere. The question is where is the money going then? Is the US intelligence machinery not able to get a whiff of millions of the crime money disappearing in some hole? It would appear that either the US agencies are incompetent or the stories of finances of the ISIS are gross exaggerations. Robin Thomas Naylor, professor of economics at McGill University, also, in his work *Satanic Purses: Money, Myth and Misinformation in the War on Terror* has challenged the existence of "billions of Islamic terrorist dollars" as a fabrication of the US government.

7

Combating Financing of Terrorism

A HISTORICAL OVERVIEW OF VARIOUS INTERNATIONAL EFFORTS

The Financial Action Task Force (FATF) on Money Laundering (1989)

The Financial Action Task Force on Money Laundering (FATF) was formed in 1989 by the G-7 countries. It is an inter-governmental body whose purpose is to develop and promote an international response to combat money laundering. In October 2001, FATF expanded its mission to include combating the financing of terrorism (CFT). The FATF's three primary functions with regard to money laundering are: monitoring members' progress in implementing anti-money laundering measures; reviewing and reporting on laundering trends, techniques and countermeasures; and promoting the adoption and implementation of FATF anti-money laundering standards globally.

The Forty Recommendations

The Forty Recommendations on Money Laundering (usually called 'The Forty Recommendations'), constitute a comprehensive framework for AML and are designed for universal application by countries throughout the world. The Forty Recommendations were initially issued in 1990 and have been revised in 1996 and 2003 to take into account new developments in money laundering and to reflect developing best practices internationally. The Forty Recommendations set out principles for action and international standards; they permit a country flexibility in implementing the principles according to the country's own particular circumstances and constitutional requirements.

Monitoring Progress

Monitoring the progress of members to comply with the requirements of the Forty Recommendations is facilitated by a two-stage process: self assessments and mutual evaluations. In 2002, the FATF, IMF, and World Bank adopted a single assessment methodology for AML/CFT Assessments to be used both by FATF in its mutual evaluations and by the IMF and World Bank in their assessments. The methodology sets out over 200 'essential criteria' that assessors should examine when carrying out assessments of an AML and CFT regime. A NCCT (non-cooperative countries and territories) country is encouraged to make rapid progress in remedying its deficiencies. And if they do not show progress, countermeasures including termination of transactions with financial institutions from such a country may be applied.

Reporting on Money Laundering Trends and Techniques

FATF keeps its members updated on new techniques of or trends in laundering of money and other developments in this area through its publication titled "Typologies Report".

Nine Special Recommendations

Since the mission of the FATF was expanded in October 2001 to include Combating Financing of Terrorism (CFT), it has adopted Nine Special Recommendations on Terrorist Financing (also known as Special Recommendations). Originally they were eight; the ninth regarding cash couriers was adopted in 2004. As part of this effort, FATF members use a self-assessment questionnaire of their country's actions to come into compliance with the Special Recommendations. In the following, I will provide a very brief overview of the Special Recommendations:

1. Pertains to ratification and implementation of United Nations Instruments;
2. Pertains to criminalizing the financing of terrorism and associated money laundering;
3. Pertains to freezing and confiscating terrorist assets;
4. Pertains to reporting suspicious transactions related to terrorism;
5. Pertains to international cooperation;
6. Pertains to Alternative Remittance Systems or hawala. It provides that each country should take actions to ensure that individuals and legal entities that provide for "the transmission of money or value" are licensed or registered and subject to the same standards, that is, The Forty Recommendations, that apply to other financial institutions. In addition, those entities that perform such services illegally should be subject to administrative, civil or criminal sanctions. Such requirements should apply to the transmission on money or value through an informal transfer system;
7. Pertains to wire transfers. It provides that each country should take appropriate actions to require covered financial institutions, including money remitters, to include accurate and meaningful originator information (name, address and account number) on fund transfers and related messages that are sent, and further requires that the information should remain with the transfer or related message throughout the payment chain. In addition, such financial institutions should conduct enhanced scrutiny of, and monitor for suspicious activity funds transfers that do not contain complete originator information;

8. Pertains to non-profit organizations. It provides that each county should review the adequacy of its laws and regulations regarding non-profit organizations, in order to determine whether they can be used for terrorist financing purposes. In particular, a country should ensure that its non-profit organizations cannot be misused by terrorist organizations posing as legitimate ones; to exploit legitimate entities as conduits for terrorist financing, including avoiding asset freezing measures; or to conceal or obscure the clandestine diversion of funds intended for legitimate purposes to terrorist organizations; and
9. Pertains to cash couriers. Persons or entities that carry cash and cash equivalents across national borders are often referred to as 'cash couriers'. Its objective is to ensure that terrorists and other criminals cannot finance their activities or launder the proceeds of their crimes through the transportation of currency and monetary instruments from one country to another.

The Vienna Convention (1990)

Due to growing concern about increased international drug trafficking and the tremendous amounts of related money entering the banking system, the UN, through the United Nations Drug Control Programme (UNDCP) initiated an international agreement to combat drug trafficking and money laundering. In 1988, this effort resulted in the adoption of the United Nations Convention Against Illicit Traffic in Narcotic Drugs and Psychotropic Substances (1988) (popularly known as the Vienna Convention) which came into force on November 11, 1990. It deals primarily with provisions to fight the illicit drug trade and related law enforcement issues; 169 countries are party to the Convention.

Security Council Resolutions 1267 (1999) and 1373 (2001)

Unlike an international convention, which requires signing, ratification, and implementation by the UN member country to have the effect of law within that country, a Security Council Resolution passed in response to a threat to international peace and security under Chapter VII of the UN Charter, is binding upon all UN member countries. The UN Security Council has acted under Chapter VII of the UN Charter to require member States to freeze the assets of the Taliban, Osama bin Laden and Al-Qaida and entities owned or controlled by them, as designated by the 'Sanctions Committee' (now called the 1267 Committee). The initial Resolution 1267 of October 15, 1999, dealt with the Taliban and was followed by 1333 of December 19, 2000, on Osama bin Laden and Al-Qaida. On September 28, 2001, the UN Security Council, in direct response to the 9/11 attacks, adopted Resolution 1373, which obligates countries to criminalize actions to finance terrorism. It further obligates countries to deny all forms of support for terrorist groups; suppress the provision of safe haven or support for terrorists, including freezing funds or assets of persons, organizations or entities involved in terrorist acts; prohibit active or passive assistance to terrorists; and cooperate with other countries in criminal investigations and sharing information about planned terrorist acts.

The Palermo Convention (2000)

In order to expand the effort to fight international organized crime, the UN adopted the International Convention Against Transnational Organized Crime (2000) (popularly known as the Palermo Convention) which came into force on September 29, 2003, having been signed by 147 countries and ratified by 82 countries. It contains a broad range of provisions to fight organized crime and commits countries that ratify this convention to implement its provisions through passage of domestic laws. With respect to money laundering, the Palermo Convention specifically obligates each ratifying country to criminalize money laundering; establish regulatory regimes; and promote international cooperation, in accordance with the FATF's Forty Recommendations on Money Laundering.

International Convention for the Suppression of the Financing of Terrorism (1999/2002)

The financing of terrorism was an international concern even before the 9/11 attacks on the United States. In response to this concern, the UN had adopted the International Convention for the Suppression of the Financing of Terrorism (1999). This, however, came into force after the 9/11 attacks on April 10, 2002, with 132 countries signing the convention and 112 countries ratifying it. This convention requires ratifying states to criminalize terrorism, terrorist organizations and terrorist acts. Under the convention, it is unlawful for any person to provide or collect funds with the (1) intent that the funds be used for, or (2) knowledge that the funds be used to, carry out any of the acts of terrorism defined in the other specified conventions that are annexed to this convention. The FATF does not specifically define the term financing of terrorism in its Nine Special Recommendations but urges countries to ratify and implement the 1999 Convention and adopt its definition for purposes of defining terrorist financing.

CFT MEASURES: ASSESSMENT, PROBLEMS AND DESIDERATA

Against Islamic Charity

In practice, even as it is eminently desirable, it is indeed difficult to distinguish between financing humanitarian networks affiliated with resistance groups and financing of terrorism. Blanket condemnation of groups providing social welfare services alienates Muslim constituencies and prevents aid from reaching those most in need. It is important to pressure Arab and Muslim countries and organizations to work as part of an international effort, but not to make them feel as if they are being hounded. Government efforts could perhaps focus on assisting charities to be more transparent, and designate independent bodies to regulate, investigate and accredit charities.

Against Hawala Transactions

Thomas J Biersteker and Sue J Eckert in *Countering the Financing of Terrorism* caution that policies made in knee-jerk reactions to some isolated terrorist incident in which hawala might have played a part may also result in reduced labour remittances to the nation or the region from where most of the workers emigrate; families of immigrants not receiving desperately needed income; harassment of innocent people at the hands of law enforcement agencies; and shift to more sophisticated IVTMs (Informal Value Transfer Methods), such as mis-invoicing or trade diversion with which law enforcement agents are likely to be even less familiar. Moreover, from a preventive point of view, reducing the number of IFTS operations drastically through harsh measures may mean far fewer opportunities to monitor suspicious activities and gather valuable intelligence about planned crimes. Gil Feiler of the Begin-Sadat Center for International Studies also argues forcefully in *The Globalization of Terror Funding* that it is counter-productive to ban the practice of hawala money transfers altogether – rather, he suggests that states should help facilitate efficient and cheap cross border remittances; work with banks and exchange houses to coordinate this; and poorer states should be encouraged to abolish dual and parallel exchange markets, which are an incentive to keep transactions underground. Following negotiation, an agreement can be reached with countries with more advanced economies to form an international regulation effort.

For the sake of completeness of the discussion, I am reproducing excerpts from an article "Black Money and Terror: Quality of Counter-Terrorism, Not Currency Crackdown, will Prevent Terrorism" by Vappala Balchandran, a former Special Secretary, R&AW, Government of India, in *The Indian Express:*

> "A 'cashless economy' need not be 'terror-free'. In November 2014, CNBC conducted a survey of the 10 top 'cashless' societies. It found Belgium to be the world's top cashless society with 93% non-cash consumer payments and 83% debit card use. France was second, then Canada, the UK, Sweden, Australia, Holland, the US, Germany and South Korea.... Unfortunately, Belgium and France were also the worst victims of indigenous and trans-border terrorism. This rampage started on January 7, 2015, with the *Charlie Hebdo* attacks in Paris. France did not detect that Amedy Coulibaly and Medi Nemmouche had bought their weapons from Brussels. Nor did Belgian agencies know that Molenbeek, a small 5.8 sq km area in their country was Islamic State's busiest terror incubating unit in the world. This long bloody spree saw 15 serious terror incidents, killing 254 innocents and 16 terrorists.... Global research has now found that terrorists seldom use tax dodgers or hawala agents of target countries as they are known to local agencies. 'Black money' is not preferred since it does not satisfy the principle of "volume, risk, convenience, simplicity, costs and speed". Terrorists never hire crime cartels because they shift loyalty. Dawood might have been used by a hostile government once, but terror cartels never 'outsource' their campaigns. Funds are moved using phoney legal means, although their origin might be through crimes like robbery, extortion or fraud."

Against FICN

The ISI knows that they can't materially harm the Indian economy by pumping say ₹130 million worth of notes a year. Their objective is therefore only to finance terrorists and keep their 'Kashmir budget' out of the purview of the Legislature.

Against Narcotics and Drug-Trafficking

At the international level there is a common legal framework consisting of 16 universal anti-terrorist instruments, as well as relevant UN Security Council resolutions. Included in the latter is a series of UN resolutions imposing sanctions, such as the freezing of assets, a travel ban and an arms embargo, on members of the Taliban, Al-Qaida and their associates. There are currently 124 entities and 226 individuals on this list.

Against Foreign Funding

Of late, the US position with regard to Saudi Arabia seems to have undergone a shift. In October 2016, Daniel Glaser of the US government, praised Saudi Arabia for its progress in blocking the flow of funds to groups such as Al-Qaida and wished that Qatar and Kuwait would also meet the same standard. Bruce Riedel concurs with him and, for evidence, cites the assassination attempts on Saudi Crown Prince Muhammad bin Nayef! G8 leaders and the UN could pressure the GCC (Gulf Cooperation Council) to transparently monitor more charities in their respective jurisdictions.

Against State Funding of Terrorism

The only way of addressing this problem is using diplomatic channels to make clear to the regimes that not being fully aware of what all its public servants and agencies are doing is tantamount to lack of control and therefore a sign of weakness and instability.

Against Terror Financing Through Legal Channels

Detecting terror financing through legal channels is an extremely onerous task, as the US Treasury and FATF reports also indicate. Many banks do not follow the US banks' due diligence practices and "suspicious activity identification" processes. Centralised inter-agency coordination is therefore essential to deal with global criminal activities like kidnapping, extortion, drug trafficking, charities, bank frauds and state sponsorship to link with funding.

Against Proceeds of Crime

Since it is intimately related to corruption in the police and other government agencies, it boils down to the insurmountable problem of combating corruption in a given society.

AN ASSESSMENT OF THE IMPACT OF THE AMERICAN ACTIONS

Besides designating the LeT and the JeM and several of their senior leaders as Specially Designated Global Terrorists (SDGTs) which blocks their properties subject to US jurisdiction and US persons are generally prohibited from engaging in transactions with them, the US has also taken similar action against their front organizations like JuD, IKK (Idara Khidmat-e-Khalq), Al-Rehmat Trust, Falah-e-Insaniyat Foundation, and Al-Muhammadia Students (AMS – the student wing of the LeT). The issue is what real effect these actions have had? In my assessment, given the State patronage by Pakistan and a host of informal channels open to them, the US actions are not likely to make much difference immediately to LeT and JeM or their various franchises inside Pakistan. *The Indian Express* investigation has found that the Falah-e-Insaniyat Foundation continues its activities unabated through bank accounts under pseudonyms even as their original accounts were ordered shut in 2015 itself. The evidence for their continued activities comes from the articles in the Lashkar-linked magazine *Jarrar* which speak of the FIF's humanitarian work all over the world; from Balochistan, Gaza and Syria to Myanmar. The American action will, however, make things difficult for them in the long run to operate at the international sphere raising funds and logistics through formal channels. They would also jeopardize their travels abroad.

Robin Thomas Naylor, Professor of Economics at McGill University, political economist, historian and author of 19 books, in fact, says that the counter-terrorist financing effort is not only ineffective, but has converted the world's banking infrastructure into "a global espionage apparatus". Naylor contends that the financial war on terror has been based on gross exaggerations and faulty assumptions, with significant costs, including converting the international financial infrastructure into a tool of governments for global espionage.

On a milder tone, the US response has been criticized widely as "profoundly state-centred", which has hampered its overall effectiveness. According to Robert J Bunker, an American academic and an applied theorist on national security and other advanced concepts, one of the main takeaways from US experiences in Iraq and Afghanistan is that "it takes a network to defeat a network." However, as Chad C Serena, Political Scientist at the RAND Corporation, argues persuasively, "this overly simplified yet widely accepted view ignores the point of organizational adaptation" because "being a network or acting like a network does not ensure that an organization can or will adapt appropriately to achieve its goals."

RECOMMENDATIONS FOR FURTHER EFFORTS

Necessity of Greater International Cooperation

Targeting as wide a range of terror groups and organizations as possible must be conducted as part of a well-coordinated international effort. As a part of greater international cooperation, for example, more pressure needs to be put on the EU to implement regulations that can keep better track of terror and criminal financing. This is admittedly likely to curtail personal freedoms and impinge on human rights, but they will have to be very wisely balanced against the risks that the threat of terror poses.

Within a nation, strong cooperation between different agencies is essential. I refrain from commenting on India. However, for illustration, at the moment, in the US, there are too many vested interests looking after different aspects of terror financing, including the Department of Treasury, the FBI, CIA, and the DHS (Department of Homeland Security). A multiplicity of agencies dealing with countering the financing of terrorism in any country undermines international cooperation because each of the liaising parties does not have access to the full picture. The General Accountability Office of the US government has issued several critical reports, noting that the US does not systematically collect and analyse data on alternative financing mechanisms, that inter-agency turf battles and lack of cooperation have hindered the effectiveness of enforcement efforts, as well as the provision of technical assistance to other countries.

Boosting the Powers of the FATF

The FATF is the closest thing to an international body on terror financing. Its powers can be boosted by increased funding and appointing a high ranking cabinet minister. One idea is to have the president or prime minister from each of the member states to sit on its board, giving its meetings top level authority, similar to the G7 and G8 summits.

Using Different Measures for Different Terrorist Groups

The terrorist groups acting trans-nationally on a global scale, like Al-Qaida and its affiliates and the ISIS, have different goals, scope of operations, needs, bases, and means of financing themselves, as compared to groups acting on a local or sub-national scale like the JeM which has a very strong anti-India and Kashmir-centric focus. James Fallows, in his article "Declaring Victory" in *The Atlantic*, drawing on a paper of David J Kilcullen in the *Journal of Strategic Studies*, agrees that –

> "Western countries should do everything possible to treat terrorist groups individually, rather than 'lumping together all terrorism, all rogue or failed states, and all strategic competitors who might potentially oppose US objectives'."

The same logic applies to other countries also.

APPRECIATING THE INTRINSIC COMPLEXITY OF THE ISSUE

Adaptation by Terrorist Organizations and the Need for Counter-Adaptation by Nation-States

Successful terrorists and insurgent organizations develop an agile organizational structure and when the opportunity arises, they turn to new technologies and other non-state actors like criminals, which in many cases can act as force multipliers. An ideal terrorist group could be functioning like a holding company, which maintains several different business lines and operational divisions, functioning independently. Furthermore, rigged transactions between two companies controlled by the same organization, the use of falsified documents, and the diversity of payment methods (personal and bank checks, transfers, payment orders, banking remittances and credits, etc) all contribute to the difficulty of countering groups adept at these processes. Even with improved financial regulations, terrorists have simply become more adept at masking these transactions and at using intermediaries to act on their behalf. In response to government counter-measures, the methods of financiers and terrorists adjust in kind. It is a continuous cycle of adaption and counter-adaptation. The more vulnerable terrorists feel in using the international financial system, the more likely they will be to rely upon more informal means of raising and moving money.

With the ever-increasing volume of trade flows, for example, the international trade system is increasingly vulnerable to abuse by terrorists, as well as other criminals, through false invoicing and the use of commodities to move funds. Nations combating terrorism must watch out for trade diversion. To detect it, governments should create trade transparency units to analyse, share, and track international trade data to identify anomalies. Greater cooperation with the private sector victimized by diversion schemes should be explored, and enhanced priority placed on inter-agency cooperation and prosecution of trade diversion cases.

We should also not lose sight of the fact that supply-side interventions, while having tactical import, also may have strategic diminishing margins of return because such efforts may bolster the popular support that these groups enjoy, creating better recruitment and funding environments for the groups. As the Canadian Ministry of Foreign Affair's website points out, destroying the links between terrorists and their financiers is akin to slaying the Hydra – cut off one head and it is replaced by two more.

Need for Constant Review of CFT Policies

The response to terrorist financing has not changed fundamentally since 9/11, nor has there been any comprehensive effort to reassess the policy. The primary focus on the formal financial sector continues, notwithstanding the fact that terrorists have turned to criminal methods and cash smuggling as major methods of raising and moving money. To be effective,

CFT policies must be recalibrated constantly, especially in light of the adaptive nature of terrorists.

Limitations Inherent in Conventional Approaches

There are certain things which nation states can address; certain things they cannot. As Tom Keatinge, analyst of terror financing and Director, Centre for Financial Crime and Security Studies, RUSI (Royal United Services Institute), London, also points out in his paper in *Foreign Affairs*,

> "Money always finds a way to its intended recipient. Restrictive regulations have simply pushed large pools of funds outside formal channels, encouraging criminals and terrorists to finance their activities in the shadows."

When dealing with combating the finances of terrorist groups, it is also important to recognize that in certain cases – as with ISIS – the international banking system will be of little help. Instead, the local economies of these groups must be the primary focus and the priority should remain developing the capacity of local and regional actors while also targeting the insurgent group's financial facilitators and local sources of revenue.

One of the main issues in CFT is that of intelligence gain/loss (IGL). In simple words, it means that when intelligence about the financing of a terrorist group is acquired and placed in the public domain, this alerts them and forces them to change their tactics, techniques, and procedures (TTPs). Severe restrictions on banks could encourage terrorists to avoid the formal financial system altogether. If banks are made to exit problematic markets and de-risk their operations completely, what entity would fill the void? In the end, nations are faced with the dilemma: Would it be better to move against an adversary the moment an opportunity arises, or would it be more beneficial to allow the adversary to continue such of his actions that are traceable? In the latter option, one could hope for even more valuable intelligence to come. But it comes with a risk that the terrorists could get wind of your infiltration and quickly change course, denying you the chance to take action against them.

Everybody clamours for more and more regulation, but we need a better understanding of the effectiveness and costs of regulation. This is important because 'moral panics' can develop at times of perceived crisis. These panics can result in excessive or counter-productive efforts with unintended consequences. This creates ever more difficult regulatory challenges and the potential pitfalls of over-regulation and other negative externalities. For this reason alone, it is vital that CFT is not viewed and carried along in isolation. Countering of the financing of terrorism must be considered within a broader framework of an integrated counter-terrorism strategy.

8

How Terrorists Procure Their Arms and Ammunition?

TERRORISTS' ARMS BAZAAR

The Pierce Brosnan-starring James Bond film "Tomorrow Never Dies" (1997) starts off with the scene of a terrorists' arms bazaar on the Russian border replete with all sorts of military vehicles, aircrafts, machine guns – the whole enchilada. We find James Bond watching the bazaar through a telescope as part of a joint Anglo-Russian mission. He gathers such frightening intelligence that despite M's insistence to let Bond finish his reconnaissance, British Admiral Roebuck orders the frigate HMS Chester to launch a cruise missile attack on the arms bazaar to wipe them all out in one go. Before the missile comes crashing in, Bond discovers that one of the planes for sale, an L-39 Albatross jet trainer (the gunrunners did not go so far as to be selling the Joint Strike Fighter F-35 – they were happy with a trainer aircraft!) for sale happens to be carrying "enough plutonium to make Chernobyl look like picnic", as the Russian military observer puts it.

With four minutes till total annihilation by the cruise missile, Bond takes matters into his own hands, pausing briefly to punch out a terrorist guard who asks him for a light ("A filthy habit,"

Bond mutters) before the carnage begins. Bond walks into an encampment of hardened terrorists who not only are carrying weapons but are there for the sole purpose of buying and selling even more weapons. As it usually happens with Bond, while he turns the whole place to Swiss cheese with grenades and a single assault rifle, nobody manages to land a finger on him. Meanwhile, the missile has moved too far along its flight to be aborted. Bond hijacks the L-39 and flies away seconds before the bazaar is destroyed. The quintessential Bond – how much we love him!

Does not matter that real life is not so simple; the arms bazaars are, however, indeed real, and arms trafficking is a real global operation. Estimates of the total value of legal exports of light weapons globally reach $5 billion, while the value of the illicit trade is estimated to range anywhere from $1 billion to $10 billion! The harsh reality of the world is that illegal arms bazaars are deeply embedded in the international landscape and the various UN arms embargoes have largely failed to limit people's access to weapons. The illegal arms trade follows the simple mechanics of demand and supply. It exists because there is a demand for it. As long as demand will be there, the illegal arms trade would flourish and manage to overwhelm the attempts to monitor and control the trade through export licensing schemes, international agreements or whatever.

THE INTERNATIONAL BLACK MARKET IN ARMS

History of Gunrunning in the World

Bond's fictional arms bazaar was on the Russian border. Many people indeed ascribe to a popular notion that it is only due to the collapse of the Soviet Union that lawlessness has come to reign in the areas bordering Russia and that's where the international black market in weapons has flourished. To their disappointment, I must tell that the international black market in arms is indeed very old. Jonathan Grant, Professor of History at the Florida State

University, has shown in his paper "Merchants of Death: The International Traffic in Arms" that starting in the 16th century, European traders began trafficking arms into African, American, and, to a lesser extent, Asian markets. Since 1945, conflicts in Africa have caused somewhere around 6.5 million deaths. Since the 1990s, West Africa has experienced some of the most devastating armed conflicts in the world. The United Nations Development Programme (UNDP) has estimated that some 8 million illicit small arms and light weapons are already present in West Africa. Nigerian sources claim that 1 million of such arms may be in Nigeria alone. Now, as we know, the African nations do not manufacture arms. If the millions of militiamen and terrorists (as against national armies) there have arms on such a staggering scale, the only source possible is illegal arms trade.

Interesting though it is, for want of space we will take up the history of black market in arms since the post-World War II era only. In the post-World War II era, arms trafficking received a huge boost thanks to the vast quantities of war surplus equipment located in depots around the world. The world's biggest arms dealer of the era, Samuel Cummings, controlled 90% of world's private trade in guns, doing business of $100 million annually. His company Interarms, with assets in both UK and USA, ultimately bought and sold more rifles and ammunition than Gen Eisenhower had needed for the invasion of Normandy and the defeat of the Wehrmacht! The beauty was that he was politically neutral. He supplied guns to overthrow the Guatemalan government in 1954, sold arms to Castro and Batista, and to both sides in the Costa Rican Civil War, and purchased the entire surplus from the Spanish Civil War.

Supply of Illegal Arms by State Actors during the Cold War

The Cold War rivalry between the Communist world and the West greatly contributed to the expansion of the global arms trade. Governments used private arms brokers also to facilitate covert arms deals. In general, the supply of arms and military equipment became one of the most powerful weapons in international diplomacy, with both the United States and the Soviet Union giving a high proportion of their foreign aid in this form. Before 1970, world military exports rarely exceeded $5 billion annually. 1978 to 1985, Third World countries ordered $258 billion worth of arms and ammunition! After the conclusion of the Vietnam War, Communist Vietnam got booty of nearly 2 million small arms (M16s) and 1,50,000 tonnes of ammunition, a legacy of the bloody war. The Vietnamese traded many of these to the Cuban government in exchange for foodstuffs. The Cubans then trafficked these weapons into Central America to support the spread of revolution by supplying the Sandinistas in Nicaragua and the FMLN in El Salvador. Some were sold directly to Mexico too.

Enter the Post-Soviet World and the 21st Century

Victor Bout, the Stuff of Legends

Following the collapse of the Soviet Union in 1991, vast numbers of light weapons were released from controls and entered the international arms market. In April 2012, Victor Bout, perhaps the single biggest private arms trader in the world at that time, was convicted in a New York court and sentenced to 25 years in prison. The case against Bout was built upon a sting operation with DEA agents posing as would-be buyers from FARC, the Revolutionary Armed Forces of Colombia. Bout was prepared to supply anti-aircraft missiles so that FARC could shoot down American pilots working with Colombian government officials.

Bout, a Russian citizen, began his private business as a military transporter and weapons supplier in the early 1990s following the collapse of the Soviet Union. He acquired a fleet of Soviet military aircraft including Antonov and Ilyushin cargo planes as surplus of the Cold War and employed them in operations to deliver weapons to various combatants in Africa. Bout used an intricate web of supply chains involving up to 30 different companies and superficially legitimate end-user certificates to deliver arms around the globe.

By his own admission, he had flown weapons to anti-Taliban forces in Afghanistan during the 1990s and aided the French government in transporting goods and UN peacekeepers to Rwanda after the genocide there. According to UN documents, in exchange for illicit diamonds Bout had supplied former Liberian President Charles Taylor with weapons to help destabilize Sierra Leone. Earlier, Bout had supplied arms to both sides in the Angolan Civil War and had also sold and delivered weapons to various warlords across Central and North Africa. Operating through Eastern Europe, Bout transported weapons through Bulgaria, Moldova and Ukraine to Liberia and Angola in the first years of the new millennium. Indeed, there were few conflicts in the world over the past two decades where Bout's weapons were not present. So spectacular was his rise as an arms dealer that his story served as the basis for the 2005 film "Lord of War".

Public-Private Partnership, So to Say

Victor Bout's case exemplifies the synergistic relationship between arms dealers and the state actors. Arms brokers have perfected techniques of circumventing national arms controls and international arms embargoes; if there is some trouble, they can always depend on official protection. It helps both – the job of the dealer is rendered easier somewhat; and the states have the option of falling back on the argument of deniability in case something went wrong. Private arms brokers use counterfeit documents or legitimate documents acquired through corrupt practices to find clandestine transport and to develop business relationships with corrupt officials. Indeed, many governments have 'allowed' notorious arms brokers to operate within their borders and are not interested in breaking up known trafficking networks or arresting habitual violators. The revelation of Venezuelan President Hugo Chavez's plans to supply militants from the terrorist organization FARC, operating in Colombia, with Russian weapons set off one of the biggest International scandals of modern time (lenta.ru/news/2008/05/12/documents). It is unlikely that this could have happened without Russian knowledge.

Life in the post-Soviet nation states in the former Warsaw Pact countries has been difficult. It is particularly difficult for the arms industries. How do they survive? Well, they survive by manufacturing arms, something they learnt well during the Soviet days. Where do they sell them? Well, to whoever needs them for conflicts of his own! The conflicts in the African continent and the Islamic terrorists, among others, provided the demand; arms from the Russian and former Warsaw Pact countries provided the supply – simple; and who cares about UN prohibitions? Since these small states could not manage the deviously complex affair of shipments entirely on their own, that's where the private arms dealers stepped in with their expertise of centuries – everybody was happy. Evolving 'suitable' mechanisms for this was just a matter of detail – some time senior government officials needed to be 'handled'; some time, the shipments had to be disguised as humanitarian goods, or whatever.

Prior to its breakup, Federal Yugoslavia was selling some $500 million worth of firearms each year, mainly to the Middle East and its fellow non-aligned members. The arms were built in keeping with the principle of 'brotherhood and unity' with key parts of the M-84 tank made in Bosnia-Herzegovina, Serbia and Montenegro and assembled in Croatia. The subsequent beginning of the war in Bosnia-Herzegovina came as a real boon for the region's black market of illegal arms. The wars fought during the breakup of Yugoslavia in the 1990s left a vast supply of small arms in the region. Bulgaria has been the arms bazaar for rebels and terrorist organizations of every political, ethnic and religious persuasion. At the centre of the trade are Kintex, the state marketing agency, and Arsenal, the country's largest arms manufacturer, which is also state-owned. Founded by Bulgaria's secret police in the 1960s, Kintex has a history of dubious arms trading. During the Iran-Iraq war, the company had sold to both sides. With the collapse of the Soviet Union, Bulgaria lost those secondary markets, as well as the Warsaw Pact. Struggling to survive economically has caused the companies to engage in shady practices.

THE CURRENT DIMENSIONS OF ARMS TRAFFICKING

The Staggering Volume of It

According to the independent works of Heath Druzin; Kiko Itasaka; Phillip Killicoat; "Havocscope: Global Black Market Information"; and 2012 'Issue Brief' by the Council on Foreign Relations, the illicit arms traffic in the world is worth about $1 billion today or more, perhaps up to $10 billion. At any rate, most scholars agree, the illicit arms trade is not less than 10-20% of the global arms trade. This may be examined in the backdrop of the fact that, as maintained by the Small Arms Survey; Nicholas Marsh; and David Kinsella independently, the global value of small arms production in the world is about $7.4 billion. That is, nearly 14% of the small arms of the world are held by non-state actors! According to Rachel Stohl and EJ Hogendoorn (the former at the Stimson Center, and the latter at the International Crisis Group, Washington), only one third of the 875 million small and light arms in circulation around the world, or 291 million, are held by legitimate security forces. The rest of the available arms are in the hands of non-security forces. At this moment, there are nearly 100 million AK-47s in circulation worldwide.

An idea of the trade in small arms can be had from the black market prices of various weapons given below.

Average price of AK-47 worldwide	$534
Price of AK-47 in Afghanistan	$1,500
Price of AK-47 Ammunition	$0.15 – $0.45 per cartridge
Price of RPG in Iraq	$100, $50 per rocket grenade
American night vision goggles in Afghanistan	$1,500

The rather high price of the AK-47 in Afghanistan is attributed to increased demand for firearms in anticipation of international forces leaving Afghanistan, and is thus is the result of a sort of 'panic buying'. A few years ago, the Chinese Type 56 PRC (Chinese copy of the AK-47) could be had for just $400. In comparison, an American M-16A2 assault rifle goes for $2,700 and the M-4 carbine goes for $6,000 in Iraq. According to an investigation by 'NBC News', supplies from the United States military are being sold in street markets in Kabul, Afghanistan. Along with whey protein powder, Oakley sunglasses and lemon-scented Pledge, hardware from US security forces are openly sold.

Mechanics of the Black Market in Arms

As Rachel Stohl has shown in several of her works, small arms can enter illicit networks from the legal trade in nine distinct ways. First, states, companies or individuals violate national, regional or international sanctions and embargoes in order to ship weapons to barred countries or parties. Second, corrupt government officials of those countries where it would otherwise be difficult or illegal to do so, may provide export licenses to those ineligible due to domestic or international laws, and corrupt customs officials may quietly allow weapons to be shipped from or through ports. Third, inadequate weapons stockpile security and management allow small arms to flow out of government arsenals into the networks of shady arms brokers or organized crime syndicates, terrorists, pariah governments, and insurgent groups. Fourth, opportunists may loot national arsenals and weapons caches during periods of instability or rampant crime. In 1997, Albanian government arsenals emptied as the country descended into chaos, and more than half a million weapons flowed into the hands of Albanian citizens. Many of these guns made their way throughout the Balkans and into other regions. Fifth, small arms could be misplaced or lost from government and military stocks.

Sixth, it is possible that some government weapons are simply sold off by unscrupulous soldiers or officers. Seventh, weapons could be stolen from legitimate private owners. Eighth, ambiguous or ineffective domestic laws concerning the purchase of small arms can contribute to the quantity of small arms available on the black market. If there are no limits to how many guns a person may own or buy at one time, 'straw purchasers' can buy several weapons at once and then illegally resell them. These illegal weapons are often sold across international borders from a country with lax regulations to one with quite strict gun laws, as is common between the United States, Mexico and Canada. Ninth, individuals or organizations can make their own weapons for sale on the illicit market, a process referred to as 'craft production'. This is, however, limited basically to shotguns or simple blowback action sub-machineguns as anything more complex cannot be made in such improvised set-ups.

Flexibility Par Excellence

If there is one thing that characterizes illegal arms trafficking, it is the immense flexibility of the operations. The traffickers make use of anything and everything that is expedient. Arms trafficking networks rely on many different actors in many different countries. The arms could have come from Eastern Europe; the cargo aircrafts used could have originated in Belgium, Ukraine, or South Africa; and the clients could be in anywhere from Africa to Afghanistan or Congo to Colombia. Weapons might be sold for cash; bartered for teakwood, hostages, heroin, or religious artefacts; or countertraded for grain and oil. The deals could be transacted by go-betweens who are equally at home in smuggling gold to India, trafficking in counterfeit computer chips to the United States, or shipping toxic waste to Somalia. The ships hauling the arms could be registered in a flag-of-convenience country boasting commercial secrecy, low registration fees, and the opportunity for rapid name and ownership changes. The payments could move through a series of coded bank accounts in the name of a global network of ghost companies and are protected by the banking and corporate secrecy laws of one or several of the many financial havens around the world. Specialists in the arms trade believe that –

> "cross-border mergers between airlines, marketing alliances, leasing, chartering, franchising and offshore registration of fleets, crews, and companies, all make it even more difficult to monitor and regulate the airspace and freighting industry".

Difficulties in Blocking the Arms Traffic

Once brokers acquire the arms, they become one part of an illicit network that deals in drugs, guns, jewels, art, humans, and anything else worth trading through unofficial channels. Actually, there is no separate black market for each commodity. While some dealers may specialize in weapons, most are plugged into the general international underground economy. Rebel groups and terrorist organizations take advantage of these illegal networks by using the commodities they have available with them to procure weapons. Those who have drugs, sell drugs to buy weapons; those who have diamonds, sell diamonds to buy weapons – the list is quite long!

In an effort to move their products without detection, brokers rely primarily on counterfeit documents, or legitimate documents acquired through bribery. Generally, they transport weapons using false bills of lading, fake end-use certificates, and incomplete manifests, etc. They adopt circuitous routes through 'friendly' trans-shipment countries which are willing to look the other way in exchange for payment, sometimes cash or even a share of the weapons. They often disguise their weapons shipments as humanitarian aid or other supplies also. A lack of concerted international cooperation and intelligence sharing has also allowed arms brokers to act without fear of being captured or punished.

HOW TERRORIST GROUPS OPERATING FROM PAKISTAN AND AFGHANISTAN GET THEIR WEAPONS?

Historical Origins of the Gun Culture in Pashtunistan

Guns exist because people love guns. George Bernard Shaw has reminisced that once as a child he was taken to watch a play. He did not like the play per se, but was greatly fascinated by the swords and guns of the actors! The fascination with arms could not have been truer than in the case of Pashtunistan. The people there simply love guns. Since a repressive colonial legacy would not allow people to possess as many guns as they needed, they fell back on illegal guns – simple! There is indeed a pronounced 'gun culture' in certain areas of Pakistan and Afghanistan. There is a saying that *"ghar ka chulha bhale thandha ho, bandook ki naal garam honi chahiye"*; that is, even if the fire in your kitchen is cold, the barrel of your gun must be hot – meaning, even if you are so poor as not to be able to afford food, you should have a gun and you should have fired it for good reasons like defending your honour or for exacting revenge. In other words, you must place your honour above your survival – this is what the gun culture is essentially about. Incidentally, Gen Musharraf himself had also spoken of the 'Kalashnikov culture' in the region. In 2001, he started a campaign also to counter it. For obvious reasons, it had no hope of succeeding. The Geneva-based research group Small Arms Survey maintains that out of some 18 million arms in Pakistan, only about 2 million are legal; the rest are all illegal!

However, let us understand one thing clearly. The sword in an earlier period and the Kalashnikov in the present era are not the cause of instability in the region; they are, rather the facilitators of instability. A complete de-weaponisation of the region which has historically lived in the shadow of some weapon – be it the *talwar* or a rifle – is unrealistic. I won't say that people there are inherently unruly; however, the Mughal and the British experience would strongly suggest that they are loath to the controls of what we consider to be a civilized society. The attempts to 'control' them came from foreigners. Foreigners had both strategic and commercial reasons to be interested in controlling the region. In the Mughal era, it was literally the gateway to India – both to protect India as well as to invade it. It was also the transit point for trade – the horse trade in particular, vital for the military. And for the British, it was, of course, the focal point of the Great Game between Britain and Imperial Russia. Russia was fearful of British commercial and military inroads into Central Asia, and Britain was fearful of Russia adding "the jewel in the crown", that is, India, to the vast empire that Russia was building in Asia.

Thus for centuries, outsiders wanted to 'control' them and they continued to resist with might and main, tooth and nail. In *Baburnama*, Babar provides a description of Afghan defensive combat techniques:

> "I first heard the word *sangar* after coming to Kabul where people describe fortifying themselves on a hill as making a *sangar*."

I am sure, all those Indians who have not studied the *Baburnama*, heard the word *sangar* for the first time in their lives in connection with the fortifications built by the terrorists/invaders from the region on the hills during the Kargil War. What a strange coincidence!

Ethnic and Cultural Roots of the People of the Region

It would be of some interest to have a bird's eye view of the issues of ethnicity of the people inhabiting the region. It is important because generally a great deal of confusion prevails about it. As Olaf Caroe writes in his famous book *The Pathans: 500 BC-AD 1957*, a clear distinction can be drawn between those who inhabit plains and open plateaus on one hand and the highlanders on the other. The former have been called Afghans. They again can be broadly divided into (i) the Western Afghans, of whom the most important are the Abdalis (now known as the Durranis) and the Ghilzais, and (ii) the Eastern Afghans, namely, the Yusufzais and other kindred tribes of the Peshawar plain and the valleys to the north of it. Of these, the Western Afghans have had considerable Persian influence in the past. In between the Eastern and the Western Afghans, and to some extent keeping them apart, are interposed the highlanders. These include most of the famous names of the North-West Frontier: Afridi, Khatak, Orakzai, Bangash, Wazir, Mahsud, and Turi.

These tribes are the Pakhtuns, or Pashtuns – or, better known as the Pathans. The word Pathan, in the opinion of Olof Caroe, is the Indian variant of Pukhtanah, the plural of Pakhtun. I agree with this etymological derivation of the word Pathan. Some scholars maintain that the word Pathan is a corrupted version of Pahtan which was derived from the word Batan.

Nirodbhusan Roy says in *Niamatullah's History of the Afghans*, that the word Batan means 'delivered', or 'set free'. Since this is a clear post factum allusion to a particular trait of their character, I find it rather far-fetched and do not agree with it. Most people are confused by the words Pakhtun and Pashtun. Pakhtu is the language spoken by the north-eastern tribes, and Pashtu by those in the south-west.

Having said this for academic interest, I must point out that, even as ethnicity and tribalism are, in popular perception, often held responsible for the disunity in the region, the fact is that in the modern context of terrorism, cultural influences are often more important than ethnic – ethnicity and tribalism are important factors but not the most important factors. The gun culture, for example, has been common to all tribes. Then, often, purely materialist considerations take over. During the Mujahideen war, the front-lines cut through almost all ethnic groups and the larger tribes. In all those groups, there were (a) sympathisers and collaborators of the regime; (b) fierce enemies of the regime; and (c) people who had decided to wait and see who would be the winner. Bernt Glatzer, the late Advisory Board member of the Afghanistan Analysts Network, says in his article "The Pashtun Tribal System" in the book *Concept of Tribal Society* that he personally knew many families whose strategy was to place one member among the communists, another one or two among the Mujahideen, and sent yet another one as a refugee to Europe or USA, while the rest of the family set up their household in a Pakistani refugee camp! Of course the family continued communicating among all its members. The issues of ethnicity are often invoked according to convenience. In the beginning, Gulbuddin Hekmatyar laid stress in his public speeches on pan-Islamism and the Muslim ummah. Later, during his campaigns for recruitment in Pashtun areas he appealed to the ethnic and tribal solidarity of the Pashtuns who, he argued, should defend their identity and honour against the rest of the world. That's why for a general overview of their cultural patterns, I would refer to them as people of the region.

Pashtunwali, or the Pashtun Way of Life

Historically, the Pashtuns have been fiercely independent people clinging to their ancient values. Scott Shane sums up their character in some simple words in a lighter vein:

> "They have a language (Pashtu), an elaborate traditional code of legal and moral conduct (Pashtunwali), a habit of crossing the largely unmarked border at will, and a centuries-long history of foreign interventions that ended badly for the foreigners."

But we must determine the reasons why they have been so fiercely independent people. The reason is that for a very large part of their existence they could be subjugated but not made subservient; defeated but not trampled at the hands of stronger and more advanced civilizations. A realization of this fact, coupled with their geographical isolation, made them hang on to their own way of life.

They knew that, in spite of their intrepidity, excellent exploitation of the terrain in combat, and their unconventional tactics; they did not stand much chance against regular armies armed with superior weaponry in pitched battles. However, they also knew that the land was so inhospitable that no conqueror would find it economically viable to maintain a large garrison there just to keep the local people under control. As such, no victor would bother to establish a proper administrative set up there replete with the state's military resources as the land would not yield much revenue. Kabul was, in fact, the poorest subah in the entire Mughal Empire and yet demanded the highest military expenditure on it. The Kabul subah typically yielded 81% less revenue than say, Agra subah or Lahore subah. Hence, in effect, all that the victors succeeded in was merely subjugating the people temporarily – it was not really worthwhile to waste resources on governing them and changing their way of life. This left them, for all practical purposes, to their old way of life. If they became more unruly than was acceptable, punitive expeditions would be sent to the interior areas. You could call them the precursors of modern-day COIN or counterinsurgency operations. But eventually, they would have to go back. And thus it continued throughout the Mughal rule. 'Insurgent-type behaviour' thus became a part of their collective psyche and value system.

To understand the gun culture better, we must have a brief overview of Pashtunwali. It is an un-written code, lifestyle or value system which they follow. It is certainly pre-Islamic. Passed on from generation to generation, Pashtunwali guides both individual and communal conduct. If one has to list all the attributes of Pashtunwali, they would be: Melmastia (hospitality); Nanawatai (forgiveness or asylum); Nyaw aw Badal (justice and revenge); Turah (bravery); Sabat (loyalty); Khegaṛa/Shegaṛa (righteousness); Groh (faith); Pat, Wyaar aw Meṛaana (respect, pride and courage); Naamus (protection of women); Nang (honour); and Hewaad (country).

Scholars have differed in their understanding of the crux of Pashtunwali. Nadjma Yassari of the Max Planck Institute and Maliha Zulfacar of the Social Sciences Department, Cal Poly, USA, for example, hold views typical of people from that ethnic background. Winston Churchill (in *My Early Life*, Chapter 11: The Mahmund Valley) was rather uncharitable about them in a way highly characteristic of the 'detached' British ruling class (as against those army officers who had happened to live amongst them and worked with them, and thus had developed a different, somewhat amusingly admiring view of the people):

> "The Pathan tribes are always engaged in private or public war. Every man is a warrior, a politician and a theologian. Every large house is a real feudal fortress.... Every family

> cultivates its vendetta; every clan, its feud.... Nothing is ever forgotten and very few debts are left unpaid."

In a modern (2005) novel *Morgen's War* by Leonard Schonberg, the character Abdur speaks of Pashtunwali:

> "It is the way of the Pathans. We have *melmestia*, being a good host, *nanawatai*, giving asylum, and *badal*, vengeance. Pashtuns live by these things."

In any case, however, 'revenge' ranks as one of the most important tenets of Pashtunwali in all its interpretations. Naturally, it goes hand-in-hand with the concepts of courage and honour. It is considered the bounden responsibility of a man to live by these values – he is not man enough if he has to look up to some 'authority', police, judicial system or the government to do justice to him. It is for him to protect his honour; the honour of his women; the honour of his country; and get justice for himself – no one else would do it for him. This is where the roots of the gun culture lie. When they could do it with swords, they did it with swords; when guns arrived, they were immediately perceived as great 'equalizers' demanding nothing unusual from bodily strength and they took to the guns like no other people in the world.

How the Mujahideen War Flooded the Region with Weapons?

Arms Pumped in the Region on an Unprecedented Scale

In the so-called Operation Cyclone, being one of the longest and most expensive covert CIA operations ever undertaken, the CIA is believed to have spent money at the rate of $20-$30 million per year in 1980 and rising to $630 million per year in 1987. It continued after 1989 also as the Mujahideen battled the forces of Muhammad Najibullah's PDPA during the Civil War in Afghanistan (1989-1992). Saudi Arabia in particular agreed to match dollar for dollar the money the CIA was sending for the

Mujahideen. And this included, besides the usual AK and M16A2 rifles, light, medium and heavy (12.7 mm) machineguns, the signature RPG-7, mortars, light artillery, the famous 107 mm MBRL rockets, Chinese Type 83 mine-clearing rockets, and Egyptian and Chinese 122 mm rockets, etc, besides the famous Stinger missiles. Mark Urban, the Diplomatic Editor of BBC TWO's 'Newsnight', estimates that by the time the Soviets withdrew in 1989, the guerrillas could have received anything between 200 and 500 Stingers most of which were unaccounted for at the time the proxy war came to an end. Tara Kartha of the IDSA has estimated that, in the end, nearly $8 billion worth of weapons were dumped into the region.

The ISI Brigadier Muhammad Yousaf, one of the most important characters in the entire operation, himself writes in his book *Silent Soldier: The Man Behind the Afghan Jihad:*

> "The system achieved levels and layers of complexities stretching half way across the world, involving six countries other than Pakistan and Afghanistan, and by 1987 was costing over a million dollars a day, while the 'pipeline' eventually had expanded to a capacity of ferrying 1,000 tonnes of armaments a week by 1986."

The sheer demand on logistics alone deserves to be taken note of.

Pilferage and Diversion

With the inflow of arms, Afghanistan became literally the warehouse for weapons in the region. While weaponry worth billions poured into the region till 1992; the pilferage on the way, mostly along the Pakistani end of the pipeline ensured that even 20 years later, the ISI was believed to have some 3,00,000 AK rifles greased and packed with it. It is from these weapons that they have been giving arms to the terrorists of different hues. During the siege of Kandahar, foreign-aid officials leaving the city at the time or shortly before fighting broke out, reported seeing grease paper everywhere as the Taliban removed the wrappings from the packed weapons. It is understood that the weapons had come directly from the ISI warehouses.

John K Cooley, American author and journalist specializing in terrorism, in his book, *Unholy Wars: Afghanistan, America and International Terrorism* cites British author and arms-trade specialist, James Adams:

> "The mixture of Pakistani corruption and the Afghan aptitude for making money by any means produced an industry that had little to do with a holy war against the infidel Soviet invaders and a great deal to do with profiteering."

In the case of a typical shipment of 100 Kalashnikov AK-47 assault rifles, it would be delivered from Egypt by ship usually to Karachi. At this point of delivery almost third was believed to be appropriated by the Pakistan military. Another point of leakage was believed to be the border checkpoints of the Pakistani army from where they were meant to be distributed under the supervision of the ISI. In the end, the Mujahideen got about 50% of the load originally intended for them." What the ISI did not keep in its warehouses, ended up eventually in the international black market.

Lawrence Lifschultz, author and journalist with *The Guardian*, says that Andrew Elva, an American advisor to the Afghan Mujahideen and an official of the Federation for American Afghan Action (FAAA) had claimed before the US Senate that

> "Pakistan's Inter-Services Intelligence, run by Maj Gen Akhtar Abdul Rehman, which oversees the transfer of money and arms to the rebels, is responsible for the theft of millions of dollars in funds and military equipment."

He alleged that $700 million out of $1.09 billion in aid earmarked by the Congress for the rebels between 1980 and 1981 had disappeared.

The Unbelievable Story and the Hoax of the Gun-Makers of Darra Adam Khel

The Front

Darra Adam Khel, a small town some 20 miles south of Peshawar city, fascinates the Westerners to no end. A large number of photo journalists have visited the place and many photo features have appeared on the place. Most readers might have seen photographs of arms shops there with all sorts of rifles hanging from the walls and cartridges kept in plastic jars like candies. Prospective buyers could fire the weapons at will – even visitors could have the pleasure of firing them for a small fee. In fact, a famous joke about Darra Adam Khel is that there are only two smells there: cordite and hashish!

A so-called 'Darra-made AK-47' could be had for as little as $125 against the world average of $534. This is cheaper than most smart phones. A copy of the Turkish/Bulgarian MP5 sub-machinegun would cost just $67. Khitab Gul, a 45 year old gun-maker told AFP,

> "In the past 10 years I have sold 10,000 guns, and had zero complaints."

The Reality

When you go there, you are shown people working with rather elementary hand tools. Since ages, everybody has been accepting this story without questioning it – simply because nobody ever applied critical mind to it. In the following, I will take this unbelievable story and the hoax of the local gun makers apart, and show that the 1,200 gun shops in Darra Adam Khel are just a ruse to cover up the truth. The simple fact is that it is impossible to manufacture an AK rifle or any other modern weapon system with hand tools. This is against basic science and engineering. Modern weapons demand great precision and that sort of precision can never be had with hand tools.

There is no way one could make a complex thing like the bolt of an AK rifle or make rifling in the barrel, without machines made specifically for the job. Making a double barrel shot gun in 'craft production' is one thing – making an automatic rifle quite another. Making the parts of a modern rifle like the rotating bolt carrier etc necessarily requires factories and sophisticated machines made specifically for that purpose. Rifling a barrel, for example, requires something called a rifle lathe. The lands and grooves in a typical rifling are cut and measured in thousandth of an inch. You cannot make such parts with a file or drill in your hands. The bullet fits the rifling of the barrel to within one-thousandth of an inch. The tolerances being so small, this sort of accuracy can come only with machines. In this book, I do not have space to discuss this issue at greater length and give photographs but I strongly suggest interested readers to go to https://www.scribd.com/doc/35165946/Ak-47-TechnicAl-Manual and download the following documents in pdf from this link and subsequent links therein for free. They are: "AK-47 Technical Description Manual"; "AK-47 Rifle: Disassembly"; and the "Service Manual 7.62 mm Kalashnikov Rifle (AK)". These documents contain a large number of detailed colour photographs and drawings of the parts of the AK-47. Even if you do not have any idea of how parts are made on a lathe or milling machine, the sheer complexity of the design would instantly convince you that no one can ever make them with hand tools or in a small workshop. Making them is an enormously complex process. In fact, getting the right steel itself is very difficult. You can also go to https://www.youtube.com/watch?v=Ad_4whlPGzU and watch the video "How Does The AK-47 Work: 3D Animation Model". The video on https://www.youtube.com/watch?v=laYMa5xhTQc will show you a documentary in which they show you the AK-47's origins, how it's made and tested, who uses it and much more. You'll be taken to the Izhmash manufacturing plant (Kalashnikov Concern – Izhevsk Machine-building Plant till 2013) where the rifles are assembled. Another video at https://www.youtube.com/watch?v=y6hNqR4K7tw will show you "How Does the M16 Work: 3D Animation Model". You can also go to Google Images and see the photographs of the interiors of Izhmash manufacturing plant. You will be amazed. And do not buy an argument that the Darra guys do not have to manufacture on that large a scale. If you have to make a certain part, you necessarily require the machine specifically required to make that part even if you have to make just one piece. The machine can, of course, make many more pieces too.

The whole story of home-making of the AK-47 and other weapons in some sort of mythical cottage industry is, therefore, an elaborate hoax which all those people in the media and academic circles (who are not highly critical scientists) have accepted for decades without questioning. It also demonstrates how a worldwide hoax (you may recall the Y2K hoax also) can be perpetrated. If the rifles are getting made there, there have to be proper factories replete with the necessary machines – no compromise is possible on the essential machines. They have to have access to the starting materials also – steel rods, ingots, sheet metal, everything. And if you have, by any chance, the requisite machinery, the story of a cottage industry automatically collapses. Any modern weapon system cannot be made with hand tools or home tools – period!

This means that either the Darra people do not show their real factories to anybody or that the entire Darra thing is an elaborate hoax to hoodwink the world – may be the rifles get made somewhere else but are just sold through these people. You can understand, it is easy to sell things with a little bit of romantic history attached to it – here are the guys who have been making guns since the past nearly 120 years – look at how skilled the poor, illiterate guys are! For all you know, the ISI itself could be making the rifles in some secret factories and selling it through the 'front' of the shops in Darra Adam Khel. Or maybe they are still selling off some of the rifles they had pilfered during the Mujahideen war.

Copies of famous rifles are made elsewhere in the world also by smaller countries. A Myanmar state-owned company makes the so-called MA-1 rifle which is based on the Israeli Galil. Copies of Colt M4 have also been found made in Myanmar. Who makes them in Myanmar? Long before the UN/USA arms embargo struck Myanmar, a German engineer, called Fritz Werner, had established a plant to manufacture G3 rifles. After the embargo, the factory was taken over by the military government. Myanmar has founded its own arms industry – the EMEC (The Electro Mechanical and Engineering Corps of the Burmese Armed Forces) is believed to have acquired the technology and the machinery to manufacture weapons illegally from Israel and Singapore. They are believed to have made a bullpup rifle also, called EMERK-1 which is based on the Chinese QBZ-97B, the Israeli Tavor and the Steyr AUG. Everywhere they have to make them in factories. Nowhere in the world have you found people making them in their backyards – then what is so magical about the Darra guys?

Let us not abandon scientific reasoning. Let us not buy the rhetoric of the locals. Aamer Ahmed Khan of the BBC was told by Haji Munawar Afridi, an arms trader (and a former MP too) at Darra Adam Khel that "There is nothing we cannot copy." He went on, "You bring us a Stinger missile and we will make you an imitation that would be difficult to tell apart from the original." This is outrageous. A Stinger is much more than a tube and a rocket. The electronics involved is so complicated that even huge nations like India have not been able to make it – and here you have a tribal boasting about making it! The journalist writes further, "but it would perhaps be unwise to dismiss it as sheer bluster." You can see that's where journalists (who are obviously not scientists) fail. Haji Munawar Afridi did not stop at that. In April 1988, a major ammunition dump in Rawalpindi used for stockpiling US and Saudi-funded arms for the Afghan fighters had accidentally blown up. The entire dump, called the Ojhri camp, was gutted in a day-long inferno during which dozens of people were killed. Haji Afridi says that the government sold all the destroyed ammunition as scrap to arms dealers in Darra Adam Khel. And, "from those destroyed weapons, we overnight acquired the technology for manufacturing mines, machine guns, small cannons and even multi-barrel rocket launchers." Acquisition of high technology from gutted, destroyed scrap – outrageous becomes a feeble word! By God, had it been true, the Afridis deserved a Nobel Prize! Give him enough rope and he will hang himself – the proverb was never truer than in the case of Haji Afridi!

Drug Money and the Illicit Arms Trade in the Region

Even in the Mughal era, most of the revenue from the region came from poppy cultivation. No wonder, poppy is still the principal support system of the region. It was natural that the warlords too would use the drug money for procuring weapons. About 88% of the world's heroin and morphine come from Afghan opium; the remaining comes from Myanmar and the Lao People's Democratic Republic. Drugs bring the money that they need to buy arms. Even in those cases where terrorism is state-sponsored, the government agencies concerned use drug (or some other crime) money to procure arms. The ISI has been financing its covert operations partly through drug trafficking. Drugs are procured from the Golden Triangle (Iran, Afghanistan and Iraq) and the Golden Crescent (Myanmar, Thailand, Cambodia and Laos). Major drug seizures on the India-Nepal border point to it.

The dynamics of drugs and illicit arms trade (narco-terrorism) is actually quite simple. Narcotics flow from east to west; that is, from the less developed to the developed. The arms flow from west to east, that is, from the more developed to the less developed. At times, even the routes adopted are the same. The Balkan and northern routes are the main heroin trafficking corridors linking Afghanistan to the huge markets of the Russian Federation and Western Europe. The Balkan route traverses the Islamic Republic of Iran (often via Pakistan), Turkey, Greece and Bulgaria across South-East Europe to the Western European market and carries about 61% of the stuff. The northern route runs mainly through Tajikistan and Kyrgyzstan (or Uzbekistan or Turkmenistan) to Kazakhstan and the Russian Federation and carries the rest of it. More than half of the global seizures take place in Iran and Turkey.

According to the "World Drug Report of the United Nations Office on Drugs and Crime", and user information submitted to the "Havocscope: Global Black Market Information", the price of heroin in some countries given below will give some idea of the money involved in the business: India $10.93 per gram; Afghanistan $2.4 per gram; Pakistan $3.0 per gram; Colombia $20.1 per gram; Belgium $31.8 per gram; Germany $48.0 per gram; United Kingdom $61.5 per gram; Italy $80.6 per gram; Ukraine $123.9 per gram; and United States $200 (UN) / $110 (User Submitted) per gram. No wonder, the illegal drug trade in the world is estimated at about 1.5% of the total global trade and was reckoned at about $435 billion a year by the UNODC in 2013. Illegal drugs trade accounts for nearly 50% of the entire business of international organized crime.

HOW DID THE ISIS GET ITS WEAPONS?

There are several theories regarding the sources from which the ISIS acquired its armament. All of them are partial truths. We will critically examine them at length.

Loot from the Retreating Iraqi Army

ISIS is claimed to have looted many weapons from Iraqi military stocks including US military vehicles and an array of internationally manufactured arms given to them, when they registered some startling military victories across northern and western Iraq beginning in June 2014. Two things argue against the hypothesis. The first is that professional armies are taught to destroy their weapon systems if they are obliged to leave them behind lest they fall into enemy hands. Naval commanders scuttle their massive ships also. Even in the raid that killed Osama bin Laden, since one of the helicopter that had made the emergency landing was damaged and unable to fly again, it was destroyed to safeguard its classified equipment (rumoured to be some sort of stealth capability). The pilot smashed "the instrument panel, the radio, and the other classified fixtures inside the cockpit" and the SEALs scuttled it with explosives. The question is why the Iraqis did not do so? They needed no time or preparation for it. Just shove the muzzle of a rifle in dirt or mud so that some of it goes into it and then fire it – the barrel will bulge beyond repair and render the rifle unusable. The second is that, even if the fleeing Iraqi soldiers had deliberately ensured that the ISIS got the weapons, the ISIS could not go on fighting with only those weapons. Ammunition is not the only consumable item in a battle; part of guns wear out, get damaged and need replacement – often the whole gun needs to be replaced. All armies maintain elaborate arms repair workshops and a reliable system of supply of spare parts. Even if we accept that the ISIS fortuitously got a large number of rifles in one go, how they were supposed to get spare parts and arms repair workshops in future?

And if we are to accept the popular narrative that the ISIS landed upon the Iraqi weapons by chance as the Iraqis fled, it means that the ISIS could not have had factored it in their strategy before they had attacked Mosul. The ISIS could not have made its strategic plans based on this. They could not have imagined that the Iraqi forces would give up without fighting and they would get all their weapons and that, with the help of those weapons, they would be able to capture further territory and further weapons caches including those from armed forces and opposition groups in Syria. This is ridiculous; they could not have foreseen the future. As we have discussed earlier, the meek surrender by the Iraqi forces remains a great unsolved mystery in the saga of the ISIS. The question is what strategic planning the ISIS must have made for the 'more likely' eventuality of the Iraqi forces offering stiff resistance? Surely, we don't mean to tell the world that the ISIS rode on its luck all the way! This means that while they got weapons from the fleeing Iraqis, it cannot be their sole source.

Purchases from the International Black Market

Considerable research has been done on the subject in a study by the Amnesty International in a report called "Taking Stock: The Arming of Islamic State"; by the Armament Research Service (ARES), and the London-based arms monitoring group Conflict Armament Research (CAR), all based on an extensive review of thousands of verified videos and photographs, besides cataloguing of thousands of cartridges. Jack Moore, Middle East reporter of the *Newsweek*, also cites this report and discloses that the ISIS is using arms and ammunition made in at least 25 countries, including the US, China, Belgium, France, Russia and Germany. The ISIS has purchased old weapons made in countries that no longer exist, such as the former Yugoslavia, Czechoslovakia and the former Soviet Union also. The other major sources of purchase are China and Serbia. Analysis of the cartridges was important as any attempt at erasing manufacturer's marks from millions of cartridges (as against the marks on guns) to conceal their origin is extremely difficult as well as risky – you cannot use an oxyacetylene torch on a cartridge, nor can you put it to a sander.

Et tu, United States of America?

Washington spent nearly $30 billion training and equipping Iraqi security forces. In the Amnesty report mentioned above, Patrick Wilcken, researcher on arms control, security trade and human rights says that arms continued to pour into the country, without proper checks and balances. What happened to the now unaccounted weapons we do not know. Whether it was corruption of some officers or collusion of some people, we do not know – what we know for sure is that the weapons have disappeared and have very likely ended up with the ISIS. However, a sizable chunk of the small arms and other weapons systems it handed over to them is now unaccounted for. Michael Kaplan (specializing in Middle East and contributor to Al Jazeera English etc) in his article in the *International Business Times*, and Eric Pianin, Washington Editor and DC bureau chief of the *Fiscal Times* claim that according to a statement of Iraqi Prime Minister Haider Al-Abadi in June 2015, some $656.4 million worth of US military equipment was taken by the ISIS. In other words, the Iraqis are claimed to be so dumb that all the American training was wasted upon them and they did not learn anything all these years!

A "2007 Report of the Government Accountability Office" in the USA had disclosed that 1,90,000 American weapons could not be located at that time in Iraq. John Holly, a retired Marine colonel who served as director of reconstruction logistics for the US-led Coalition Provisional Authority and the US Army Corps of Engineers in Iraq admitted in an interview to the "Center for Public Integrity" that the most fatal Shakespearean flaw was that there was no centralized database of what the Americans had procured for the Iraqis. The question is why? Does the

United States of America not know the importance of keeping a database? Are they so inept? They are the people who keep on tom-tomming in the whole world about the dangers of arms proliferation through their government policies, orders, statements, think-tanks and other publications. Even if someone comes up with a contrived (and patently unbelievable) plea that they had to deliver the arms in such a tearing hurry that they got no time to take receipts from Iraqi commanders, they could have kept at least a centralized pre-delivery database of the serial numbers and other crucial details of the weapons! And did they trust the receivers so implicitly with regard to managing and securing their weapons' stock that they did not consider it necessary for a moment to devise some means of monitoring the end use? If Iraqi military's poor management of arms was well known to all states that transferred weapons to Iraq post-2003, why had they not taken precautionary steps all these years?

Moreover, if we are to believe in the precise figure given by the Iraqi Prime Minister Haider Al-Abadi with regard to the weapons taken from them by the ISIS, what does it indicate? It proves that the Iraqis had accounted for every single weapon that was given to them – whereas the Americans say that they were not accounted for. How do we reconcile the discrepancy? Obviously, one or both of them are telling a lie. Was it, therefore, a deliberate case of 'give and forget'? Or, as many critics believe, the acts of omission were done on purpose. And that would lend credence to all the theories regarding American hand with regard to the ISIS that we have discussed earlier.

Prof Michael Chossudovsky in his article, "US 'Military Aid' to Al-Qaida, ISIS-Daesh: Pentagon Uses Illicit Arms Trafficking to Channel Enormous Shipments of Light Weapons into Syria" minces no words:

> "The US and its allies (including Turkey and Saudi Arabia) have relied on the illicit trade in light weaponry produced in

> Eastern Europe, the Balkans, China, etc for delivery to rebel groups inside Syria, including ISIS-Daesh and Al-Nusra. In turn, operating out of the occupied Golan Heights, Israel's IDF has provided weapons, ammunition, and logistical support to Al-Qaida rebels operating in Southern Syria.... These shipments of weapons are not conducted through internationally approved weapons transfers. While they are the result of a Pentagon (or US government) procurement, they are not recorded as 'official' military aid. They use private traders and shipping companies within the realm of a thriving illicit trade in light weapons.... America's weapons shipments to Syria's rebels are commissioned by the Pentagon (and/or a US government agency) through several intermediaries via private weapons trading and shipping companies from the Black Sea port city of Constanta."

Joseph Christoff, who directed international affairs and trade issues at the US Government Accountability Office between 2000 and 2011, admitted to the "Center for Public Integrity" that monitoring or keeping track of the weapons supplied was extremely difficult. Mark Mazzetti (a Pulitzer Prize-winning journalist) and Ali Younes (veteran columnist and journalist, and contributing analyst for several Arabic, American and International news channels) cited both American and Jordanian officials and claimed in *The New York Times* that weapons shipped into Jordan by the Central Intelligence Agency and Saudi Arabia intended for Syrian rebels had been systematically stolen by Jordanian intelligence operatives and sold to arms merchants on the black market. From the black market, they were there for anybody who could pay for them.

The *Jane's Defence Weekly* (Jane.com April 2016) laid bare the entire process by which the USA supplied weapons to rebels in Syria. The Pentagon (or the relevant government agency) instructs the US Navy MSC (Military Sealift Command) with details and specifications of the light weapons to be purchased and shipped to Syria's 'freedom fighters' via Turkey and Jordan. The ports of delivery are specified. The final destination of the weapons is purposefully not mentioned. The MSC places the order with the FBO [US Government's Federal Business Opportunities (FBO); commercial trading entity acting on behalf of the US Navy MSC]. The FBO in turn transacts with private companies for the procurement and shipping of the weapons and 'explosive materials' out of the Romanian Black Sea port of Constanta: first, to the Turkish Eastern Mediterranean facility of Agalar-Limani near Tasucu in support of rebels in Northern Syria, to be smuggled into Syria with the support of the Turkish authorities. The remainder of the shipment to the Jordanian Red Sea port of Aqaba (for rebels in Southern Syria) via the Suez canal. From Aqaba, the weapons were to be smuggled into Syria through the Southern Syria-Jordanian border.

Arms from Ukraine

Jack Losh, a British foreign correspondent based in eastern Ukraine, wrote in Vice.com, reported that Kuwait's Interior Ministry claimed to have arrested six people in an extremist cell that was aiding the Islamic State (IS) by brokering arms deals, recruiting fighters, and raising money that was then sent to IS-related bank accounts in Turkey. According to the report, the arrested ringleader – a Lebanese man named as Osama Khayat – had admitted to closing weapons deals at an undisclosed location in Ukraine. These arms allegedly included Chinese-made FN-6 MANPADS also. These, the report claimed, were shipped to Turkey and smuggled to IS fighters in Syria. An accomplice, a Syrian national named as Abdulkarim Muhammad Selem, was even said to have owned a Ukraine-based arms company. Losh says that possible gateways to Turkey and the alleged smuggling route lie upon stretches of shoreline along the Azov Sea that are outside of government control, or in the famous port of Odessa, where bribery has been as constant as the tide.

Eastern European Countries, the Usual Suspects

Louise Ridley, assistant news editor of *The Huffington Post* says that James Bevan, the director of Conflict Armament Research (CAR), had told *The Huffington Post* (UK) in September 2016 that the ISIS was purchasing directly from Eastern Europe and the weapons were moving from Eastern Europe to Islamic State in Iraq and Syria within weeks through a 'very rapid' transfer through several countries. Despite signing an 'End User' agreement saying it will use the weapons itself and not sell them to any other countries, Saudi Arabia sent them 'straight to Turkey', from where they got into Islamic State's hands. The Eastern European governments actually knew that Saudi Arabia would pass on the weapons to someone else because, as Bevan said, the Saudi army does not use Soviet calibre weapons – they use NATO calibre American weapons! Jeremy Binnie, Middle East/Africa Editor of the *Jane's Defence Weekly*, concurs completely.

The Guardian reported in its article "Revealed: The £1bn of Weapons Flowing from Europe to Middle East" in August 2016 that since 2012, Eastern European countries have had approved 'discreet sale' of $1.28 billion of weapons to Saudi Arabia, Jordan, the United Arab Emirates and Turkey that are known to ship arms to Syria and Yemen. Citing a team of reporters from the Balkan Investigative Reporting Network (BIRN) and the Organised Crime and Corruption Reporting Project (OCCRP), it claimed that arms export data, UN reports, plane tracking, and weapons contracts examined during a year-long investigation revealed how the munitions were sent east from Bosnia, Bulgaria,

Croatia, Czech Republic, Montenegro, Slovakia, Serbia and Romania. By tracking the movement of aircraft and ships, BIRN and OCCRP were able to follow the flow of arms in real time also. According to Robert Stephen Ford, the US ambassador to Syria between 2011 and 2014, arms bought by the Saudis, Turks, Jordanians and the UAE for Syria are routed through two secret command hubs – called military operation centres (MOCs) – in Jordan and Turkey. The weapons are then transported by road to the Syrian border or airdropped by military planes.

The Turkey Connection

Some journalists have travelled to the region and have video recordings of the endless convoys of trucks supplying the terrorist army. These trucks were travelling from deep within Turkey, crossing the Syrian border with absolute impunity, and headed on their way with the implicit protection of nearby Turkish military forces. Attempts by the Syrian government to attack these convoys and the terrorists flowing in with them were met by Turkish air defences. Germany's international broadcaster 'Deutsche Welle' (DW) published the first video report from a major Western media outlet illustrating that ISIS was supplied not by 'black market oil' or 'hostage ransoms' but billions of dollars worth of supplies carried into Syria across NATO member Turkey's borders via hundreds of trucks a day.

Geopolitical analyst Tony Cartalucci also argues in his article in the *Global Research* that if the supply lines of the ISIS were solely confined within Syrian and Iraqi territory, then surely both Syrian and Iraqi forces could utilize their one advantage – air power – to cut the front-line ISIS fighters from the source of their supplies. But this is not happening and there is a good reason why. The supply lines of the ISIS run precisely where Syrian and Iraqi air power cannot go – that is, to the north and into NATO-member Turkey, and to the southwest into US allies Jordan and

Saudi Arabia. There is no other plausible explanation of the ISIS's ability to wage war within Syria and Iraq besides immense resources being channelled to it from abroad. Turkey has created de facto buffer zones within Syrian territory which would require a direct military confrontation with Turkey itself to eliminate.

If you believe the Russians, Vitaly Churkin, the Russian envoy to the UN, as reported by RT.com, has categorically stated in his submission to the UN Security Council,

> "The main supplier of weapons and military equipment to ISIL fighters is Turkey, which is doing so through non-governmental organizations. Work in this area is overseen by the National Intelligence Organization of Turkey."

He mentioned several NGOs by name, including the Besar Foundation and the Iyilikder Foundation.

THE ISIS'S REPERTOIRE OF WEAPONS AND THEIR UTILITY

The ISIS has a motley mix of weapons which includes even decades old weapons. This fact, by itself, confirms two things. First, that the sources are diverse. Second, that the buyers, that is, the ISIS, were either fooled by the arms dealers; or they were not very discerning, not to speak of being knowledgeable, customers – in effect, they took whatever they got without any planning and strategy for their employment. From the studies mentioned above, it has been determined that the important weapon systems being used by the ISIS in significant numbers included the following:

1. **Rifles:** Iraqi-manufactured 'Tabuk' M70; Chinese CQ assault rifle; American Bushmaster XI5-E2S semi-automatic rifle; American M16 and M4; German H&K G-36; Russian Dragunov SVD; American Mk 14

Enhanced Battle rifle; Austrian Steyr SSG 69; and older rifles like the Belgian FN FAL, Czech VZ 52, Russian SKS and German Walther KKJ etc.

2. **Machineguns:** Russian PKM; Russian DShK; Chinese Type 80 PK/PKM analogues; Hungarian KGK; Russian and Iraqi variants of the Russian RPK light machine gun; and the German Rheinmetall MG3.
3. **Anti-materiel Rifles:** Iranian Sayyad-2 AM5015; and the Chinese M99 rifle.
4. **Auto Cannons:** Russian 2A14.
5. **Anti-Aircraft Guns:** Russian ZU-23-2; Chinese Type 65.
6. **Anti-Tank Weapons:** RPG-7 with PG-7V, PG-7VT and OG-7V anti-tank and anti-personnel munitions (or analogue designs); Russian 9K135 Kornet ATGW (anti-tank guided weapon); Chinese-designed HJ-8 (Red Arrow 8); besides older and less effective 9M17M Skorpion-M and the 9M14 and 9M14M Malyutka.
7. **Mortars:** Iraqi Al-Jaleel 60 mm light mortar and World War II era Russian 82-PM-41 and 82-BM-37 types; and home-made mortars in the 80-100 mm range. IS captured an unknown quantity of 155 mm M198 towed howitzers from Iraqi military stocks during its capture of Mosul, along with the older Chinese Type 59-1.
8. **Artillery:** Russian 85 mm D-44; Russian 122 mm howitzers D-30 and M-30; Type 59-1 field gun; and American M-198 155 mm howitzer captured from the Iraqis.
9. **MANPADS:** In one instance in 2015, IS attempted surface-to-air attack using an old SA-7 Strela system against US aircraft that were supporting the Iraqi army and Kurdish forces. In another incident, IS employed the Chinese FN-6 system against an Iraqi military helicopter near Bayji.

10. **AFVs and Tanks:** Most armoured fighting vehicles currently in use by IS are Russian-designed or US types captured from Iraqi military stocks: the Russian BMP-1, MT-LB Infantry Fighting Vehicle, and the US M113A2 Armoured Personnel Carrier, M1117 Armoured Security Vehicle, and up-armoured HMMWV (Humvee) variants. The main battle tanks deployed by IS are the Russian T-54/T-55 and T-62; IS has been able to capture some Chinese Type 69-II tanks and US M1A1M Abrams in Iraq. It appears, however, that all captured M1A1M tanks were later destroyed by IS, and there is no evidence of their use in further combat.

From a professional perspective, the question is, are all of them useful in the type of combat they envisage? The answer is a categorical no and rather affirms the lack of higher level military knowledge in the commanders of the ISIS, a fact that we have discussed earlier. They seem to be using anything and everything, including bolt-action rifles which the arms dealers dumped on them. But not all of their weapons lend themselves to be used profitably by a terrorist organization. For example, they might have landed some old tanks. The question is what do you or what can you do with just a couple of tanks? You are not a conventional army. If you want to fight in the fashion of a conventional army, you should have the requisite numbers of tanks – and that you do not have. Hence while posing with the tank or taking them out in some parade in a town may look good to the uninitiated, there is not much one could do with it – moreover, they are an easy target for the warplanes of Russia, America, Britain and France. Then, most importantly, how would they manage the complex task of repairs of the tanks which the tanks need so frequently; typically, one breakdown every 250 km?

So is the case with heavy artillery being used in the open. The photo op might be good for recruitment purposes, but the poor prospective recruits would be in for some rude surprises once they land in the field. A terrorist ought to remain a terrorist; the moment he tries to become an army, he would be playing the game on the terms of the enemy and shall be decimated. The ISIS is obsessed with a medieval imagery of reckless charges. This happens – they are not alone in living such fantasies. *The Hindu* had reported in July 2000 that some arrested members of an organization called Deendar Anjuman in Vijaywada had admitted to have directives to create communal disturbances and 'prepare the ground' so that their guru Hasan, with nine lakh 'Pathans' on horses, could invade and capture India sometime next year and spread Islam. Pathans on horses in the 21st century!

CAN ANYTHING BE DONE REGARDING THE ILLEGAL ARMS TRADE?

Wishful Thinking and Reality

In the context of Pakistan and Afghanistan in particular, it is customary in academic circles (such as Michael Bhatia and Mark Sedra) to speak in platitudinous terms, such as:

> "The potential for small arms reduction and control programming is dependent on the presence of a number of conditions that can be grouped under the headings of security, development and political. In the security sphere, a base level of security and stability is required to advance small arms collection and control efforts. Steps must be taken to break previous cycles of violence and imbue the population with the confidence to abandon their arms.... Deployment of a robust peace support mission capable of providing a security buffer for the process, and the successful implementation of a security sector reform process to entrench the rule of law across the country."

It needs no explanation that such wishful thinking is best left to the seminar/conference circuit – we cannot imagine 'imbuing the population with the confidence to abandon their arms'. Obviously, they do not know the people of the region. What could not be done in 2000 years cannot be done in 20 years. Given the very strong cultural life force of the gun culture, nothing can be done, at least in that region, to address the problem of the innate lawless, irrepressible, uncontrollable nature of the people. India must accept this reality and plan accordingly.

The problem of illegal arms in the world is too complex and enormous to lend itself to simplistic solutions. Trafficking in arms is not a problem one could solve outright; it is a problem which, at the very best, one can only hope to manage somewhat. Logically, the objective should be to reduce the supply of, and demand for, the weapons. Well over a 1,000 companies manufacture light weapons and ammunition in nearly 100 countries. Let us face it. As long as there would be conflict in the world, there would be demand. And as long as there would be demand, there would be somebody to supply. The arms dealers are only the middlemen between the producers and the consumers of arms. The real 'culprits' are the consumers and the producers. We do not have any control on the consumers. As for the producers, they too are affairs of sovereign nation states. As such, neither the factories can be shut down nor can the nations be asked to restrict their sales. The social cost of any such misadventure will be too heavy. After all, profits generated by the arms factories are not for the government alone; the factories directly support a large number of workers and their families, and indirectly constitute an important part in the entire complex economic machinery of the nation. We cannot envisage a situation where the arms factories keep on producing full blast but are unable to sell to anybody. Finally, we must realize that a world which could not carry out even nuclear disarmament, how could it even think of dispensing with conventional weapons? It would not be even a pipe dream; it would be a madman's fantasy. Frequently touted measures like enacting strong export and border controls; safeguarding (or destroying) stockpiles; dismantling trafficking networks; and addressing the root causes of the civil conflicts and soaring urban crime rates, etc would require a Herculean effort in the first place and, second, pro-active willing cooperation of all states. That is not going to happen. Similarly, addressing the root causes of conflicts is yet another childish dream – we cannot eliminate conflict from the world!

A Critique of the Suggested Measures

The United Nations Conference on the Illicit Trade in Small Arms and Light Weapons in All Its Aspects (July 2001) adopted the "Programme of Action to Prevent, Combat and Eradicate the Illicit Trade in Small Arms and Light Weapons in All Its Aspects" (PoA), the first comprehensive global agreement on such arms. The PoA calls for 10 pillars: national points of contact and coordination agencies; legislation, regulations, and administrative procedures; criminalization regimes; stockpile management and security; weapons collection and disposal; export, import, and transfer controls and regulations; brokering; marking, tracing, and record-keeping; disarmament, demobilization, and reintegration of ex-combatants; assistance and international cooperation. It has, not produced any result at all.

For the sake of completeness of the narrative in the book, I will briefly discuss the measures suggested by Rachel Stohl also. Her recommendations include:

> Regional and international arms embargoes with stringent punishments; developing a common international system for the marking and tracing of weapons so as to be able to track weapons to their sources; creation of an international clearinghouse, where weapons can be registered, recovered and traced, allowing states to identify seized small arms and

> to verify the legality of the trade; adoption of an international treaty, or at the very least common international standards, regarding the practices of arms brokers so as to prevent arms brokers from changing locations to avoid prosecution under one country's laws by doing business in and through other, less-regulated countries; instituting an international treaty or, at the very least, agreed-upon common international export criteria and fixing international standards that determine eligibility requirements for arms exports so as to prevent arms from entering the legal market and falling into the hands of those likely to divert them or use them for unintended purposes; strengthening of end-use monitoring (EUM) by arms-exporting states in order to prevent legal sales from being diverted into the black market; developing a common, international end-user certificate that cannot be easily forged or duplicated; providing adequate security and management of arms stockpiles; destroying surplus and obsolete weapons, particularly in conflict areas, to ensure that these weapons are not diverted to the black market; enhancing international cooperation and information exchanges to assist in the apprehension and prosecution of illicit arms brokers and the recovery of illicit weapons; and strengthening of oversight of weapons issued to individuals – both civilian and military – to avoid the temptation of selling weapons on the black market.

These measures cannot be effective because they ignore the fundamental realities of the business in arms discussed above. As such, they are wishful thinking at best and a puerile academic exercise at worst. These measures cannot work unless the world is reduced, for all practical purposes, to something before which an Orwellian state of the worst type would pale. Moreover, who can imagine this sort of mutual cooperation in the world when there is so much discord?

9

Radicalization, Salafism and Jihad: Facts and Fallacies

WHY CERTAIN MUSLIMS HAVE TAKEN TO TERRORISM?

Islamic precepts have been there in the world for a long time – if it were to be argued that there is something such in Islam that drives the Muslims inexorably towards committing acts of terrorism, why did we not have the problem of terrorism earlier? The answer is that the very premise of there being "something such in Islam that drives the Muslims inexorably towards committing acts of terrorism" is wrong. Those who say so are trying to find a religious explanation for a political problem and that's just not possible.

Michael Scheuer, a former CIA intelligence officer, author, foreign policy critic, political analyst and currently an adjunct Professor at Georgetown University's Center for Peace and Security Studies, argues in his book *Imperial Hubris* that Islamic terror attacks against America are motivated by a perception that the US foreign policy is a threat to Islam:

> "The focused and lethal threat posed to US national security arises not from Muslims being offended by what America is,

> but rather from their plausible perception that the things they most love and value – God, Islam, their brethren, and Muslim lands – are being attacked by America."

He has further condensed his argument down to the phrase "They hate us for what we do, not who we are." Scheuer acknowledges that American culture and religion are offensive to many Muslims, but claims that these factors have very little role as motivators of Islamic terrorism. Rather, he cites the following US foreign policy actions as fuelling Islamic terror:

- The presence of US troops on Muslim holy ground in Saudi Arabia;
- US support for 'apostate' police states in Muslim nations such as Saudi Arabia, Egypt, Pakistan, Algeria, Morocco, and Kuwait;
- The US invasions and subsequent occupations of the Muslim nations of Afghanistan and Iraq;
- US support for the creation of the Christian state of East Timor from territory previously held by Muslim Indonesia; and
- US approval or support of:
    - India against Muslim forces in the disputed region of Kashmir;
    - The Philippines against separatist Muslims in Mindanao;
    - Russia against Muslim Chechens in the Second Chechen War;
    - China against Muslim Uyghur separatists in western China; and
    - Israel against Muslim Arabs in the Palestinian territories.

Albert J Bergesen and Omar Lizardo, both at the University of Arizona, also conclude in their work "International Terrorism and the World-System" that –

"Terrorism should be seen as a strategic reaction to American power, an idea associated with the 'blowback' thesis. In this view, the presence of empires – both at the end of the last century and today – and the analogous uni-polar military position of the United States today provoke resistance in the form of terrorism. The Russian, Ottoman and Habsburg Empires – which controlled multiple ethnic, religious, and national peoples – led to a backlash, or blowback, by Serb, Macedonian, and Bosnian terrorist organizations (the Black Hand, Young Bosnia, Narodnaya Volya). By analogy, the powerful global position of the United States, particularly in its role of propping up repressive undemocratic regimes, constitutes something of a similar condition with Arab-Islamic terrorism as a result. The causal mechanism here is that the projection of military power plants seeds of later terrorist reactions, as 'retaliation for previous American imperial actions'."

RADICALIZATION AND DE-RADICALIZATION

If it is claimed that extreme religiosity of a rabid kind has suddenly increased to dangerous proportions amongst a section of the Muslims and that it is driving them towards terrorism, a reason must be found for it. Radical Islam, radicalization and the need for de-radicalization have been the buzzwords in the official circles of the world and the usual seminar/conference circuit. Radical Islam has been described as having a nihilistic fury. But what makes them nihilistic? All religious texts are liable to be interpreted in different ways. But there is no reason to believe that a certain interpretation (call it Salafist, Wahabi, jihadi or whatever) is so powerful, so irresistible that those exposed to it would come to believe in it so fanatically, so uncompromisingly that they would be prepared to kill innocent people for that. What is there in it which makes people embrace certain death (for example, in a suicide bomb blast) and have no remorse at all in killing people with whom they had no direct enmity? What is so unique to it that other religious philosophies do not have? Can other religions or even their 'deviant' interpretations produce such men? If not, why? Every race, every religion, every civilization has had a medieval or ancient past and parts of it could have been glorious. But not all of them get obsessed with a desire to return to that glorious past. And even if they do, how does it translate into killing innocent people?

As we know, not all of the terrorists are the products of brainwashing or intense indoctrination in some dinghy, desolate madrisa in the outback of Afghanistan. There are many who went to the West, studied subjects like engineering and medicine and yet got 'radicalized'. Would someone blow himself up merely because he is such a staunch supporter of the *purdah* system that he cannot tolerate women going about the marketplace showing their faces? There may be what the Westerners describe as a "toxic mix of religion with tribalism", but that does not translate into acts of terror or a 'war on the West' by itself. Analysing the phenomenon would demand both intellectual and moral courage as it could lay open some uncomfortable truths about the society in question. Policy-makers may have to stare in the face of some cracks, incongruities, and ugly truths about the society they represent.

Incidentally, dying in a bomb blast or in a shootout in some *fidayeen* attack is not easy – it hurts before you breathe your last. How do they overcome it? Those who flew the two huge commercial airliners into the WTC towers flew it with great precision. It amounted to landing the plane in a strip of the width of the towers and that too without the aid of the Instrument Landing System – even their speed was far in excess of the normal landing speed. This means that they did it with simple visual control. This means that the tower was very much in sight and grew in size with every moment. How would have it felt to find a rock solid massive concrete tower before your eyes and knowing that you are going to crash into it? How they would have felt before the collision and immediately after it? They must have known that with the thousands of gallons of aviation fuel on board, the plane would not only disintegrate with the impact, it would burst into a fireball. How would have been the feeling of imminent death by the shock of collision and fire? The hijackers were certainly not drugged like some of the assassins (the *hashshashin*) of yore – they could not have flown the plane in a drugged state. This means that were perfectly in their senses. Determined people can make themselves willing to die and refuse to scream; even they can, however, not say that they enjoy the process of death. There is much pain in it. How do they prepare themselves to overcome it? Would the West like the world to believe that those few lines in a certain interpretation of the Qur'an have some such magical power that they enable a man to overcome the pain of death?

If there is even a modicum of truth in the popular narrative of radicalization, the human race will have to re-examine all the theories it has developed over the centuries regarding human behaviour and rational faculties in the Homo sapiens. We should not start treating a disease without diagnosing it first. The so-called 'radicalization' might be leading to terrorism, but we must first find out what makes these people susceptible to radicalization in the first place. Unless we address those susceptibilities and vulnerabilities, any attempt at 'de-radicalization' would amount to symptomatic treatment at best and hogwash at worst.

This is a complex thing and we cannot afford to be simplistic about it. The fundamental question is very sensitive:

> "Are the Muslims who are susceptible to the so-called radicalization so dumb that all their technical and secular

> education notwithstanding, they are taken in by a motivator in just a few minutes?"

What is so special and mesmerizing about the 'talk' of the motivator? What is the secret of his persuasive skills even as he could not be a guy with a formal secular college education? Is the so-called radicalization so easy? If someone really believes that radicalization through brief personal contacts, websites, or videos posted on the YouTube is indeed possible then would they not be indirectly implying that there is something fundamentally wrong with the susceptible people and which cannot be helped by giving them secular education? If someone argues that the content of the talks during personal contacts, websites or videos is so captivating that it changes the entire worldview of the listener or viewer, it should theoretically be possible to create similarly captivating content arguing in the opposite direction of de-radicalization also. Why has someone not done that so far? And if it has been done, why it has been unsuccessful? We must know, what is so fascinating about essentially a medieval world-view that the susceptible people get prepared to leave the comforts of their homes, kill and get killed for that? What is in the modern world which, in their subjective perception, is unjust, unfair, immoral or ungodly?

There is a term called *takfir* and it has been touted in the West at the root of all the executions of Shi'ites, Christians, Yazidi and members of other ethnic and religious communities by the ISIS. The Hezbollah leader Hassan Nasrallah frequently referred to Salafist-jihadi Islamic organizations (the most prominent of which are ISIS and the Al-Nusra Front) as '*takfir* groups' (*jama'at takfiriyya*). But, once again, to blame everything on a disputable concept is utterly simplistic. According to the dictionary of Muhammad Mustafa Khan 'Maddah', *takfir* means "to accuse a Muslim of *kufr* through a *fatwa*". Now *kufr* is another frequently misunderstood word. Its correct meaning is "non-acceptance, not accepting, rejection, ungratefulness". *Kafir* means one who is not grateful to God for His mercies and all things good, one who conceals the truth, etc. Fatwa means a written order on a religious matter by a religious authority. *Takfir* also means to give *kaffara*. *Kaffara* means an act to purify oneself or redeem oneself of a sin by repentance. Now, it would be stretching it a bit too far to claim that *takfir* means to denounce a person as an infidel and thereby approve his execution.

Do we mean to say that the susceptible people not have any rational faculties of their own? And if they really do not have rational faculties, would it not mean that in spite of all the progress which mankind has made in all these centuries, we have not yet been able to evolve an education system which would enable people to think rationally? What have we been producing – just zombie-like people with some skills in some field – 'software coolies', for example? A too heavy and exclusive emphasis on radicalization as the root of all evils amounts to denying that the susceptible people could be becoming terrorists for some other reasons also. It is imperative that we address those reasons and take corrective or even punitive measures if necessary. But I must caution that there are no simplistic explanations of the 'reasons of terrorism'. Different peoples in different societies (even within a given society) might have different reasons to take to terrorism. For some, there could be personal reasons like some personal loss or atrocity suffered; for some, a persecution complex or perceived unfair discrimination; for some, the reasons could pertain to something common to the whole community. For some, it could be a desperate exercise to redeem what they perceive to be their self-respect; for some, it could indeed be some political issue. There are myriad reasons of people taking to terrorism and oversimplification or the desire to find a single 'real reason' or common 'root cause' must be ruthlessly eschewed.

The world will have to face complexity. Let us not be frightened of complexity. One who does not have the moral courage to face a complex truth, invents simpler falsehoods. Frederick Forsyth, in his novel *The Afghan*, offers a simplistic explanation of how someone had become a terrorist:

> "The cruise missiles were aimed at the training camps of Al-Qaida, and the caves of the Tora Bora. Among those that went astray was one that entered the mouth of a natural and empty cave high in the mountain above Maloko-zai. The detonation deep inside the cave split the mountain and an entire face peeled away. Ten million tonne of rock crashed into the valley below.... When Izmat Khan reached the mountain there was nothing to recognize. The entire valley had been buried. There was no stream any more, no farm, no orchards, no stock pens, no mosque, no stables, no compounds. His entire family and all his neighbours were gone. His parents, uncles, aunts, sisters, wife and child were dead beneath millions of tonnes of granite rubble. There was nowhere to dig and nothing to dig for. He had become a man with no roots, no relatives, no clan.... In the dying August sun he knelt on the shale high above where his dead family lay, turned west towards Mecca, bowed his head to the ground and prayed. But it was a different prayer this time; it was a mighty oath, a sworn vendetta, a personal jihad unto death and it was against the people who had done this. He declared war on America."

How simple! How melodramatic! It might have happened to one person or some persons. But what about those thousands of others who had not suffered any personal loss and yet who have also taken up arms against the USA? How do we explain their cases?

Some could simply have been 'used' by powers bigger than them. Evan F Kohlmann, an American terrorism consultant, reveals in his paper for the Swedish National Defence College:

"Indeed, some of the most important factors behind the contemporary radicalization of European Muslim youth can be found in Bosnia-Herzegovina, where the cream of the Arab Mujahideen from Afghanistan tested their battle skills in the post-Soviet era and mobilized a new generation of pan-Islamic revolutionaries. The CIA decided that bin Laden's 'Arab Afghans' (or the other Mujahideen they had helped create) were too useful an ally to abandon after the Soviets left Afghanistan, and in a meeting at Green's Hotel, Peshawar, Pakistan, in late 1991, between their local representatives, Prince Turki bin Faisal (head of the Saudi intelligence service) and the 'Arab Afghans', they decided to continue links. The 'strategic' position of Afghanistan vis-a-vis Central Asian oil was also a factor in this decision. The Islamist connections were employed in Bosnia during the break-up of Yugoslavia. Using the Pakistani ISI as an intermediary once more, the CIA channelled weapons and 'Arab Afghan' and other Islamic fighters to the Bosnian Muslim Army. As it was done in the past in Afghanistan, this time too Chinese, North Korean and Iranian arms were supplied in order to maintain deniability."

HOSTILITY TO THE WEST AND WESTERN VALUES

From ISIS to Boko Haram, a feature common to all terrorists is their hatred of the West in general and the USA in particular. The US is increasingly identified with the political, social and economic forces that are responsible for the misery of the community. Contrary to popular perceptions, anti-Americanism and hostility to the West and Western values are not limited to the hardliner Salafis/Wahabis or other Sunni groups. Shi'ite groups such as Iran's Khomeinist regime also hated America. In my view, this hostility has rather complex psychological and cultural dimensions. Prima facie, they may appear irrational but that's what human nature is.

Psychological Dimension

A plausible source of hostility is a sense of their having lost in a 'competition of civilizations' with respect to the West (and not the much-touted 'clash of civilizations'). This has led to the development of some sort of inferiority as well as persecution complex and a feeling of dejection. It is not merely a question of ruing the glory that the Islamic Empire once was. They know that the Muslim nations, in spite of Pakistan being a nuclear power and Iran having developed some good missiles, would find it difficult to cope with even Israel, not to speak of other major Western powers. For the present, somewhere deep down their hearts, they realize that in the materialistic, technological or intellectual race, they have lost out to the West. And this is what hurts them. In their perception, the attitude of the West towards them is condescending at best and overbearing at worst, if not outright hostile. Troubles in life force one to seek the shelter of religion. Religion is a great comforter when everything else fails you. Religiosity amongst people of all races tends to increase when they are passing through difficult times. It is a historically established fact and is not unique to Islam. A desperate man, seeking solace in religion, is susceptible to certain provocative interpretations of religion which offer him a ready, easy-to-understand, even simplistic explanation of all his miseries. People tend to latch on to an idea which paints a certain entity as the root of all their problems – it saves them the trouble of exercising their own critical faculties.

Cultural Dimension

American or Western culture is perceived as a dangerous temptation threatening to poison the Islamic world and the values they cherish – that's why, for example, there are so many issues about the way the terrorists perceive women. They believe the Western culture is a temptation. Muslims are liable to become addicted to and therefore is perceived as dangerous. The name 'Boko Haram' is variously translated as "Western education is forbidden", "Western influence is a sin" and "Westernization is sacrilege". The Hausa word *boko* means 'fake', from the sense it was used earlier in *'ilimin boko'* to describe the kind of schooling the colonialists had brought with them. *Haram* means 'forbidden' or 'sin'. In other words, Boko Haram is thus basically opposed to Western education or Western cultural influences. The way they have developed a complex with respect to the West in the matter of their material progress; they have developed a complex with respect to the West's cultural progress (or dissimilarity) also. They believe that an Islamic revival would result only when the Muslim communities are 'purged' of the 'morally' corrupting Western cultural influences.

Never mind that there are many other non-Muslim countries and societies also which do not approve of the so-called Western culture and the so-called Western influenced cultural norms. In our own country, don't we have millions of people who have serious issues with girls wearing jeans or what they consider as 'revealing Western clothes'; drinking in pubs; going out with boys; sitting together in public parks; celebrating the Valentine's Day; solemnizing a 'love marriage'; or eloping with a boy of a different caste or religion; amongst a thousand things of the type. This might have resulted in criminal acts by those who object to the influence of Western culture, even rapes and murders; but not acts of terrorism. However, for one who has other sources of disgruntlement with respect to the West, the allegedly corrupting influence of Western culture becomes yet another factor to add to his hatred.

JIHAD AND JIHADISTS

For the average Westerner, the words 'jihad' and 'jihadist' conjures up images of wild-eyed, bearded religious fanatics, brandishing swords, attacking the 'infidels' wherever they find them, and forcing them, virtually at knife-point (or, these days at the point of the AK-47), to recite the Kalimah or face a cruel death. Generally, in the West, they think that jihad translates into Holy War. In other words, jihad, to them, means offering the non-Muslims only two choices: conversion or death. They could be pardoned for not knowing better. But, even the terrorists think that they are out on waging a 'global jihad'. That's how you find names like the United Jihad Council and so on. The irony is that other than using the word in its popular sense, they too do not know what they are talking about and can they really accomplish what Islam, even at its peak, could not accomplish? The truth is, however, quite complex. Since the concept of jihad is associated with Muslim theology, it can only be analysed with the requisite knowledge of theology. Of course, there are bound to be disputes and differences of opinion even amongst scholars of the religion over such matters, and there cannot be any unanimity. I can therefore present only an overview of several opinions or interpretations.

The Western notion of a Holy War comes from the Crusades and the etymology of the very word crusade never had any doubts about it. In the late 16th century, the word was originally '*croisade*'. It came from the French word *croisade* which in turn, was an alteration influenced by the Spanish word *cruzado*. *Cruzado* came from *croisee*, literally meaning "the state of being marked with the Cross". The origin of the word crusade may therefore be traced to the Cross made of cloth and worn as a badge on the outer garment of those who took part in these enterprises. In the 17th century the form *crusado*, closer to the Spanish *cruzado* was introduced. The blending of these two forms led to the current spelling, first recorded in the early 18th century. Thus 'crusade' literally meant 'war for the Cross'. The word jihad has never had any such an etymology or meaning.

Amir Hussain, a Canada-based renowned author and scholar of Islam, faculty member at the Loyola Marymount University, USA, and editor of the *Journal of the American Academy of Religion*, points out in his book *Oil and Water: Two Faiths: One God*, the word *'jihad'* appears only four times in the Qur'an. *'Jahada'*, the root verb of the word *'jihad'*, occurs about 25 times and the word *'mujahid'* (one who makes jihad) appears another four times. The word *'jahd'*, according to the celebrated dictionary of Muhammad Mustafa Khan Maddah, means striving, effort, attempt, hardship, etc. In the first place, the correct and the full term for *'jihad'* is *'jihad fi sabilillah'*. In view of the above, it means "to strive in the way of Allah" (SWT). It does not mean a Holy War. War in Arabic is called *'harb'* and holy is called *'muqaddas'*. Thus 'Holy War' in Arabic is called *'harb muqaddas'*! The plural of *'harb'* is *'muhaarbaat'*. A battlefield is called *'harbgaah'*. Since a normal 'war' is called *'harb'* in Arabic, as Maddah also says, a 'warrior' or 'fighter' is therefore called *'muhaarib'*. The plural of *'muhaarib'* for 'warriors' is *'muhaaribun'*. *'Muhaarib'* and *'mujahid'* are quite different things. A *muhaarib* has mundane objectives; a *mujahid* has loftier objectives.

Sayyid Abul A'la Maudoodi, the world-famous scholar of Islam with some 120 books to his credit, in his famous works *Jihad fi Sabilillah* and *Al Jihad fi Islam*, also agrees with the above line. He says that any act or deed which is done for the collective well-being of mankind, by a person who has no vested interest in this world, but seeks only to earn the pleasure and favour of Allah (SWT), is regarded in Islam as a deed done "in the way of Allah (SWT)". It is the sacrifice of life, wealth and carnal desires; the objective of the 'struggle' should be to free one completely from the taints of selfish motives and ambitions for wealth, fame and glory. As an obligation of the individual it is known as *'fard ayn'*; and as an obligation of the community it is known as *'fard kifaya'*. Along this line, Majid Khadduri, Visiting Professor of Islamic Law and Middle East specialist at universities like

Harvard and Columbia, founder of the Paul H Nitze School of Advanced International Studies at Johns Hopkins University, and author of more than 35 books, describes four kinds of jihad:

- Jihad of the heart (*jihad bil qalb/nafs*) is concerned with combating the devil and in the attempt to escape his persuasion to evil. This type of jihad was regarded as the greater jihad (*Al-jihad Al-akbar*).
- Jihad by the tongue (*jihad bil lisan*) is concerned with speaking the truth and spreading the word of Islam with one's tongue.
- Jihad by the hand (*jihad bil yad*) refers to choosing to do what is right and to combat injustice and what is wrong with action.
- Jihad by the sword (*jihad bis saif*) refers to armed fighting in the way of Allah (SWT).

To these four, some people add one more, namely, jihad by the pen and knowledge (*jihad bil qalam/ilm*) is a struggle for good against evil through scholarly study of Islam, *ijtihad* (legal reasoning), and through sciences. Ibrahim Ibn Abi Abalah, one of the Successors, is quoted having said:

> "We have returned from the lesser jihad (*Al-jihad Al-asghar*, meaning battle) to the greater jihad (*Al-jihad Al-akbar*, meaning jihad of the soul)."

Sufis and Shias also classify '*jihad*' into two; the 'Greater *Jihad*' and the 'Lesser *Jihad*' or '*Jihad* of the Sword' and a '*Jihad* of the Spirit', with the former being the 'lesser' *Jihad* and the latter the 'greater' *jihad*.

On the other hand, the historical and so-called 'mainstream' view of *jihad* is articulated by the Hanbali jurist Ibn Taimiyya (d 1328). He says:

> "Since God's word is uppermost, therefore according to Islam, those who stand in the way of this aim must be fought."

The popular interpretation says that the world can be divided only into two conceptual entities: the *Dar-ul-Islam*, that is, the realm of Islam, refers to the places where Islam reigns supreme and its laws are strictly obeyed. The rest of the world becomes, by default, the *Dar-ul-Harb*, that is, the realm of war. The ultimate objective of the true believer is to transform the entire world into *Dar-ul-Islam* (also called *Dar-ul-Iman*). Until that is done, those living in the *Dar-ul-Harb* must either keep on striving to convert that into *Dar-ul-lslam*, or flee from the *Dar-ul-Harb* to some *Dar-ul-Islam* as *'mohajirs'*.

As the readers might be aware, the eighth surah of the Qur'an, the Surah Anfal, and the ninth surah titled Tauba have been described in the West as 'jihadic' surahs and there is great dispute amongst scholars over their true meaning. So is the case with the verses 8:39 and 2:193,

> "Fight them until persecution is no more and religion is all for Allah (SWT)."

Some scholars point to the use of the words 'persecution' and 'fighting'. It has also been pointed out that the Prophet Muhammad (SAW-PBUH) could not have declared a 'Holy War' even before the so-called 'Holy War' of the Crusades had come into existence! Persecution could refer to all that was unjust, and fighting could allude to the 'struggle' Maudoodi speaks of. I will leave it at that as a further semantic and theological discussion is likely to confuse most readers. However, by now, it should clear that the prevailing notions of jihad and jihadists are utterly simplistic.

It needs to be kept in mind that several concepts of many religions may appear to be quite at variance with modern value systems or even legal systems. But one cannot denounce a religion itself for that. All that is expected of the followers of that religion is that they must abide by the laws of the land they live in – what they believe in is immaterial; believing is an internal process for which an offence cannot be defined or created – we do not have the Orwellian concept of thought crime anywhere in the world. This is a fine legal point and needs to be understood clearly.

It should also be clear that even if the popular interpretation of jihad is accepted for a moment for the sake of argument, it still does not equate jihad with acts of terrorism. Terrorism in general and terrorism by some Muslims in particular is not about the Muslims making a bid for the conquest of the world with the help of a few AK-47 rifles and bombs/IEDs. Surely, they are aware of the terribly advanced weapon systems that the armies of the world have made and also their massive resources. They also know that nations can withstand a great deal of punishment, even casualties running into tens of millions. One could kill several thousand people in a single terrorist strike (such as in the 9/11 attack) but anyone who has studied history knows that when it came to the crunch even small nations like England could put up with casualties running as high as 60,000 in a day at the Battle of Somme in the World War I! Nations cannot be terrorized into submission by a few thousands of casualties – it would require either a 'soft' nation or something different to force them to capitulate. Let us be realistic. Does anyone really believe that even the craziest amongst the terrorists would dream of defeating the massive armies of the nations of the world with the help of nothing but a few AK-47 rifles, a few RPG-7s and some bombs/IEDs?

We have Muslim terrorists alright in the world but they could not be driven by a desire to conquer the world; the grandiose 'vision' of the ISIS notwithstanding. They are terrorists not because it is 'ordained' for them to exterminate the non-believers; they are terrorists not because they ascribe to 'radical' Islam; they have become terrorists because of some more mundane problems and issues – some of them could be real; some could be perceived. What the ISIS says can be dismissed as bluster, pure propaganda, an attempt to mock the world, or sheer stupidity. Nations must be addressing those mundane problems and issues. For God's sake; for the sake of peace in the world, let no one speak in terms of jihad being inevitable and Islam being incorrigible in so far as living with non-Muslims is concerned.

THE HOURIS IN HEAVEN

The West is completely baffled by the phenomenon of Muslim terrorists who display absolute disregard for others' and even their own lives, particularly in the context of suicide terrorism. A popular explanation is that acts of terrorism are committed by some crazy Muslims who, driven by their desire to acquire the title of a *'Ghazi'* (warrior of the faith) and the reward of 72 beautiful virgin *Houris* and young boys (*Ghilman*) in heaven, commit acts of terrorism and even get killed in the process. Once again, it is too simplistic to be true.

The Islamic paradise is described in considerable detail in the Qur'an and the Hadis; for instance, in Qur'an surah 56 verses 12-40; surah 55 verses 54-56; ND surah 76 verses 12-22. I will quote the translation of surah 56 verses 12-39 by NJ Dawood:

> "They shall recline on jewelled couches face to face, and there shall wait on them immortal youths with bowls and ewers and a cup of purest wine (that will neither pain their heads nor take away their reason); with fruits of their own choice and flesh of fowls that they relish. And theirs shall be the dark-eyed houris, chaste as hidden pearls: a guerdon for their deeds.... We created the houris and made them virgins, loving companions for those on the right hand...."

The Qur'an is silent about the exact number of houris. But in the Hadis we find reference to 72 virgins in heaven specified. In a Hadis collected by Al-Tirmizi (d 892 CE) in the Book of Sunan [Volume IV, chapters on The Features of Paradise as described by the Messenger of Allah (Prophet Muhammad), chapter 21, About the Smallest Reward for the People of Paradise, (Hadis 2687)]. The same hadis is also quoted by Ibn Kathir (d 1373 CE) in his Qur'anic commentary (Tafsir) of Surah Al-Rahman (55), verse 72:

> "The Prophet Muhammad was heard saying: 'The smallest reward for the people of paradise is an abode where there are 80,000 servants and 72 wives, over which stands a dome decorated with pearls, aquamarine, and ruby, as wide as the distance from Al-Jabiyyah (a Damascus suburb) to Sana'a (Yemen)'."

The most important thing which the popular perception fails to understand is that the houris in paradise are available for all Muslims, not just martyrs. Every pious Muslim is supposed to go to paradise anyway. Thus it cannot be argued that houris in paradise are a special inducement for those who seek to become martyrs. A claim that those Muslim terrorists are prepared to die fighting because they are sexually deprived on the earth and they want to satiate themselves in paradise instead, is preposterous at best and outright slanderous at worst. If a terrorist claims that it was indeed his motive, he can only be pitied for having committed an offence against humanity so that he could satiate his lust in heaven! Rewards in heaven are promised in all religions – they must be taken as metaphorical devices to encourage the believers to follow the religion. They are not meant to be taken as the sole driving force of one's existence or one's belief. If they were to be taken literally, why did other religions not produce such desperate characters?

SALAFISM/WAHABISM: CRADLE OF ALL EVIL?

Origins

Like jihad and the houris, the popular perception regarding Salafism/Wahabism and the madaris (plural of madrisa meaning a school; usually mis-spelt as madarsa and made into madarsas for plural) is that they are the font of all evil; and that they are the fountainheads from which terrorists spring forth into the world to unleash mayhem. However, we must keep in mind that the religious beliefs of a terrorist are immaterial – his evil deeds are. It is therefore necessary to dispel the popular myths regarding Salafism/Wahabism and the madaris.

Wahabism is the dominant form of Islam in Saudi Arabia and Qatar, and is also popular in Kuwait, Egypt, UAE, Bahrain, Morocco, Algeria and Mauritania. The words Wahabism and Salafism are often used interchangeably – there are indeed fine differences but they would confuse most readers. Wahabis, as the name itself indicates, are followers of Shaikh Muhammad Ibn Abdul Wahab (1703-1791, born in the town of Uyayna). The House of Saud has had been not only a follower of Wahab but also had cemented the association by marriage since 1744.

Salafi (from *Salaf al Salih*, meaning 'righteous predecessors', 'pious ancestors' or 'early generations'), is a Sunni Islamic school of thought that takes the pious ancestors (*Salaf*) of the patristic period of early Islam (the first three generations of Muslims: the *Sahaba*, who were Prophet Muhammad's (SAW-PBUH) companions, and the two succeeding generations after them, the Tabi'in and the Taba'at-Tabi'in) as exemplary models of the practice of Islam. They believe that an Islamic revival will result through the emulation of the three early generations and the purging of foreign influences from the religion. Salafism, as we find it today, had started in Egypt in the mid-19th century amongst intellectuals at the Al-Azhar University, the prominent centre of Islamic learning in Cairo. Prominent among them were Muhammad Abduh (1849-1905), Jamal-ud-din-Afghani (1839-1897) and Rashid Rida (1865-1935).

Wahabis and Salafis in general are opposed to both Sufi and Shi'a doctrines, which they regard as having many aspects of shirk, *bid'ah* and impermissible intercession of religious figures, and thus treat them as apostates. This tenet is generally held to be responsible for the sectarian violence. But the very fact that Wahabism and Salafism are endorsed, sponsored and patronised by several nation states means that even the West does not regard them as the font of terrorism – otherwise, they would have been under an obligation to declare them supporters of terrorism. Several of these countries are allies of the USA.

Wahabism in India and the Wahabi Revolt

Many readers would perhaps not be aware that there was a significant Wahabi movement in India against the British in the early 19th century – years before the well-known Mutiny of 1857. The movement was led by Saiyyid Ahmad of Raibareli (1786-1831), who was actively helped by a band of zealous and staunch followers, notably Shah Muhammad Ismail [known as the *Shaheed* (martyr)] and Maulana Abdul Hayy who took up arms first against the Sikhs in the Punjab and then against the British. As Allen Isaac says in his work *Revival of Islam*, the Wahabis fiercely advocated a return to the "simplicity of faith (and society) of the Prophet's Arabia" and rejected "all accretions to and declensions from the pure Islam". The Wahabi revolt, though bold in spirit, failed as a military venture for the simple reason that Saiyyid Ahmad was no match for the generalship of the British – Peshawar was recaptured by the Sikhs, and Saiyid Ahmad himself was killed in a battle at Balakot in 1831.

However, in the meantime the views of the sect had spread very rapidly. While Vilayet Ali and Inayet Ali preached in Kabul and Frontier provinces, Shah Muhammad put the organization on a sound footing in Bengal and Bihar, where he opened a number of branches. The British, however, forced surrender on them in 1847 at Haripur. Vilayet Ali died a natural death in 1852. Inayet Ali suffered heavy losses in a battle in 1853 and though he managed to escape, eventually died in 1858. Though victorious, the British were quick to perceive the potential strength of the Wahabi revolt. According to the "1872 Proc Home-Judl", the Wahabis were "the first to spread, if not to originate, the idea of greased cartridges amongst the sepoys at Barrackpore," and according to JH Reily, District Superintendent of Police on Special Duty (later promoted as DIG), "the story had its origin in the Misre Ganj Masjid at Calcutta." Reily maintained that there existed a very serious and widespread conspiracy, with its headquarters at Patna, for the purpose of carrying on war with the English. According to the *Proceedings of the Trial of Muhammad Bahadur Shah*, Gen Bakht Khan, the leader of the mutineers at Delhi, was also described a Wahabi, and it was stated that the Wahabis came to the capital in large numbers from Jaipur, Bhopal, Hansi, and Hissar to join the mutineers.

This background establishes that Wahabism is not new to India and we have had a strong Wahabi tradition – the Al-Qaida, ISIS or the madaris in Pakistan/POK do not have a monopoly on Wahabism.

Ahle-Hadis and Deobandis

The Wahabi/Salafi influence in Punjab was responsible for the emergence of two *ghair-muqallid* (non-conformist) schools of theology. These became known as *Ahl-e-Hadis* (people of the apostolic tradition) and the *Ahl-e-Qur'an* (people of the Qur'an), because they regarded, respectively, the Hadis of the Prophet (plus, of course, the Qur'an) or the Qur'an alone to be the final authority for the correct interpretation of Muslim rituals and dogmas.

The Deobandi movement, on the other hand, developed as a reaction to the British colonialism in India, which was believed by Muslim theologians to be corrupting Islam. Inspired by the spirit of the great scholar Shah Waliullah of Delhi, it was started by several prominent ulema, headed by Al-Imam Muhammad Qasim Nanautawi. The other prominent founding scholars were Maulana Rashid Ahmed Gangohi and Haji Syed Abid Hussain. The Dar-Al-Ulum at Deoband was established in 1866.

FIDAYEEN AND 'SUICIDE' TERRORISM

Why Some Terrorists Resort to Suicidal Missions?

Suicide terrorism is a Western term to describe the use of such operations by the terrorists in which the death of the attacker is almost certain. As we all know, it is not unique to Muslim terrorists. It has been witnessed in Sri Lanka, India, Lebanon, Kuwait, Israel, Panama, Algeria, Pakistan, Argentina, Croatia, Turkey, Tanzania, Kenya and the USA. The LTTE in fact had conducted a large number of suicide operations in the world; so had Hizbullah, Hamas and the PKK (Kurdistan Workers' Party, Turkey).

Etymologically, the word *'fidayeen'* has a fairly respectable origin. Its root word in Arabic is *'fida'* which means enamoured of, in love with, captivated by, or totally devoted to. From *'fida'* we get *'fidayee'* which means a lover, devotee, faithful or one who would even give up his life for another person or for a cause. *'Fidayeen'* is the plural of *'fidayee'*. In a political context, the word *'fidayeen'* has been in use since the late 11th century when Hasan Sabbah had divided his fraternity into *murshids, da'is* and *fidayeen*. However, it drifted back into popular usage in the 1950s when it was used to describe Arab guerrillas, especially those operating against Israel. A *fidayee* is one who is prepared to sacrifice even his life for his love. If his love is for a cause, he should be prepared to lay down his life, if it comes to that, for the cause. The emphasis is on his willingness, his preparedness to sacrifice his life; it does not mean that he shall or he should necessarily sacrifice his life. The simple idea is that his devotion ought to be of such a high degree that he should not hesitate from paying the highest price for it. It does not say that he has to commit suicide in the process. Islam values martyrdom but there is no religious approbation for achieving martyrdom in a suicidal fashion. It is a fine point and must be understood carefully. Thus, a terrorist who goes into an attack that could be very dangerous or one in which he has kept the option of killing as many of the opponents as possible open by giving up his own life, is more concerned with the efficiency of the operation in terms of the costs involved. He is merely a more motivated fighter; not a more skilled fighter! As such, any special invocation of the halo of 'martyrdom' in suicidal terrorism is essentially rhetorical for propaganda or motivational purpose. Surely, even the terrorists would not want to lessen the value of the lives of those of their ranks who are killed in operations other than the so-called fidayeen operations. Anyone who sacrifices his life for his cause, contributes towards the success of his cause and is thus valued by his organization as a martyr. Suicide is for losers; taking great risks is for the daredevil.

Islam condemns suicide by a man who is say, for example, under debt or is suffering pain for that indicates a weakness of character and personality. Suicides of that type are different from certain death embraced in the course of action. One who dies this way is not a weak-kneed person, weary of life, or one who has accepted defeat in life from his circumstances; rather he is a man who is prepared to lay down his life for a cause. He is not dying because he is unable to carry on living – he is dying because he decides to give up his life. There is subtle difference between the two. In ordinary suicides one takes his own life because he cannot get on with life anymore; in martyrdom one voluntarily gives up his life because the cause is dearer than hanging on to life. There is despair in suicide, but determination in martyrdom.

(Interested readers may refer to my treatise *Urban Terrorism: Myths and Realities* for details.)

That in some attack a terrorist may seek to escape is not regarded an act of cowardice for the terrorist knows it too well that one who fights and runs away, lives to fight another day. It also boosts the morale of the group. His larger strategic objective is more important. He is not fighting to give up his life but he is always ready to give up his life should the need arise. If he survives, it's good enough; if he does not survive, even then it is good. In an era when large armies used to fight, people could afford to suffer casualties on a large scale – even thousands in a day. The ranks of the terrorists are, however, much smaller. They cannot afford large scale casualties. Hence the concepts which were developed in the bygone era are not strictly applicable today. Once upon a time, Islamic fighters were encouraged to wear white clothes so that the blood of their sacrifice would be seen easily and clearly. The modern terrorist who sneaks into attack in the dead of the night does not have this luxury – he has to wear camouflage pattern only.

In conventional warfare, suicidal attacks have never paid off. No decisive victory could ever be clinched by a suicidal charge. The French Marshal Pierre Bosquet had very rightly observed for the Charge of the Light Brigade at Balaclava: "It is magnificent, but it is not war!" The charge of the Light Brigade was suicidal only in its consequence – it was never 'intended' to be a suicidal charge! Then we know how the tactic of kamikaze aircrafts also had failed. The situation, however, is materially different for unconventional warfare or terrorist strikes. Suicidal attacks do pay off for terrorists.

Terrorists resort to suicide terrorism for a variety of reasons. Agreed, that all of them stem from an implicit admission that they are desperate. Nobody loves to blow himself up. They are obliged to do so when, at a military or operational level, they find that their usual repertoire of numerous terror tactics or other tactics of unconventional warfare is not proving sufficiently effective. In other words, suicidal attacks tend to tilt, at least temporarily, the balance in their favour in the asymmetric warfare they are waging.

Terrorists who use suicidal techniques do it simply because they have, at that particular juncture in their 'struggle' (or business if you call it), found it expedient to do so. Expedience is the most important consideration; the alleged influence of some fundamentalist indoctrination or some sort of religious brainwashing comes later as a post facto attempt to justify it. It is just another technique in the repertoire of the techniques of asymmetric warfare used for reasons of expedience. The cause comes first, the religion later. It should be obvious that the very use of the term 'suicide terrorism' for the phenomenon is actually a misnomer. Still, we are obliged to use it for the simple reason that it has become so popular that a technically correct usage would confound most readers.

Efficacy of Suicide Terrorism

The following are the reasons due to which a person or group decides that it would be expedient to resort to suicide attacks.

- Suicidal attacks have got a certain shock value attached to them. They send the target into a state of psychological shock much beyond the actual damage inflicted upon him.
- Suicidal attacks are sure-fire methods. The chances of the attacks succeeding and inflicting considerable damage on the enemy are quite high.
- As such they are very cost-effective. Inflicting the same damage conventionally would demand heavy commitment of resources. In suicidal attacks, all that they stand to lose is a couple of men.
- They are also a cost-effective means of countering sophisticated weapons at the disposal of the state, particularly air force, armour and heavy artillery, things which

non-state actors or terrorists lack, either in the combat zone or outside it. The destruction of more than a dozen aircraft including eight military and some civilian aircrafts by the LTTE in a single suicidal attack on the Katunayake military airbase is a good example.

- Car bombs have been called 'the poor man's air force' because a very heavy explosive payload can be delivered without having aircrafts. Similarly, explosive laden boats can attack much larger ships.
- Suicidal attacks are much simpler to plan. They do not have to concern themselves with making an escape plan, often the most difficult part of an operation. They have only to worry about penetration.
- The suicide device itself is much simpler than other devices as one does not have to bother about making a remote-controlled device or a delayed action device.
- Since the attacker is a human, making last-minute changes in the plans is easy. A time bomb placed somewhere becomes totally useless if the target changes his programme and does not come there at the time when the device is set to go off.
- Since the attacker is a human, he can use deception and guile to penetrate a heavily defended target that may not be penetrated easily by mechanical means alone.
- They do not have to worry about some member getting caught and revealing sensitive information in the course of interrogation or torture.
- At times, if properly executed, it can even result in strategic advantage to the non-state actor particularly if they have taken out some important leaders, vital for the conduct of operations against them.
- It also makes the state waste its manpower and material resources in strengthening the security of its top functionaries, vital installations and public places.

- In fact the non-state actors can force the state to squander its resources merely by propagating a 'hit list' of their real or imaginary targets. Once that list is out, there are few governments which can afford to think rationally and most of them are forced to protect even those things which they would have never protected otherwise.
- Not only that, it forcefully introduces widespread panic and feeling of insecurity amongst the people. They get a larger-than-life image at a very low cost.
- They can deliver maximum shock to the enemy in a single attack. That is to say, they do not have to worry about conserving their resources for some other day.
- The fact that, in a suicidal attack, even high security places can be attacked, serves as a great morale booster to them. It has great propaganda value too.
- Even young boys and girls can inflict as much damage as grown-up soldiers – as such, if the terrorists have suffered casualties in the ranks of their soldiers, they need not 'waste' more of them.
- Suicide attacks are living examples of the supreme sacrifice. They constitute the most convincing proof of the dedication and devotion of those who took part in it for their 'cause'. Thus, they act as a source of inspiration to all those who find their resolve wavering and that they are lacking in the fervour which they had once.
- They can hope to gain some sympathy amongst their covert or half-hearted supporters by such acts of daring and 'bravery'. Every movement looks for and eulogizes its martyrs.

10

Preparing for Worst-Case Scenarios

NECESSITY OF PARADIGM SHIFT

Presently, the whole gamut of security at the premises of any of our vital installations or buildings (the so-called VIP locations, if that pleases someone) or even protected persons is designed for and geared towards a most trite and conventional method of attack, namely, attack made in the fashion of the 2001 attack on the Parliament or the 26/11 Mumbai attack – in other words, attacks made primarily with small arms and perhaps grenades using just brute force for gaining entry. There was no clever stratagem used in both these instances. Better and deadlier attacks have been made elsewhere in the world. Hence one should not, even unknowingly, come to regard them as some great attacks. In the following I am going to describe some of the possibilities that exist; and some of the ingenious ways which the terrorists could employ or have already employed but usually people are unaware of them so that the security system may prepare accordingly. I cannot be accused of giving the terrorists any fresh idea – similar attacks have already taken place in the world and while intelligent terrorists would certainly know them, knowledgeable security planners must also know them. It is really unfortunate if our security planners do not know them.

My contention is that the current Indian security establishment has actually been preparing for and responding to yesterday's threat and threat perception. It would simply collapse in the face of innovative methods of attack for which it is just not prepared. If at all the security system of the premises of any of our vital installations or buildings is to be improved, a paradigm shift needs to be introduced to cater for the hitherto unimagined methods of attack.

The Importance of the Psychological Impact of an Attack

In the case of a vital installation or building housing some protected person or any important institution like that, the actual damage or casualties which could possibly be inflicted in any attack, is actually of little consequence to the terrorists. The very fact that an attack could be made, is enough to grab headlines and grant them the psychological advantage they seek. The actual physical damage caused or casualties caused by an attack are just a bonus – what really matters is its psychological impact. Even if a bomb (say, for example) does not result in many casualties or extensive damage to property, the very fact that a bomb could be detonated at a certain heavily guarded place goes on to show that the terrorists could breach the security of an important institution of the state, and thus the act damages the credibility of the state significantly.

Towards this purpose, it is not at all necessary that the terrorists should be able to physically gain entry into the premises or be able to physically harm the occupants or damage any part of the structure. Even a failed attack would gain almost equal publicity. Therein lies the intrinsic advantage of the terrorist. For this issue to be properly appreciated and understood, it is necessary that the security forces carefully observe and analyse the video footages and still photographs of the behaviour of the crowds following any terrorist attack. Utter confusion and panic are the hallmarks of crowd behaviour anywhere in the world. This means that the 'field of choice' for the terrorist is wide open. He can try anything as long as the 'attempt' succeeds – the actual outcome of the 'attempt' is not so important. The methods which a terrorist or urban guerrilla can adopt are limited only by his imagination. Those in the establishment, who think only in terms of conventional methods of attack, are therefore destined for a rude surprise.

An Outline of Some of the Feasible Innovative Methods of Attack

In the following, I will discuss some of the unconventional but very much feasible methods of attack which have not yet been considered or incorporated into the security systems in India. When I use the word feasible, I do not mean merely theoretically feasible – I mean methods which have been used in the past by other insurgent/terrorist groups in the world and for which there is no reason to believe that they are beyond the technological capabilities of the insurgents/terrorists in India. As such, they are very much feasible. They include, but are not limited to:

(a) Attacks made using NLOS (Non-Line-Of-Sight) weapons as the primary means of attack from a 'safe' distance and delivering explosive payloads inside the premises. (In this method, the terrorists' basic concern would be to increase the possibilities of their abandoning the vehicle used for the actual discharge of the weapon and getting out safely using getaway vehicles, etc.)

(b) Attacks made using NLOS (Non-Line-Of-Sight) weapons as an 'opening' or 'diversionary' attack while another team tries to gain entry taking advantage of the confusion and panic created. After that, they may indulge in shooting sprees inside the premises and use grenades etc and be prepared to eventually get killed.

(c) Attacks made as above but in which no attempt at entry is made. Rather, casualties are inflicted by firing from a distance on the panicked mob exiting the gates. (It may be kept in mind that intelligent terrorists shall not commit the mistake of engaging the security forces in a gun battle. One who is firing on a mob, can fire from even inside a moving vehicle. The vehicle need not be a proper bullet-proof vehicle. Improvised bullet-proofing (they need not bother about procuring proper armour steel – in a pinch, a lamination of even two sheets of 4 mm mild steel would do) on the most vulnerable parts and obvious targets of incoming fire, such as the door panels of the vehicle can be easily done. Further, even if the terrorists inside a vehicle are neutralized or the vehicle rendered incapable of escaping further, they can still cause more damage by blowing up the vehicle as it is approached by the security forces.)

(d) Exploding a vehicle (VBIED – Vehicle Borne Improvised Explosive Device) which is brought near one of the entry gates. The vehicle could be running and manually stopped in case it is a suicide attack.

(e) The explosion could serve two purposes. If sufficient quantity of explosive is used, they need not make any attempt at ramming anywhere, thus rendering all the access-control devices useless. Timothy McVeigh had used as much as 2.3 tonnes of homemade explosive in the Alfred P Murrah Federal Building Bombing in Oklahoma in 1995 and after lighting the fuse, had calmly walked away to his getaway vehicle parked several blocks away. It inflicted 168 casualties in dead and over 680 in injured. Let no one think that the cost of such a device would be prohibitive or beyond the financial resources of terrorists and their financiers. In an interview with the 'MSNBC', McVeigh had disclosed that the total cost of the explosive material, other systems and even the rental of the truck that he had used in planting his device was below $5,000. Many people do not know that in India, factory-made emulsion explosive costs just about ₹62,000 a tonne! Even criminals are able to purchase one 180 gram cartridge of the emulsion for about ₹100. Given the authorized production of as much as nearly 1.89 million tonnes of emulsion in this country in a year, availability of explosives has not been found to be a problem at least for the left-wing extremists from whom recoveries running into tonnes of explosives have been made.

(f) If the IED is not a stand-alone device as discussed above, it can still be used to create confusion and panic. In other words, the impact could be purely psychological or it could be used as a 'diversionary' tactic to gain forcible entry and then indulge in mayhem inside. Such an IED need not be mounted on a vehicle – it can be concealed in a myriad and perfectly innocuous-looking ways.

(g) Equally possible is the option of detonating a suicide bomber's bomb right in the process of security checking so as to inflict casualties preferentially on the security personnel and then sending in a second wave of attackers.

(h) It may be noted that confusion and panic can be increased manifold by using smoke and irritant gases also along with any explosion. Once again, they need not bother about procuring Sarin or a similar nerve agent. That is for the un-intelligent. The simple fact is that the very sight of a couple of men choking by even a simple pulmonary agent like chlorine would be enough to spread the word that some 'chemical' has been used.

Then panic would take over the masses – nobody would bother to or could afford to verify whether it is a nerve agent or a much simpler agent.

(i) Many other novel methods of attack are possible but the terrorists will have to keep their destructive potential, psychological impact and cost in mind and balance them against the overall objective. The payload of most drones of affordable cost, for example, is very low and this reduces their combat potential significantly. Ducted fan Quadcopter drones which can lift the payload of a sub-machine gun have been made and demonstrated in Russia by a private civilian innovator – a YouTube video is also available (https://www.youtube.com/watch?v=SNPJMk2fgJU). But the number of rounds they can carry on-board is obviously limited. They can also drop small loads of explosive, though correct triggering by a reliable impact or time fuze may be a bit difficult for most terrorists to make.

Factory-Made or Improvised NLOS Weapons

Mortars

The simplest NLOS weapon is a mortar. Mortar fire is preferred by the intelligent terrorist as it is extremely difficult to ascertain the firer's position and mount a pursuit and search operation. Factory-made mortars may be difficult to obtain but improvised ones have been around for a long time now. Mortar rounds are fired from improvised tubes/barrels and with improvised propellant charges. The Irish Republican Army (IRA) had done it very systematically. In the latest phase of the Al-Aqsa Intifada the Gaza Strip witnessed a significant development with the use of improvised mortar systems against Israeli Defense Force (IDF) bases and Jewish settlements in the Gaza Strip. The latter were well protected with secure perimeters but could not defend themselves against indirect fire from nearby Palestinian areas. The IRA had been successful in firing mortars on reinforced police and military compounds, British military facilities outside Northern Ireland, Heathrow airport outside London, and once even the British Prime Minister's official residence at 10, Downing Street on February 7, 1991. The mortar mounted on a van and the British prime minister was obliged to vacate the residence for several days.

The Irish Republican Army deployed several types of homemade, throwaway mortars to devastating effect. The IRA used its homemade mortars on average of once every ten days in the six months prior to the 1994 cease-fire. Although the IRA was able to field up to 17 different mortar variants, they were all constructed in basically the same way. A number of homemade mortar tubes (usually cut from commercial gas cylinders) were mounted on the back or inside of a hijacked/stolen truck or van. These tubes were sealed on one end and fitted with an electrically detonated charge that launched the projectile out of the tube. The 'Mark 10' could heave 24 pounds of explosives well over 300 yards. Three such mortars using a mixture of ammonium nitrate and nitrobenzene – known as 'Annie' – as warhead explosive were used in London against British Prime Minister John Major and his War Cabinet during the first Gulf War. It was fired from a Ford Transit van. Should anyone have any misgivings about the range of the improvised mortars, it may be noted that the Mark 11 had a range of 550 yards. The Mark 6, 7 and 8 which fired the lighter 60 mm bomb, had a range of 1200 yards – much more than the factory-made mortar of the same calibre. Coming to the warhead, the Mark 15 which became famous as the 'Barrack Buster' had a calibre of 320 mm and was loaded with 196–220 pounds explosives with a range of 275 yards or so. The Mark 15 barrel was an adaptation of a commercial 'Kosangas' gas cylinder for heating and cooking gas used in rural areas in Ireland. Two British helicopters, one Lynx from the Army and an RAF Puma, were brought down by this type of mortar between March and July 1994.

The purpose of describing all the above is that technologically there is nothing so difficult about making mortars similar to the above or even better than them. Therefore, there is no reason to believe that intelligent terrorists in India cannot do it.

Improvised Small Unguided Rockets

Rockets of the 107 mm Type 63 MBRL have been used several times in the past in Kashmir, fired from improvised launch pads in the absence of a factory-made launcher tubes. Even if this famous rocket is not available, terrorists have been making rockets of their own. Even the Naxals have made a very credible attempt at manufacturing their own rockets and improvised launch pads. They can, in fact, have much greater stand-off range than mortars, though the warhead would not be that heavy. They can also be conveniently fired from trucks and vans in the same way as mortars were fired.

At this moment, the Qassam rocket of the Palestinians is the best in this category of improvised unguided rockets. There is no reason to believe that insurgents/terrorists elsewhere in the world cannot emulate them or make similar rockets of their own. The invention of the Qassam rocket is attributed to Adnan Al Ghoul, known as the "Father of the Qassam". The rocket gets its name from Sheikh Izz ad-Din Al Qassam, a militant Syrian preacher who advocated rebellion against European colonial powers in the Middle East during the 1920s and 1930s. The beauty of the rocket lies in its essential simplicity. Incidentally, the solid motor of the Qassam uses a fuel as elementary as a mixture of potassium nitrate and sugar. Lest anyone have any doubt about the capabilities of such simple propellants, it may be noted that there is a whole programme of amateur scientists and rocket enthusiasts called SS2S (Sugar Shot To Space) which intends to launch a rocket powered by this to exactly 100 km up in the atmosphere, recognized as the beginning of space. Black powder rocket motors are equally good for terrorists. The Qassam-3 is capable of achieving a range of approximately 10-12 kilometres, and carries a payload of 10-20 kilograms of explosives.

It does not require a PhD in aeronautical engineering to make a rocket as elementary and yet as effective as the Qassam. The Palestinians could have, in fact, fired many more rockets on Israeli territory but for the relentless bombing of their manufacturing locations by the Israelis – an option which is perhaps not open to us for domestic terrorism. The implications of developing a similar rocket or even an inferior version with a smaller range and payload are serious – it would mean that the terrorists would be able to fire from a very safe distance and get away.

UBGL Grenades

Similar effects, though on a much smaller magnitude, can be achieved by the use of UBGL (Under Barrel Grenade Launcher) grenades which are available aplenty and which have been successfully fired in NLOS mode several times in Kashmir and elsewhere. UBGL grenades can be easily used to fly over the perimeter fences, walls and view cutters so ceremoniously installed in conventional security systems. This is their intrinsic advantage over RPGs. The RPG is likely to expose the firer whereas the UBGL firer can easily take advantage of any cover – body of a truck, trees, winter fog, and smoke, whatever.

Attacks Involving VBIEDs and the Issue of VIP Security

VBIEDs have been described as "poor man's air force" in view of the great payload that they can carry. In the attack on the US Marines barrack in Beirut in 1983, the terrorists' truck was carrying about 12,000 to 18,000 lbs of high explosive – almost as much as a Daisy Cutter bomb and inflicted 307 casualties in dead and 75 in injured. Using a VBIED to blow through the barriers and create enough confusion, however, does not require a huge quantity of explosive. Even 200 lbs of emulsion would do – one does not require any military-grade high explosive like TNT or RDX for that. The task of infiltration in a diversionary attack will be made much easier if they incorporate some deception or impersonation into it. In the confusion arising out of a VBIED blast, nobody is going to ask as to who is running where.

In the context of VIP security, it may be kept in mind that terrorists could use VBIEDs against a protected person's car on the other side of the road across a road-divider in situations where traffic on the other side is not held up for movement of the protected person's car. The protected car being armoured would not make much difference because if the VBIED has about 100 kg or more of explosive, it is enough to physically lift and throw away even the 20,000 lbs 'The Beast' of the US president from a distance of 25 feet, not to speak of lighter vehicles. Their structural integrity may not be compromised as a result of their armouring but the very fact of being hurled away in an armoured vehicle would seriously injure the occupants. In about 11 successful attacks on the 12 tonne MPV (26,448 lbs Mine Protected Vehicle) by the Naxals, they have used nothing but emulsion for the purpose and every time they have succeeded in toppling the vehicle. The 'V'-shaped hull was never ruptured but casualties were caused by occupants banging their bodies inside the steel box.

INSTANCES OF INNOVATIVE AND INTELLIGENT METHODS OF ATTACKS IN INDIA AND ABROAD

Some of the instances of terrorist attacks in India where some ingenuity was exercised by the terrorists in attacking facilities are discussed below. It would show that, if the terrorists apply professional mind, they can mount very deadly attacks. The problem with the security planners is that they do not care to analyse the past to learn what exactly the adversary is capable of doing. Even at the cost of quoting a cliché, I must re-emphasize that those who fail to learn from history, are doomed to repeat it. Not only that, their surprise would be worse.

Kashmir: Attack on the Badami Bagh Cantonment, Srinagar (November 3, 1999)

In this attack, taking advantage of the confusion and panic created by hand grenades, the terrorists entered through the elaborate security arrangement at the gate.

Kashmir: Attack on the SOG Complex, Srinagar (December 27, 1999)

In this attack, it was entry by impersonation – the terrorists came in police uniform. After entering the complex the two terrorists informed the sentry on duty, who came out from his bunker, that they wanted to meet 'saheb'. As soon as the sentry came out of the bunker; the terrorists shot him and then rushed inside the building.

Kashmir: Attack on the Rashtriya Rifles Sector HQ, Khanabal, Anantnag (January 12, 2000)

This attack was mounted in a direct fashion with brute force sans any stratagem. It is significant because brute force of grenades, smoke bombs and bullets succeeded.

Kashmir: Attack on the Badami Bagh Cantonment, Srinagar (April 19, 2000)

In this attack, a car bomb was used at the barrier. But for the fortuitous presence of a parked vehicle that had effectively blocked the road after the barrier, the VBIED would have gone inside the camp and taken the explosive to wherever it had intended.

Kashmir: Attack on the Srinagar Airport (January 16, 2001)

In this attack, they used deception of a hardtop jeep that appeared to be a government jeep and managed to get into the convoy of a minister. The terrorists could reach some distance short of gate number 1 of airport when they were stopped and started firing.

Kashmir: Attack on the Police Control Room, Srinagar (February 9, 2001)

This attack involved impersonation. One of them was allowed to go and see the station writer. He started firing there and in the ensuing confusion, the other terrorist waiting at the gate was also able to enter inside the PCR.

Kashmir: Attack on the Legislative Assembly, Srinagar (October 1, 2001)

This attack used several clever and innovative techniques simultaneously. This included the use of impersonation; a VBIED to destroy the barrier; a 'suicide' bomber; and three others who had got out of the VBIED car just about 100 m before it exploded, and sneaked into the premises taking advantage of the confusion. For the attack, they had hijacked a Tata Sumo vehicle belonging to the Telecom department from Jehangir Chowk in Srinagar earlier during the day. Explosives were packed in it and they drove it towards the Assembly. In all, a copybook attack by the Jaish-e-Muhammad in which they killed 34 and injured 70 persons.

Jammu: The Kaluchak Massacre and the Attack on the Army Camp (May 14, 2002)

In this incident, three terrorists attacked a tourist bus coming from Himachal Pradesh. When the bus reached near Kaluchak, they shot the driver and the conductor and opened fire on the passengers killing seven passengers. The terrorists then entered the nearby army camp of 196 Field Regiment, firing and throwing grenades.

Afghanistan: Attack on Army Base (April 21, 2017)

In this deadly attack on an army base near Mazar-e-Sharif, the Taliban killed at least 140 soldiers and injured about 160. In this attack, according to Aljazeera (http://www.aljazeera.com/news/2017/04/taliban-attacks-key-military-base-north-afghanistan-170421134021613.html) they seem to have used almost every trick of the trade: first, the use of deception through all the 10 terrorists wearing military uniforms and moving in three military vehicles; second, use of forged documents to pass through checking points; third, one suicide bomber blowing himself up to create diversion and then the others entering taking advantage of the confusion; fourth, another suicide bomber blowing himself elsewhere; fifth, firing of a rocket on the entrance of the base to gain entry; and sixth, choosing the targets at their most vulnerable, namely shooting at the soldiers near a mosque as they were leaving Friday prayers, and in the dining facility. The Taliban claimed total casualties of about 500 and also that four of the attackers were former soldiers intimately familiar with the layout of the base – that is, seventh, the use of subversion, giving them an edge.

Afghanistan: Assassination Attempt on the Afghan President Ahmed Karzai (April 27, 2008)

The attack was made when he was reviewing a parade to celebrate the National Day. The attack was made with a NLOS weapon – mortar fire in this case. After the first four or five volleys of the artillery gun-salute, a mortar bomb slammed into a main street outside the parade ground. It was followed by gunfire and then a second mortar. Later an eyewitness claimed that the attackers were firing from a third-floor room of a three-storey hotel about 500 yards away! The most revealing part of the incident was that the hundreds of soldiers present there ran off in the parade ground in disarray for their lives – as simple as that. *The New York Times* commented that the assassination attempt had turned into a moment of national embarrassment for the government.

Afghanistan: Attack on the Indian Embassy in Kabul (July 7, 2008)

An explosive-packed Toyota Camry, driven by the suicide bomber, rammed into two Indian diplomatic vehicles entering the embassy and detonated. The casualties could have been higher but for the sand filled blast barriers called HESCO barrier or HESCO bastion.

Russia: The Moscow Theatre Hostage Crisis (October 23, 2002)

In this attack, about 40-50 armed Chechen rebel fighters took 850 hostages including members of the audience and performers. All the hostages were kept in the auditorium and the orchestra pit was used as a lavatory. After a two-and-a-half day siege, Russian OSNAZ forces pumped an unknown chemical agent into the building's ventilation system and raided it. Officially, 39 of the terrorists were killed by Russian forces, along with at least 129 and possibly many more of the hostages. Afterwards, it was found that the terrorists had no explosives with them. If they had explosives with them, the casualties could have been very high.

IMPLICATIONS FOR THE SECURITY OF OUR VITAL INSTALLATIONS

There is no reason to believe that in a future attack on an important facility of the nation like some vital installation or building which is intimately linked to the sovereignty and prestige of the country, the terrorists are under any obligation to resort to such methods of attack for which the security system has already catered for. The terrorists can reasonably be expected to keep themselves informed of the techniques developed and methods used elsewhere in the world as the information is in the public domain. As such, they may use several unconventional methods of attack which will defeat the existing security systems.

None of the existing systems can deter an attack made using anyone of the unconventional methods discussed above. Moreover, they would not be able to do anything to prevent damage or casualties once the attack is made. They are suited to prevent and deal with conventional methods of attack only. Since the terrorist or the aggressor has a wide field of choice to achieve his objectives, the security systems must be designed to protect against each one of them. They would necessarily include observing some fundamental principles like maintaining exclusive and non-exclusive stand-off distances; re-locating the facility if such stand-off distances cannot be found; hardening the facility against blast; use of HESCO bastions; use of Bremer Wall Sections; and installing electronic intrusion detection systems, etc. The list is, by no means, exhaustive. Physical security of threatened facilities has been developed into a complete science and in a chapter of a book on a different topic; I do not have space to include that here. However, the innovative countermeasures are discussed at length in my treatise *Ultimate Handbook of Urban Warfare* and interested readers may refer to that.

11

Terrorist Violence in India

ATTACK ON AMARNATH YATRA PILGRIMS IN 2017

During the writing of this book, the latest terrorist attack that took place in India was on the pilgrims of the Amarnath Yatra (pilgrimage to the Holy Cave at Amarnath) on July 10, 2017 in Jammu and Kashmir. In this attack, late in the evening, terrorists fired on a bus carrying the pilgrims back from the Amarnath Shrine. Eight persons were killed in the attack and 19 were injured. The terrorists managed to decamp after the attack.

The usual round of blame-game and mutual incriminations ensued after that, and the media was abuzz with the talk of it having been a security lapse. It was, for example, claimed that the bus was not registered and was not moving along with the security convoy. An impression was sought to be conveyed that had it been following the rules, an attack would have been impossibility.

However, such notions are grossly mistaken, and belie a dangerously poor understanding of the intrinsic advantages that terrorists enjoy over intrinsic limitations of a practical and feasible security system. It is extremely difficult to prevent hit-and-run type of terrorist attacks. In the following, I will elaborate on it. In first place, it must be clearly understood that it is not humanly possible to secure every inch of a route that is hundreds of kilometres long. Even with the massive deployment of security forces that is made every year for this purpose, terrorists can always find gaps. That an attack of this type took place in Kashmir after years is not really to be attributed to the security arrangements but to the compulsions of the terrorists. This time, the terrorists had apparently sought to make it into a communal issue, hammering on the idea of their nefarious activities being a part of some sort of Islamist effort against a secular nation-state. They summarily failed in their motive as the sheer mindlessness and brutality of the attack was condemned from every section of the Kashmiri society.

Coming to the preventive aspects, it must be kept in mind that the security men are usually deployed in buddy pairs on either side of the road—this is for two reasons. The first is that they should be able to watch both the road and the sides of the road. The second is to ensure that a man standing alone is not surprised from his own rear. Now, if two such buddy pairs were to be deployed such that the distance between them is about 50 yards, one would need 352 such pairs for a mile (1,760 yards), that is, a total of 704 security personnel per mile.

The distance from Jammu to the Amarnath Cave Shrine via Khanabal and Pahalgam through Chandanwari is a total of 327 km or 204 miles. This means that for the buddy pairs of security personnel to be deployed at every 50 yards, we would need 1,43,616 security personnel for lining of the route alone! Clearly, getting such a large number of men is impractical because you need them for many other purposes also, such as providing security to the camps of the pilgrims, traffic management, and providing static security to vulnerable points, etc. For every vulnerable point that needs round-the-clock security, you need three times the manpower deployed at a given moment because men have to be deployed in three shifts of eight-hours each. All this adds heavily to the burden on the manpower needed.

Since the state cannot mobilize so many men, in practice it results in a much thinner deployment on the roads than the hypothetical scenario of two buddy pairs every 50 yards. Quite often, it so happens that two buddy pairs deployed cannot even see each other either because of distance or because of turns on the road. In such a situation, it is not at all difficult for a couple of terrorists to hide somewhere, emerge suddenly on the road and fire a magazine of 30 rounds each from the AK-47 rifle in 3 seconds flat in an automatic mode. Hitting a target as large as a bus is not a problem at all. By the time the security personnel, even if they happen to be present somewhere within 100-150 yards of the pace of incident, hear the shots and realize what is happening, the terrorists would have run away. In this attack, the terrorists were obviously in a tearing hurry to run away to safety otherwise with, say four men firing 30 rounds each, they should have been able to kill many more people in a tightly packed bus.

We must also keep in mind that even if the security persons do hear the gunshots, it is not advisable for them to simply rush in that direction blindly. In the first place, they must be in sufficient strength themselves—a few men are likely to be both outgunned and outfought. Secondly, even if they gather in strength, they cannot barge into a place just like that. The gunshots could well be a ruse to divert them to some place so that an attack could be made somewhere else, or it could be a device to lure them into a trap or ambush. Proper planning and thought must be applied to assess and understand the situation before they launch a counter-strike.

Now, even if this ill-fated bus was a part of a security convoy with security elements riding in front, rear and the middle in their own vehicles, it could still be attacked. You cannot expect a convoy of buses to ride in a tail-to-bumper fashion. They have to make allowance for a safe ride and braking distances. As such, in practice, convoys are therefore large, very conspicuous objects that move ponderously. A convoy of even 50 buses would become some one-and-a-half mile long. A convoy is therefore never safe from a terrorist ambush. As I said earlier, all that a terrorist needs is just three seconds. Moreover, in this era of saturation news coverage pining for sensational tidbits, even the mere fact of having fired some rounds on a convoy becomes big news and helps the terrorists in their propaganda war.

There is no set pattern for a likely area for an ambush. Usually, they would prefer places which by their very topography provide them both cover and concealment. However, as the history of counterinsurgency operations shows, ambushes on convoys have been made even on flat terrain or near populated areas. In fact, an ambush in a populated area ensures that the security forces are constrained from using their full firepower lest they cause unacceptably high collateral damage. Particularly in low or failing light situations, by the time the security elements realize from which direction the fire came (and nothing prevents the terrorists from firing from more than one direction to confuse the forces) or what effect it had, the terrorists have already turned around to go home. There have been situations where, after the attack, they have simply abandoned their weapons somewhere and become normal-looking persons who could coolly walk away.

There are thus practical and intrinsic limitations in security that can be provided against terrorist attacks. This is the dilemma of the Indian state in dealing with terrorism. Before they launch into an exciting blame-game and shouting match on the TV channels, the Indian people, the media and all stakeholders must understand that there is no way the state can protect every target from terrorist strikes. In the following, we will first take an overview of terrorist violence in India and then discuss the complexity of countering terrorism successfully.

AN OVERVIEW IN FIGURES

According to the authoritative South Asia Terrorism Portal (satp.org), in Jammu and Kashmir alone, since 1988 till September 10, 2017, there have been as many as 47,246 terrorist incidents in which at least 14,782 civilians and 6,331 security forces personnel have been killed.

Earlier, during the days of the Khalistani terrorism in Punjab from 1981 onwards till date, as many as 11,787 civilians and 1,761 security forces personnel were killed.

In terrorist violence in the north-eastern states, from 1992 onwards till date, as many as 10,272 civilians and 2,743 security forces personnel have been killed.

The Naxal movement is now exactly 50 years old but has picked up serious momentum since 2005 following the merger of two rival outfits, namely the MCC (Maoist Communist Centre) and PWG (People's War Group) into the CPI-Maoist (Communist Party of India-Maoist). The left-extremist Naxal insurgency, since 2005 onwards till date, has taken a toll of 3,009 civilians and 1,918 security forces personnel in killed.

Islamist violence in India (taking only those incidents that have taken place outside J&K, Punjab and the north-east), from 2000 onwards till 2017, reflected itself in the form of 64 incidents in which 873 civilians lost their lives and 53 security forces personnel were also killed.

The list of major terrorist strikes in the country is very long. We can mention only a few major ones by way of refreshing the memory of readers. In Jammu and Kashmir, we have had the

Wandhama massacre of 1998; the massacre of Amarnath Pilgrims in 2000; the Chattisinghpora massacre in 2000; the 2001 attack on the Legislative Assembly; the 2002 Raghunath Temple attack; the Kasimnagar massacre in 2002; the Kaluchak massacre in 2002; the Nadigram killings in 2003; the 2006 Doda massacres; and various attacks on the army camps, including the fateful attack on the Uri camp in 2016 which eventually led to the surgical strikes.

Elsewhere in the country we have had notorious incidents like the 1987 massacre of bus passengers in Punjab; the 1991 massacre of train passengers in Punjab; the 1998 Chamba massacre in Himachal Pradesh; the Akshardham attack in 2002; the Varanasi Sankatmochan Temple and Railway Station bombing in 2006; the Hyderabad Lumbini Park and Gokul Chaat Bhandar bombings in 2007; the Ajmer Dargah bomb blast in 2007; the Jaipur bomb blasts in 2008; the Ahmedabad bombings in 2008; the 2013 Hyderabad blasts; and the 2015 Gurdaspur attack.

In Delhi, the capital of India and the seat of national power, there have been as many as 32 terrorist attacks since 1997 till date in which 134 people were killed and 884 injured. These included the Sarojini Nagar/Paharganj/Govindpuri bomb blasts in 1997; the Red Fort attack in 2000; the Parliament attack in 2001; the 2008 attacks in Karol Bagh/Connaught Place/Greater Kailash; and the High Court attack in 2011. On the other hand, in Mumbai, the commercial capital of India, there have been 14 terrorist attacks since 1993 in which 719 people were killed and 2,393 injured. These included that the 1993 serial blasts; the 2003 Gateway of India and Zaveri Bazar attacks; the 2006 local train blasts; the 26/11 attacks on 2008; and the serial blasts in 2011. This shows that even such heavily guarded and heavily policed places are not immune from terrorist attacks.

THE COMPLEXITIES OF ANTI-TERRORIST OPERATIONS

Anti-terrorism or counterinsurgency is a very complex affair. Robert Taber, an American scholar who had analyzed the Cuban insurgency very closely, in his seminal work *War of the Flea: The Classic Study of Guerrilla Warfare* had famously stated:

> "The guerrilla fights the 'war of the flea', and his military enemy suffers the dog's disadvantages: too much to defend; too small, ubiquitous, and agile an enemy to come to grips with."

Fact is, every terrorist group, irrespective of its ideological, nationalistic, or religious inclinations, has used similar tactics to advance their cause and the governments have always suffered from the same disadvantages. Terrorists use all available tools – political, informational (including appeals to religious, ethnic, or ideological beliefs), military, and economic – in their attempt to carry the movement forward to its logical conclusion. The governments usually have an initial advantage in resources; however, that edge is counterbalanced by the requirement to maintain order and protect the population and critical resources. Terrorists often succeed by sowing chaos and disorder anywhere; the government fails unless it maintains a degree of order everywhere.

The terrorist derives his strength almost entirely from the psychological impact of his strikes on the government through the reactions amongst the people and most importantly, in the media. In terms of efficiency, therefore, a terrorist movement is much more efficient than an insurgency. All that he requires is the will to hurt the system and be prepared to face the consequences should he be caught. Collecting the means of committing acts of terrorism is no problem at all – even individuals can do that. In modern situations and particularly with consumerist societies having traditionally selfish and politically indifferent people, running an insurgency successfully is very difficult and the governments can indeed exploit the natural weaknesses of the insurgents and the target population to apply brakes to the progression of an insurgency, if not stamp them out completely. Terrorism, on the other hand, is much harder to handle. The perpetrators are so very few and their potential targets so immensely large in number. It is impossible to protect the myriads of targets that any modern society presents. Insurgencies, because they take upon themselves a grand objective and cumbersome means, have a higher chance of failure than terrorists. One of the great strengths of terrorists is that they take small tasks and small objectives upon themselves. An ideal terrorist would never overstretch himself nor provoke the governments beyond a point that could result in an all-out action against it.

Rational people must admit that it is difficult to make a modern society completely impervious to terrorism. A modern complex society offers such a large degree of anonymity and an infinite number of places to hide, that the law and order machinery faces an uphill task in keeping a tab on what every citizen is doing, thinking and planning. Let us, those who live in urban societies, ask ourselves, do we really know every family that lives in our society? It is only after a terrorist attack has taken place that we come to notice that the guy who was living in a rented room, and who never appeared out of place or suspicious, is now missing and is a suspect. India is not a small country like the former East Germany and unlike their secret police, the Stasi, we could possibly not have file on almost every citizen. Carlos Marighella, the well-known Marxist Brazilian writer, politician and guerrilla fighter, in his famous book *Mini Manual of the Urban Guerrilla* had also agreed that the increased size and the socio-economic differentiation of the urban areas made them especially vulnerable to terrorism and sabotage. It is infinitely easy for the urban terrorist to hit and simply disappear in an urban area. In fact, now we have the very disturbing phenomenon of the 'lone wolf' terrorist. If there is a large group, the police and the intelligence agencies can hope to penetrate it somehow. For one who is operating alone, there is nothing to penetrate!

Let us realize that we are a massive country of 1.34 billion people. It is not possible for a CCTV to watch every place; it is not possible to check every single bag which people might be carrying in markets; it is not possible to check every train passenger's luggage; it is not possible to watch what every resident of a colony or slum is doing, what time he goes to work, when does he come back, and what sort of people come to his room to see him; it is not possible to intercept and listen to every mobile telephone call or VOIP (Voice over Internet Protocol) call or Whatsapp chat or Telegram conversation; and it is not possible to peep into the mind of every subverted element.

The USA and European countries have a very large number of CCTVs installed. Yet it has not prevented terrorists from attacking them. Terrorists utilize novel methods to beat security systems. If they cannot take rifles or explosives to some place, they use a bus or truck to ram into crowds and simply crush scores of people, as it happened in the 2016 Nice, France attack. In the 2017 Manchester attack, the terrorist knew that he could not possibly penetrate the security ring and attack people inside the arena. He bypassed the security systems by attacking the people after they were coming out of the arena.

We should also realize that, at least in the context of modern terrorism, acquiring the implements of terrorism is not a difficult task. Nor does it require great money. An intelligent terrorist need not get his implements from the ISI. In many States in India, even criminals have a large number of AK-47 rifles. How do they get them? In this book, we do not have space to dwell upon this topic but readers must understand that terrorists can exploit the same channels which criminals have been exploiting since long. Above all, intelligent terrorists would swear by explosives and not by rifles. And please note, for most of the terrorist strikes except those acts of sabotage which would require high detonation velocity explosives, most of the anti-personnel bombs can be made with widely available civilian explosives. Most readers would not know that, we being a very large country, produce a whopping 1.89031 million tonnes of emulsion explosives every year for legitimate activities like mining, quarrying, road construction, tunnel construction etc. It is not possible for any system to keep track of such a vast quantity. There is no pilferage or theft of any significance – basically, it is diversion. Police and investigation can only reach up to the licensed user. If he decides to divert a part of his legitimate purchase, there is nothing which can be done. For example, a mine owner could note in his registers that he charged a bore hole with 10 kg of emulsion. In reality, he could have used only 2 kg and diverted the rest. Very good bombs can be made with only a few kg of emulsions. The Naxals know this and have been using nothing but emulsion explosives. In fact, they have such plentiful supply of emulsion that often they do not bother to carry it away when security forces approach their hideouts. As a result, the recovery of emulsion explosives from Naxals, according to the Ministry of Home Affairs Annual Report 2016-2017, is close to 12,000 kg!

WHAT MAKES THE TARGETS WEAK?

Since, as explained above, countering terrorism in a direct fashion, is very difficult, we must think along the line of hardening; the target itself. The target of the terrorist is the state comprising the people. Now States could indeed be 'soft'. Soft states are characterized not only by weak-kneed governments; they are also characterized by a highly immature public and an utterly irresponsible media. A soft State not only lacks resolve, it also lacks proper understanding. The people and the media fail to understand that in a modern State it is impossible to protect the myriads of targets that it presents. They expect that the government should be able to protect everything by a magic wand. In soft States, the government becomes the default target of every terrorist activity because an immature society and an even more immature media blame the government for every terrorist act by over-reacting. Terrorists know that killing a few people or damaging some property is not going to take them anywhere near their objective. But they know it well that all such acts make a dent on the credibility of the government in the eyes of the people and the media who expect the impossible from the government. Terrorists bank on this and hope that a beleaguered government would go out of the way to grant them some concessions. It is with this belief that they kidnap important personalities or hijack a plane.

Brian Crozier, a historian, strategist and journalist, had described the terrorist's mission against the State in the following words in his book, *The Rebels: A Study of Post-War Insurrections*: "A common purpose is to make life unendurable for the enemy." Terrorizing the key institutions of the government and thus bringing about a paralysis in the functioning of the administration has manifold results. If the police are the target, terror causes a sort of disillusionment to set in, leading the force to a state of shock and inactivity. Readers may recall the reactions in the media that poured in following the brutal lynching of the DySP Mohammed Ayub Pandit outside the Jama Masjid in Srinagar, J&K in June 2017.

Conversely, if the government persists in trying to stamp out terrorism under the pressure of the people and the media, the resources of the police and the army are greatly stretched, making them even less effective. At the same time it imposes a heavy financial burden on the system as extra security measures are put in place. Moreover, there is a clamouring from a large section of the people, the media and even the ruling group for what they perceive as a panacea in the days of participative democracies, that is, a dialogue, which is essentially nothing but a tacit admission that the regime has buckled up and is prepared to grant some concessions. As the Governor General of Algeria Jacques Soustelle had described it,

> "Terror is a psychological weapon of unbelievable power. Before the bodies of those whose throats have been cut and the grimacing faces of the mutilated, all capacity for resistance lapses; the spring is broken."

Precisely for this reason, terrorists prefer to attack targets which will evoke an emotive reaction from the people and the media. The Mumbai 26/11 attacks led to such a furore and outrage because, among other reasons, it was for the first time that people of the upper classes, those who frequented five-star hotels and posh restaurants were attacked. That's why they attack pilgrims and devotees who have gone to some temple. For a terrorist, the selection of the target is as important as the manner of attack. Please remember that the first thing a terrorist does is to abandon any pretence to heroism, popular support, or fair play. Terrorism is for the cold, calculating, ruthless men who do not mind if they are called cowards. To him only the impact of his strikes matters. They strike at the softest targets; if they have to make a selection they make it according to the psychological impact it would produce and not by the considerations of the material damage caused.

He is the ultimate predator who attacks only the soft underbelly of his target however large or powerful it be. He plays upon the weaknesses of the target people. He brings their hidden fears to the fore. The upper-middle and the upper classes fear nothing more than any damage to their privileged positions and possessions. Urban terrorism threatens them right there. Shopping may no longer be enjoyable because a bomb could explode there. Somebody may start shooting at a hotel or crash a car bomb; somebody may fire at some party. Worse, political instability may result as a result of the brouhaha and the stock market may plunge. In short, urban terrorism threatens to screw their happy and cocooned existence.

THE SOLUTION TO COMBATING TERRORISM SUCCESSFULLY

Terrorism is thus found to be a particularly potent tool against regimes which lack resolve, which are weak-kneed, and which lack the moral courage to face some of the harsh realities built in their socio-political system. The people, the pseudo-intellectuals amongst them and the media of a soft State are frequently responsible for making it even softer. That we, as a people are what we are; to be fair, there is a historical reason also for this characteristic of ours. Since unlike most of the countries of Europe and even some of Asia which have gone through a horrific amount of human suffering and bloodshed in the wars of the twentieth century and earlier too, this country has not had a real baptism through blood, the Indian society has developed a morbid fear of violence and the great middle-class reacts to it in a most irrational manner.

Hence for a terrorist who understand the psyche of a nation, its people, its media and its ruling class, urban terrorism makes eminent sense. The returns of urban terrorism are certainly disproportionately higher than its innate worth. Its strength lies in two words: anytime and anywhere. The fear that they can strike you anytime and anywhere makes them larger than life. The secret of the power of urban terrorism lies in the fact that they are able to create a climate of fear, panic, disorientation and capitulation out of all proportion to their actual strength courtesy an irresponsible media and an effete population under its influence.

This has made the Indian society particularly vulnerable to acts of terrorism – intelligent terrorists can certainly extort more out of the Indian State than they can ever expect from a principled and resolute State. Terrorist attacks take place almost everywhere in the country. But, in India, they lead to a catastrophe – self-styled experts and arm-chair theorists in TV studios dissect it from every possible angle; TV reporters obtain bites from survivors and even relatives who wail and put the viewers and the government under tremendous strain; emotionally surcharged scenes from the families of the victims are shown non-stop; and scenes of funerals of soldiers in their native places with young children saluting dead fathers literally rend our hearts.

We need to realize that if we do not address our traditional weakness of character, intelligent terrorists have only to maintain a certain level of terrorist violence to make the people, the pseudo-intellectuals, the media and the leaders sick of it. That would usher in the 'climate of collapse' much before it actually arrives. In other words, while our security apparatus and its capabilities would remain intact even after much of terrorist onslaught, the reactions in the media and amongst the people would make the situation appear extremely grave and even hopeless.

After that the developments would take care of themselves. For example, foreign investors would lose no time in running away the moment their interests start getting systematically targeted. Then at isolated places there may be such police or army excesses as to lead to mass protests. In short, if the insurgents or terrorists are able to use terrorist violence in such a manner as to act as a catalyst for the innate disruptive tendencies in the country or goad certain important people into taking certain decisions, an uncontrollable and unpredictable chain reaction may result which will bring us perilously close to a 'climate of collapse'. Then they may take advantage of it in bargaining from a position of strength and extracting concessions or acceptance of demands which they could have never hoped for otherwise.

None of the above should be misconstrued to mean that we should not commiserate with the unfortunate victims of terrorism. Yes, we must. But it is also imperative for us to remain strong. There is a difference between feeling sad and breaking down, you see. Intelligent terrorists know that Indian society and political system have inherent cracks that stand to get magnified under the stress of a determined and sustained phase of terrorism. Our strategy must be to deny them this advantage.

Terrorism becomes effective only if the target makes it so. Terrorism, to be successful, expects that the target must respond in a certain manner. The fact of responding in an expected manner is such that it weakens the target, both in image and reality. Deny the terrorist the pleasure of the expected response and you have beaten him. One should always keep in mind that while the root causes of terrorism could be political, sociological or whatever, the impact of terrorism is determined to a great extent by the target's behaviour, which is largely psychological in character. The design of the terrorist is to manipulate the target's psychological perceptions to induce it to act in the way it is predisposed to act.

The effort of those who have to combat terrorism must be to refuse to act in a predictable or expected manner, and least of all in a manner that serves the purpose of the terrorists. Prudent targets must not behave as automatons. For example, if the terrorists perceive a target as powerful and self-righteous, they should expect it to over-react; certainly they would not expect it to suffer from power deflation, repress moderates, appease moderates, or be intimidated. Now if the target, despite being powerful and self-righteous, has over-reacted, it has played into the hands of the terrorists. To avoid this, the target must not over-react. It is only through knowledge of one's own perceptions and how they can be manipulated that one learns to avoid the propensity to make particular mistakes.

INDIAN SUCCESSES IN BATTLING THE MENACE OF TERRORISM

Even as the security forces have paid a high price for an admittedly difficult job of battling the terrorists hiding amongst the people, they have neutralized a very large number of them over the years. According to the data compiled by the South Asia Terrorism Portal (satp.org), the security forces have killed as many as 23,284 terrorists in Jammu and Kashmir since 1988 till September 10, 2017. This gives an average rate of neutralization of terrorists at about 814 terrorists per year. Incidentally, the highest number of terrorists killed in one year was in 2001 when as many as 2,850 terrorists were killed. The next highest was in the year 2000 when 1,808 terrorists were killed. The third place is held by the year 1994 when 1,651 terrorists were killed. The fourth position went to the year 2003 when 1,546 terrorists were killed.

In 2017, till September 10, the security forces have killed as many as 151 terrorists while suffering casualties of 57 in killed amongst their ranks. The figure also compares well with the figure of 165 terrorists killed in 2016 at a loss of 88 men amongst their ranks. In 2015, they had killed 113 terrorists at a cost of 41 soldiers. In 2014, 110 terrorists were killed while 51 soldiers made the supreme sacrifice. Of the 111 terrorists killed so far, 68 terrorists have been killed in the two-and-a-half months since April when it was resolved by the Government to go whole hog against the terrorists. Instructions have been given to the security forces to mount a relentless offensive against them and make it difficult for them to sustain operations in the valley.

The success in 2017 is therefore attributed to the revised strategy that has been adopted this year. The media has described it as 'Operation All-Out' in which the security forces are targeting the terrorists systematically and meticulously. A list of as many as 258 terrorists belonging to various groups has been made and the intelligence community has been furnishing information about their hide-outs for precise operations against them. Of late, the intelligence inputs seem to have improved and even those terrorists like Abu Dujana who had been giving the slip to the security forces since long, were caught napping.

The large number of terrorists killed and the majority of them are local Kashmiris is an indicator of the degree of subversion that has had gripped the society. However, the number of active terrorists has gone down considerably since what it used to be some 14-15 years ago. This can be attributed partly to the neutralization of terrorists on such a large scale. It has also applied brakes to the number of youth crossing over the LOC for receiving arms training in the camps run in the POK. The aggressive approach has made it difficult for infiltrators to take advantage of the summer months when the hilly routes used are more negotiable. There are clear indications that the terrorists are facing an acute shortage of arms and ammunition also.

The string of successes against the terrorists has gone hand-in-hand with India being able to bring Pakistan-sponsored terrorism into international focus. It is because of these efforts that the USA is now increasingly aligning with India's stance on Kashmir. Towards the end of June 2017, India's old bête-noire Syed Salahuddin of the Hizbul Mujahideen was declared a Specially Designated Global Terrorist. The position of Salahuddin as the co-founder of the Hizbul Mujahideen; his heading the United Jihad Council; his avowed objective of Kashmir's merger with Pakistan; and his openly addressing press conferences and rallies in POK has been well-known since long. However, in diplomatic terms, the timing of the declaration was deemed to be particularly important because it came in the process of the build-up to the meeting of the Indian prime minister with the US president. A month before that, the US president had spoken of India as a 'victim of terror' during an Islamic Summit in Riyadh. The informal stance was thus formalized by the declaration in respect of Salahuddin. This is incidentally the very first time that a Kashmiri terrorist has been designated a "global terrorist". By doing so, the United States has accepted that Salahuddin's Hizbul Mujahideen is not an "indigenous terror group" in Kashmir and poses a greater threat to the world at large. Since he has been staying in Pakistan/POK since long, the US move is perceived as a recognition of India's longstanding position that trans-border terrorism is behind the crisis in Kashmir.

12

Global War on Terror

HOW THE GLOBAL WAR ON TERROR HAS FARED?

The Sheer Cost of It

The so-called Global War on Terror was launched with much fanfare on September 20, 2001. According to "War on Terror Facts, Costs and Timeline" of the authoritative *The Balance*, the War on Terror has, till March 23, 2017, consumed as much as a whopping $2,016.5 billion or over $2 trillion! At the rate of ₹64.81 per dollar conversion rate on April 1, 2017, this comes to a staggering figure of ₹1,30,68,936.5 crore or nearly 131 lakh crore. To get an idea of what this figure means, you may like to view it in the backdrop of the Union Budget of India 2017. According to "Highlights of Union Budget" in *The Hindu*, the total expenditure of the Government of India in one year is just 21.47 lakh crore!

Spending for the War on Terror includes three major components. First, is spending for Overseas Contingency Operations. Congress appropriates these emergency funds, and they aren't subject to budget limits such as sequestration. Second are the significant increases in the base budget for the

Department of Defence. Third are the additions to the Veterans Administration budget to treat wounded soldiers. Spending rises along with the number of boots on the ground for these two wars. It also beefs up the domestic force that supports foreign operations. It develops new technology, such as the F-35 fighter jet and drones. It also includes supporting departments, such as Homeland Security, State Department and the National Nuclear Security Administration.

The year-wise break-up of the expenditure of the War on Terror is as follows:

($ billion)

2001	– 31	2007	– 192.5	2013	– 49.6
2002	– 59.1	2008	– 235.6	2014	– 88
2003	– 111.9	2009	– 97.1	2015	– 67
2004	– 105	2010	– 181	2016	– 89.5
2005	– 102.3	2011	– 162.4	2017	– 97.9
2006	– 127	2012	– 119.6	2018	– 96.4

The War on Terror added $2 trillion to the $19 trillion US debt. That's over 10%. The real cost of the War on Terror is not just what it has added to the debt. It's also the lost jobs that those funds could have created. Every $1 billion spent on defence creates 8,555 jobs and adds $565 million to the economy. That same $1 billion given to the citizens as a tax cut would have stimulated enough demand to create 10,779 jobs and put $505 million into the economy as retail spending. $1 billion in education spending adds $1.3 billion to the economy and creates 17,687 jobs. That $2 trillion spent on the War on Terror created 17 million jobs. But if it had gone toward education instead, it would have created almost 36 million jobs. That would have helped end the recession sooner.

The Drone War

Since June 18, 2004, the United States government has attacked thousands of targets in Northwest Pakistan using unmanned aerial vehicles (drones) controlled by the Central Intelligence Agency's Special Activities Division. The drones have been pounding relentlessly on targets in the Federally Administered Tribal Areas along the Afghan border in Northwest Pakistan. Till the end of January 2017, that is in a little less than 13 years, the 'drone war' claims to have killed some 2,000 to 3,000 terrorists. Estimates of civilian deaths range from a low of 158 to a high of 965. The American position is that the identities of collateral victims are usually not investigated by US forces, who systematically count each male military-age corpse as an "enemy killed in action" unless there is clear proof to the contrary, as long as the male was in a militant facility at the time. The New America Foundation has estimated that 80% of those killed in the attacks were militants. On the other hand, several experts have stated that in reality, far fewer militants and many more civilians have been killed. In a 2009 opinion article, Daniel L Byman of the Brookings Institution claims that drone strikes may have killed "10 or so civilians" for every militant that they killed.

There is considerable dispute on the actual impact of the 'drone war' even in the West. Barbara Elias-Sanbon, for example, claims that,

> "as much of the literature on drones suggests, such killings usually harden militants' determination to fight, stalling any potential negotiations and settlement."

On the other hand, Patrick B Johnson and Anoop Sarbahi argue that "drone strikes are associated with decreases in the incidence and lethality of terrorist attacks" in Pakistan. I do not think that whoever has been reading the newspapers or watching the TV since 2012 (the year they wrote this) would agree with this.

But even if we do not indulge in the debate, the very fact that the 'drone war' is being continued even now means that there are still enough terrorists on the ground to warrant their use 13 years later too.

Where Does the World Stand in Spite of all this?

In spite of this frightful expenditure and killing, the world is as much worried of terrorism in 2017 as it was in 2001! Isn't it? Had it not been so, you would not have had diplomats of all hues battling it out in every possible international forum and speaking of incisive things like 'toxic curriculum', and the 'Ivy League of terrorism'; and some international conference on the subject taking place somewhere almost every day? A whole army of think-tanks and research institutions across the world are flourishing courtesy this very subject and are churning out such a massive amount of literature that, if dropped from a C-130 Hercules like the legendary Daisy Cutter bomb, could bury the terrorists alive under their sheer weight; If they are not absolutely farcical and making a fool of the whole world, it would mean that terrorism is still a very potent threat. Al-Qaida might have been decimated; the ISIS might be on the brink of being wiped out; the drones might have killed thousands of people believed to be terrorists; the fact is that the world is nowhere near getting rid of terrorism.

Seth Moulton is a US Congressman who represents Massachusetts' Sixth Congressional District. He opined in the *Boston Globe* that although ISIS disciples act like medieval thugs, we must not underestimate them. That means recognizing that they innovate and adapt to our efforts to stop them. And that's why, counterintuitive though it may seem, the reactionary policies, some think will protect us, could actually put us all at greater risk. He went on to add:

"Whatever the political and economic cost, the US must disengage from all sides in the Middle East, before it is too late."

THE FUTURE OF TERRORISM IN THE WORLD

By the time of writing this book, US officials and analysts foresee the demise of the ISIS 'Caliphate' after the eventual recapture of Mosul and Raqqa, perhaps within the next six months, but warn that the group may revert to a more traditional terrorist organization. The ISIS attack on the Christians in Egypt in April 2017 must be seen in this light – 45 people perished in the Palm Sunday church bombings. The cabinet declared a state of emergency. A newspaper was pulled off news stands after it criticized the government. As Declan Walsh, the Cairo bureau chief of *The New York Times*, said in his article "Attacks Shows ISIS' New Plan: Divide Egypt by Killing Christians" in *The New York Times*, it was just the reaction the ISIS wanted. The harsh reaction was an affirmation of sorts for the Islamic State, which until recently struggled to have any impact in Egypt outside of North Sinai. Routed from its stronghold on the coast of Libya, besieged in Iraq and wilting under intense pressure in Syria, the militant extremist group urgently needed to find a new battleground where it could start to proclaim victory again.

In my considered opinion, once the ISIS's stupid medieval dream of 'conquest' is shattered; once they realize their inherent limitations vis-à-vis the massively resourceful and modern militaries of the nation states; they will also realize that the only way of their survival is as terrorists. Terrorism is likely to exist for an indefinite period; insurgencies may be wiped out. Terrorism has a future; insurgencies do not have one. There is no target in the world which is safe from terrorist attacks – provided the terrorists know their job. A lot of people involved with the idea die, but the idea doesn't die.

Terrorism presents a complex problem. Complex problems demand complex solutions. Those who want to run away from complexity, present platitudinous, wishful thinking as solutions for the benefit of the intellectually-challenged in the seminar/ conference circuit. Platitudinous, simplistic thinking, for example, is epitomized in the suggestions of Christine Fair in her article "Lashkar-e-Tayiba and the Pakistani State":

> "The United States, India, the United Kingdom and other states victimized by LeT and similar groups should forge closer cooperation on intelligence and counter-terrorism initiatives to interdict planned attacks and to identify and prosecute individuals after the fact. Such prosecutions will likely present evidence that will incriminate others who remain active in the organization, contributing to further efforts to downgrade their efficacy. Greater contacts must be forged with immigration, treasury and other government agencies in those states in North America, Europe, the Middle East, South and South East Asia that LeT/JuD uses for logistical purposes, movement of recruits into and out of Pakistan, transfers of funds, and other materials to sustain operations. The goal of these engagements is to deny Pakistani militant groups freedom of movement of all assets and disrupting potential cells and plots."

Such wishful thinking borders on the juvenile. Let us face it. The reality is that, as long as Pakistan wishes to continue it, they can continue it. Appealing to them or trying to starve them would not work in the long run.

THE NECESSITY OF AN HONEST INTROSPECTION

The problem of terrorism will not be solved by television debates, articles and seminars of the pseudo-intellectuals; it will not be tackled by 'kinetic force' either. The former cry themselves hoarse and yet fail to explain what keeps the terrorists going; the latter fire millions of rounds of ammunition for years altogether, kill thousands and yet wonder why they are not able to eradicate the problem. Taliban, Al-Qaida and ISIS are no better than 'savages' for the ultra-modern, ultra-sophisticated American war machine. Yet, the returns for the Americans have not at all been commensurate with their investment. They killed people by the thousands, and bombed places back to the Stone Age; yet, the problem was not solved. Something should have been missing, isn't it?

Otto von Bismarck had said,

> "Fools learn from their own experience. I prefer to learn from the experience of others."

We never learnt from the Americans' follies. They might have the best tactical doctrines in the world – they are failing because their very strategy is wrong. The world has had spent enough of 'sweat and blood'; it has not solved the problem. Countering terrorism effectively demands a perfect combination of sound strategy and tactics both – tactics without strategy is an empty noise; and strategy without proper tactics is only mental extravaganza – one must master both in order to succeed.

In general, terrorism thrives in soft States that are characterized by a highly immature public and an utterly irresponsible media besides weak-kneed governments. They fail to understand that in a modern state it is impossible to protect the myriads of targets that it presents. They expect that the government should be able to protect everything by a magic wand. When that does not happen, they blame the government, bringing them under pressure and hence more prone to the characteristic knee-jerk reactions. As the Governor General of Algeria Jacques Soustelle had described it,

> "Terror is a psychological weapon of unbelievable power. Before the bodies of those whose throats have been cut

> and the grimacing faces of the mutilated, all capacity for resistance lapses; the spring is broken."

Public opinion in this age, anywhere in the world, is determined largely by the trash which is fed to them by the print and electronic media. Since they are often the most irresponsible and intellectually the most bankrupt lot, they take the lead in softening the resolve of the people and making them think irrationally. The media can always hire self-proclaimed 'experts' or pseudo-intellectuals (usually retired officials dying for some publicity) who react to terrorist strikes either by going hyper-ballistic, demanding red-hot revenge in nothing but blood, or by an effeminate wailing. Both situations tend to preclude rational thinking and decision-making. The behavioural pattern of the reactions often exhibits itself in extremes. This may include demanding and/or instituting extensive and ostentatious protective measures or very harsh laws; a furious revenge; or simple 'stupefied inaction' which is exalted as signs of maturity, restraint, responsible behaviour or whatever. In the end, nations too become emotional and irrational like ordinary human beings. Intelligent terrorists therefore need only to 'calibrate' their actions according to the reactions of the target to make the people, the pseudo-intellectuals, the media and the leaders to bend to their will. Hence for those who understand the psyche of a nation, its people, its media and its ruling class, terrorism makes eminent sense. Terrorists seek to elicit a certain type of response from their targets. If the targets of terrorism are fully aware of the perceptions that eventually lead to the response that corresponds with the purpose of the terrorists, they can be made to alter their perceptions and respond in a different way. The mere act of doing this will be tantamount to a defeat of the terrorist because then he would have failed in eliciting the desired response from the target.

In the Indian context, a direct implication of the dilemmas faced by the ISI is that the ISI cannot raise the level of terrorism in India to some cataclysmic proportions; nor, at the same time, they would be able to abandon it completely. Therefore terrorism not exceeding a certain level will therefore continue to beset us for a long time, may be indefinitely, and we must be emotionally, intellectually, physically, financially, and militarily prepared for it.

Realistically, it should not be expected that Pakistan would ever 'reform' itself or that we would be able to do something such by way of chastisement or punishment to it that would make it a 'good boy' in the class. On September 17, 2017, the government submitted before the Supreme Court that the Rohingya refugees posed a big security threat as many of them had links with terror organisations like the ISIS, and the Inter Services Intelligence of Pakistan. Organised Rohingya Muslim influx had started in 2012 and there are around 40,000 such refugees in the country currently. Militant elements among them are found to be active in Jammu, Delhi, Hyderabad and Mewat region. Some of them are using the hawala route also to raise money for illegal activities. In other words, Pakistan's proxy war has now found another front.

Of course, I am very much aware that, given our military strength, the option of war is always open to us, but that is left to the policy-makers. We should neither wail like widows (using phrases like *dhamakon se shahar dehla; charon ore maatam hee maatam*, etc or repeatedly showing visuals of bloodied bodies, crying family members etc) nor should we rush to kill, shouting 'you bloody murderers'. **Let us face reality – terrorism is here to stay, not only in India but in the world. It is an unfortunate consequence of the historical 'sins' of the human race; we can neither disown history nor wish the 'sins' away without catastrophic upheavals in the world. Once again, nothing**

prevents us from those upheavals; but those who clamour for it, must be prepared for it.

The ISIS as a military force can be beaten and perhaps will be beaten shortly – no doubt about it. But that's only one head of the Hydra. All those things which explain its intrinsic appeal to the susceptible people are the other 'uncut' heads of the Hydra. Military defeat would not defeat the ideology or the sentiments. They are likely to survive and may be even serve as a rallying point for like-minded people across the world in future for revival in various shapes and forms. As long as there would be discontent and dissatisfaction against the overbearing attitude of the USA in world affairs, there would be people willing to take up arms, kill and get killed. Brutus had spoken in Shakespeare's *Julius Caesar*:

> "As Caesar loved me, I weep for him; as he was fortunate, I rejoice at it; as he was valiant, I honour him; but as he was ambitious, I slew him.... Who is here so base that would be a bondman? If any, speak; for him have I offended.... Who is here so vile that will not love his country? If any, speak; for him have I offended."

Ancient Indian mythology understood it only too well. We have all heard of the *rakshasas* (demons) tormenting humanity it every *yuga*. Had the Omnipotent *Bhagwan* (God) deemed it fit, He could have finished them off with his 'will' alone. Yet, He chose to descend repeatedly to the land of the mortals in His human *avatars* to slay the demons because that was the correct way of doing things. *Bhagwan* had to restore the faith of the humanity in the power and capabilities of *dharma*, and a righteous, pious, and virtuous human being. Similarly, terrorism too demands a correct way of handling it. The demons will be coming back to haunt the world in every age because no question is ever settled unless it is settled right.

Select Bibliography

21st Century Wire, "Aiding ISIS: Israel Bombs Syria for Fifth Time in 18 Months, Gives Arms, Medical Aid to Militants", December 8, 2014. http://21stcenturywire.com/2014/12/08/aiding-isis-israel-bombs-syria-for-fifth time-in-18-months-gives-arms-medical-aid-to-militants/

_______, "Israel Joins Forces with ISIS? Tel Aviv Bombs Syria for Sixth Time in 18 Months", January 20, 2015. http://21stcenturywire.com/2015/01/20/israel-joins-forces-with-isis-tel-aviv bombs-syria-for-sixth-time-in-18-months/

_______, Patrick Henningsen, "Truth Revealed: McCain's 'Moderate Rebels' in Syria are ISIS", January 22, 2015. http://21stcenturywire.com/2015/01/22/truth-revealed-mccains-moderate-rebels-in syria-are-isis/

_______, "UN Report Reveals How Israel is Coordinating with ISIS Militants Inside Syria", February 19, 2015. http://21stcenturywire.com/2015/02/19/un-report-reveals-how-israel-is coordinating-with-isis-militants-inside-syria/

A Comprehensive Note on Jammu and Kashmir (Government of India). http://www.indianembassy.org/policy/Kashmir/Kashmir_MEA/introduction.html

Quoted also in Association for Communal Harmony in Asia, Archive of Kashmir Resources.

http://www.asiapeace.org/acha/kashmir112.htm

Aamer Ahmed Khan, "Pakistan's Flourishing Arms Bazaar", BBC News, June 21, 2006.
http://news.bbc.co.uk/2/hi/south_asia/5066860.stm

ABC News, "Syria Decries 'Aggression' as US Launches Cruise Missiles", April 6, 2017.
http://abcnews.go.com/International/wireStory/mounting-confidence-nerve gas-syria-attack-46615057

Adolf Hitler, Speech, September, 1935.

AFP, "Guns Cheaper than Smart Phones – Pakistani Tribal Town".
http://www.france24.com/en/20160728-guns-cheaper-smartphones-pakistani tribal-town

Ahmed Rashid, *Descent into Chaos: The US and the Disaster in Pakistan, Afghanistan, and Central Asia*, Penguin Books, 2009.

———, *Taliban: The Story of the Afghan Warlords*, Pan Books, 2001.

Akbar Shahid Ahmed, "3 New Findings on ISIS Weapons that You should Know About", *The Huffington Post*, October 7, 2014.
http://www.huffingtonpost.com/2014/10/06/isis-weapons-report_n_5942334.html

Al Jazeera, "A Century On: Why Arabs Resent Sykes-Picot".
http://interactive.aljazeera.com/aje/2016/sykes-picot-100-years-middle-east-map/

Alan Taylor, "The Soviet War in Afghanistan: 1979-1989", *The Atlantic*, August 4, 2014.
https://www.theatlantic.com/photo/2014/08/the-soviet-war-in-afghanistan-1979-1989/100786/.

Albert J Bergesen and Omar Lizardo, "International Terrorism and the World-System", *Sociological Theory*, 22:1, March 2004.
https://www3.nd.edu/~olizardo/papers/st-terrorism-world-system.pdf.

———, "Theories of Terrorism: A Symposium", *Sociological Theory* 22 (1): 38-52, March 2004, doi: 10.1111/j.1467 9558.2004.00203.x.

Alexandra Homolar, "Rebels Without a Conscience: The Evolution of the Rogue State Narrative in US Security Policy", *European Journal of International Relations*, November 2010.

Allen Isaac, "Revival of Islam", *CR*, LVIII, 1874, p 2.

Amir Hussain, *Oil and Water: Two Faiths: One God*, CopperHouse, 2006, ISBN 13: 978-1896836829.

Amir Mir, *The Fluttering Flag of Jehad*, Lahore: Mashal Books, 2008.

———, *The True Face of Jehadis*, Lahore: Mashal Books, 2004.

Amir Rana, "Jamat-ud-Dawa Splits", *The Fact*, Issue No 11, August 2004. http://fact.com.pk/archives/august/feng/dawa.htm

Amnesty International, "Iraq: Taking Stock: The Arming of Islamic State", 7 December 2015, Index number: MDE 14/2812/2015. https://www.amnesty.org/en/documents/mde14/2812/2015/en/

Andrew Bacevich, "Tailors to the Emperor", *New Left Review*, May-June 2011, Vol 69, 101-124.

———, "The Pretend War: Why Bombing ISIL won't Solve the Problem: The Deployment of Our Military Might in Syria will Exacerbate Regional Disorder – and it will Solve Nothing, *The Spectator*. https://www.spectator.co.uk/2015/11/sorry-but-just-bombing-isis-in-syria-wont help-anyone/

Andy Beckett, "The Making of the Terror Myth, *The Guardian*, October 15, 2004. https://www.theguardian.com/media/2004/oct/15/broadcasting.bbc

Angel Rabasa, Robert D Blackwill, Peter Chalk, Kim Cragin, C Christine Fair, Brian A Jackson, Brian Michael Jenkins, Seth G Jones, Nathaniel Shestak, and Ashley J Tellis, "The Lessons of Mumbai", Occasional Paper, Rand Corporation, 2009.

Animesh Roul, Lashkar-e-Taiba and the Strategy of "Encircling" India, *Terrorism Monitor*, October 21, 2010. http://www.jamestown.org/programs/gta/single/?tx_ttnews[tt_news]=37056&cHash=b2f2164427.

———, "Lashkar-e-Taiba's Financial Network Targets India from the Gulf States", *Terrorism Monitor*, Vol 7, Issue 19, July 2009.

———, "Pakistan's Lashkar-e-Taiba Chooses Between Kashmir and the Global Jihad", *Terrorism Focus*, Vol 6, Issue 3, January 28, 2009, Jamestown Foundation. https://jamestown.org/program/pakistans-lashkar-e-taiba-chooses between-kashmir-and-the-global-jihad/.

———, "Punjab Government Financing Front Group for Lashkar-e-Taiba Terrorists", *Terrorism Monitor*, Vol 11, Issue 13, June 27, 2013.

Anthony H Cordesman; Arleigh A Burke and Varun Vira, "Pakistan: Violence vs Stability", Burke Chair in Strategy, Washington, DC: Center for Strategic and International Studies, (25 July 2011).

Appendix C – "Statement of Reasons – Jaish-e-Mohammad (JeM)", Parliamentary Joint Committee on Intelligence and Security. Parliament of Australia.
http://www.aph.gov.au/Parliamentary_Business/Committees/Joint/Completed_In uiries/pjcis/grouped/report/appendixc.

Arif Jamal, *Call for Transnational Jihad: Lashkar-e-Taiba 1985-2014*, AvanteGarde Books LLC, 2014.

_______, *Shadow War: The Untold Story of Jihad in Kashmir* (Brooklyn, NY: Melville House, 2009).

Asad Durrani, "CT Made Easy", *Dawn*, March 30, 2017.
https://www.dawn.com/news/1323674.

Ashley J Tellis, "Bad Company – Lashkar-E-Tayyiba and the Growing Ambition of Islamist Militancy in Pakistan", Congressional Testimony, United States House of Representatives, Committee on Foreign Affairs, Subcommittee on the Middle East and South Asia, March 11, 2010.

_______, "Pakistan and the War on Terror: Conflicted Goals, Compromised Performance", Carnegie Endowment for International Peace, Washington, 2008.

_______, "The Menace that is Lashkar-e-Taiba, Policy Outlook", Carnegie Endowment for International Peace, March 2012.

Assange Reveals that the West is Behind ISIS and Ukraine Crisis and Israel Behind Hamas.
http://secretsofthefed.com/assange-reveals-that-the-west-is-behind isis-and-ukraine-crisis-and israel-behind-hamas/.

Asthana, NC, *Next War: India, Pakistan, China*, Manas Publications, New Delhi, 2017.

_______, *The Ultimate Handbook of Urban Warfare*, Manas Publications, New Delhi, 2012.

Asthana, NC and Anjali Nirmal, *India's Wars and Warfare*, Pointer Publications, Jaipur, 2012.

_______, *Indian Defence: Crisis and Challenges*, Pointer Publications, Jaipur, 2011.

_______, *Intelligence and Security Management*, Pointer Publications, Jaipur, 2003.

_______, *The Ultimate Book of Explosives, Bombs and IEDs*, Pointer Publications, Jaipur, 2008.

_______, *Urban Terrorism: Myths and Realities*, Pointer Publications, Jaipur, 2009.

B Muralidhar Reddy, "Acting Under Pressure", *Frontline*, Vol 19, Issue 1, Jan 5, 2002.

_______, "Jaish behind Parliament Attack: Ex-ISI Chief", *The Hindu*, July, 3, 2004.

B Raman, "Jaish-e-Mohammed (JeM) – A Backgrounder", Paper No 332, 3.10.2001, South Asia Analysis Group.

Barak Ravid, "UN Reveals Israeli Links with Syrian Rebels", *Haaretz*, December 7, 2014.
http://www.haaretz.com/israel-news/.premium-1.630359

Barbara Elias-Sanbon, "The Pakistani Taliban's Coming Divide", *Foreign Affairs*, February 2, 2012.
https://www.foreignaffairs.com/articles/afghanistan/2012-02 02/pakistani-talibans-coming-divide

Barbara Slavin, "US Treasury Official Praises Saudi Cooperation Against Terror Funding, *Al-Monitor*, October 14, 2016.
http://www.al-monitor.com/pulse/originals/2016/10/us-treasury-official-saudi-combat-terror funding.html

BBC News, "Afghan Taliban Capture Crucial Town of Sangin", March 23, 2017.
http://www.bbc.com/news/world-asia-39365330

_______, "Indian Fury Over Freed Militant, 14 December, 2002.
http://news.bbc.co.uk/2/hi/south_asia/2575199.stm

_______, "Masood Azhar: The Man Who Brought Jihad to Britain", 5 April 2016.
http://www.bbc.com/news/magazine-35959202

_______, "Pakistan Denies Militant Arrested", 18 December 2008.
http://news.bbc.co.uk/2/hi/south_asia/7789056.stm

_______, "Who are Britain's Jihadists?", February 22, 2017.
http://www.bbc.com/news/uk-32026985

BBC, "Syria Crisis: 'Only Four or Five' US-Trained Syrian Rebels are still Fighting", September 17, 2015. http://www.bbc.com/news/world-middle-east-34278233

Ben Swann, "Reality Check: Proof US Government Wanted ISIS to Emerge in Syria", Wake Up World'. https://wakeup-world.com/2015/11/24/reality-check-proof us-government-wanted-isis-to-emerge-in-syria/

Bernt Glatzer, "The Pashtun Tribal System", Chapter 10 in G Pfeffer and DK Behera (eds), *Concept of Tribal Society* (Contemporary Society: Tribal Studies, Vol 5), New Delhi: Concept Publishers, 2002.

Bill Roggio, "US Designates Lashkar – Taiba's Charitable Front as Terror Group", *The Long War Journal*, November 24, 2010. http://www.longwarjournal.org/archives/2010/11/us_treasury_designat.php

Bloomberg, Stepan Kravchenko, "Russia Digs Ditches to Slow Inflow of Arms and Men from Ukraine", May 26, 2015. https://www.bloomberg.com/news/articles/2015-05-26/russia-digs ditches-to-slow-inflow-of-arms-and-men-from-ukraine

Bremner, Charles, "'Pakistani Army Ran Muslim Extremist Training Camps', says Anti-Terrorist Expert", *The Times*, 14 November 2009.

Brian Wood and Johan Peleman, "Making the Deal and Moving the Goods – the Role of Brokers and Shippers", in Lora Lumpe (ed), *Running Guns: The Global Black Market in Small Arms*, London: Zed Books, 2000.

Bruce Cumings, Ervand Abrahamian and Moshe Maoz, *Inventing the Axis of Evil*, New Press, 2004.

Bruce Golding, "US to Arm Syrian Rebels with High-Tech Gear for Airstrikes", *New York Post*, February 18, 2015. http://nypost.com/2015/02/18/us-to-arm-syrian rebels-with-high-tech-gear-for-airstrikes/

Bruce Hoffman and Fernando Reinares, *The Evolution of the Global Terrorist Threat – From 9/11 to Osama bin Laden's Death*, Columbia Studies in Terrorism and Irregular Warfare, Columbia University Press, 2016.

Bruce Riedel, "Blame Pakistani Spy Service for Attack on Indian Air Force Base", *The Daily Beast*, 5 January, 2016.

———, "Deadly Embrace: Pakistan, America and the Future of Global Jihad", Brookings.edu.

———, "Terrorism in India and the Global Jihad", Brookings, November 30, 2008.
https://www.brookings.edu/articles/terrorism-in-india-and-the-global-jihad/

C Christine Fair, "Bringing Back the Dead: Why Pakistan Used the Jaish-e Mohammad to Attack an Indian Airbase", *The Huffington Post*, January 7, 2015.
http://www.huffingtonpost.com/c-christine-fair/bringing-back-the-dead-wh_b_8955224.html

———, *Lashkar-e-Taiba Beyond Bin Laden: Enduring Challenges for the Region and the International Community*, Testimony prepared for the US Senate, Foreign Relations Committee, Hearing on Al Qaeda, the Taliban, and Other Extremist Groups in Afghanistan and Pakistan, May 24, 2011.

———, "Lashkar-e-Tayiba and the Pakistani State", *Survival*, Vol 53, Issue 4, 2011.

———, *The Counterterror Coalitions: Cooperation with Pakistan and India* (Santa Monica, Calif.: RAND, 2004), pp 21-27.
www.rand.org/pubs/ monographs/2004/RAND_MG141.pdf

———, "The Lashkar's Empire of Jihad", *India Today*, September 11, 2015.
http://indiatoday.intoday.in/story/the-lashkars-empire-of-jihad/1/470905.html

C Christine Fair and Peter Chalk, *Fortifying Pakistan: The Role of US Internal Security Assistance*, USIP, Washington DC, 2006.

CJ Chivers and Eric Schmitt, 'Arms Airlift to Syria Rebels Expands with Aid from CIA', *The New York Times*, March 24, 2013.
http://www.nytimes.com/2013/03/25/world/middleeast/arms-airlift-to-syrian rebels-expands-with-cia-aid.html?pagewanted=all&_r=0.

Carl Conetta, "An Undisciplined Defense", Project for Defense Alternatives, Jan 18, 2010.

Center for Public Integrity, Julia Harte and R Jeffrey Smith, "Investigators Find Islamic State used Ammo Made in 21 Countries, including America", October 5, 2014.
https://www.publicintegrity.org/2014/10/05/15827/investigators-find islamic-state-used-ammo-made-21-countries-including-america

Chad C Serena, *It Takes More than a Network: The Iraqi Insurgency and Organizational Adaptation*, Stanford: Stanford University Press, 2014, p 143.

Chakravarty, S, "The Plot Unravels", *India Today*, December 31, 2001.

Chalmers Johnson, *The Sorrows of Empire: Militarism, Secrecy and the End of the Republic*, Metropolitan Books, 2004.

Charlotte Alfred, Putin Is Rewriting History: There Would Be No ISIS Without Assad, *The Huffington Post*, January 6, 2017. http://www.huffingtonpost.com/entry/putin-assad isis_us_560d7db0 e4b0dd85030b2368

Christelle Rigual, "Armed Groups' Holdings of Guided Light Weapons", Research Note No 31. Geneva: Small Arms Survey. June, 2013.

________, "Guided Light Weapons Possession by Non-State Armed Groups: Mapping the Issue", Unpublished background paper, Geneva: Small Arms Survey, March, 2013.

Christopher M Blanchard, "Afghanistan: Narcotics and US Policy", CRS Report for Congress No RL32686 (Washington DC: Congressional Research Service, June 19, 2007).

CNSNews, "Assad: ISIS was Created in Iraq, Under the Supervision of the Americans", April 21, 2015. http://www.cnsnews.com/news/article/patrick goodenough/assad-isis-was-created-iraq-under-supervision-americans

Colin P Clarke, *Terrorism, Inc: The Financing of Terrorism, Insurgency, and Irregular Warfare*, Praeger Security International, 2015.

Conflict Armament Research, London, "Islamic State Ammunition in Iraq and Syria" (Dispatch from the field), October 2014. http://www.conflictarm.com/wp content/uploads/2014/10/Dispatch _IS_Iraq_Syria_Ammunition.pdf

Council on Foreign Relations, "The Global Regime for Transnational Crime", Issue Brief, July 2, 2012.

D Kumar, "Tracing a Puppet Chain", *Outlook*, December 31, 2001.

Daniel L Byman, "Do Targeted Killings Work?", Brookings Institution, July 14, 2009.

Daniel Markey, "A False Choice in Pakistan", *Foreign Affairs*, Vol 86, No 4 (July/August 2007), pp 90-92.

Darius Shahtahmasebi, "A Brief History of ISIS and the Problem with the West's War on Terror", *Speakout*, Op-Ed, 5 November 2015.

David Coleman Headley, "Interrogation Report of National Investigation Agency", June 10, 2010, p 14, cited in Rath, SK, 2012, "Lashkar-e-Taiba of Pakistan: An India Centric Threat Projection", *Journal of Terrorism Research*, 3(2).
http://doi.org/10.15664/jtr.406

David Gibbs, *The Political Economy of Third World Intervention*, University of Chicago Press, 1991.

________, "Pretexts in US Foreign Policy: The War on Terrorism in Historical Perspective", *New Political Science*, Vol 26, No 3, 2004, 293-321.

David Grudge, "Bigger Than ISIS – There's a hidden power behind ISIS and it's so big and so powerful, you won't believe this Massive Shocking fact about it!", 28.11.2015.
http://www.catholic.org/news/national/story.php?id=65577 and https://www.youtube.com/c/californianetwork

David Ignatius, "How ISIS Spread in the Middle East and How to Stop It", *The Atlantic*, October 29, 2015.
https://www.theatlantic.com/international/archive/2015/10/how-isis-started-syria-iraq/412042/

David J Kilcullen, "Countering Global Insurgency", Vol 28, Issue 4, 2005, pp 597-617.

David Kinsella, "The Black Market in Small Arms: Examining a Social Network", Contemporary Security Policy, Vol 27, No 1 (April 2006), pp 100-117.

David Mizner, "Don't Blame Islam: Al-Qaeda and ISIS are Products of US and Saudi Imperialism", *Jacobin*, 30.1.2015.
https://www.jacobinmag.com/2015/01/united-states-saudi-arabia-isis/

David S Cohen, "Attacking ISIL's Financial Foundation", speech at the Carnegie Endowment for International Peace.
http://carnegieendowment.org/2014/10/23/remarks-by-u.s.-treasury-under secretary-david-s.-cohen-on-attacking-isil-s-financial-foundation

Dawn, "Banned Outfits Raise Cash from Sacrifice Day", November 24, 2010.
http://www.dawn.com/2010/11/24/banned-outfits-raise-cash-from-sacrifice day.html

________, "Jaish's Masood Azhar under 'protective custody', confirms Punjab Law Minister", January 15, 2016. https://www.dawn.com/news/1232967/jaishs-masood azhar-under-protective-custody-confirms-punjab-law-minister

Dean Nelson, "WikiLeaks: Pakistan Continues to Support Mumbai Terror Attack Group", *The Telegraph*, Dec 1, 2010.

Decaln Walsh, "WikiLeaks Cables Portray Saudi Arabia as a Cash Machine for Terrorists, *The Guardian*, 5 December 2010.

________, "Attacks Shows ISIS' New Plan: Divide Egypt by Killing Christians", *The New York Times*, April 10, 2017. https://www.nytimes.com/2017/04/10/world/middleeast/egypt-christians-isis-palm sunday-attacks-sisi.html?_r=0

Deutsche Welle, "'IS' supply channels through Turkey". http://www.dw.com/en/is supply-channels-through-turkey/av-18091048

Dev Goswami, "Kashmir: 3 civilians killed, 63 jawans hurt in clashes after Budgam encounter-what you need to know", *India Today*, March 28, 2017. http://indiatoday.intoday.in/story/kashmir-budgam-encounter-civilian-clashes stone-pelting/1/915157.html

Diego Gambetta and Steffen Hertog, *Engineers of Jihad: The Curious Connection Between Violent Extremism and Education*, Princeton University Press, 2016.

Dominic Tierney, "Bashar al-Assad and the Devil's Endgame", *The Atlantic*, September 28, 2015. https://www.theatlantic.com/international/archive/2015/09/assad-syria-devil endgame-putin-obama/407635/

Don Melvin, Susannah Cullinane and Mohammed Tawfeeq, "Russia's Lavrov on Syria targets: 'If it looks like a terrorist, walks like a terrorist ...'", CNN, October 1, 2015. http://edition.cnn.com/2015/10/01/middleeast/russia-syria/

Don Rassler, C Christine Fair, Anirban Gosh, and Nadia Shoeb, "The Fighters of Lashkar-e-Taiba: Recruitment, Training, Deployment and Death", Occasional Paper, West Point Combating Terrorism Center, 2013.

Doris Buddenberg and William A Byrd, eds, "Afghanistan's Drug Industry: Structure, Functioning, Dynamics, and Implications for Counter-Narcotics Policy" (Washington DC: United Nations Office on Drugs and Crime and the World Bank, 2007).

Dr Noorhan Abbas and Dr Eric Atwell, The University of Leeds: The Qurany Concepts Tool.
http://www.comp.leeds.ac.uk/nora/html/8-41.html

Dr Sanchita Bhattacharya, "Terror-Financing in Pakistan", Society for Public Studies (SPS), *Insight*, February 2016.

Drone Strikes in Pakistan, Wikipedia.
https://en.wikipedia.org/wiki/Drone_strikes_in_Pakistan

Eben Kaplan, The ISI and Terrorism: Behind the Accusations, Backgrounder, Council on Foreign Relations, New York, October 19, 2007.
www.cfr.org/publication/11644/.

Emmanuel Sivan, The Clash within Islam [Hebrew] (Tel Aviv, Am Oved/ Ofakim Library, 2005), the chapter entitled: The Roots of anti-Americanism, pp 57-65.

Eric Pianin, "US Shoots Itself in the Foot by Accidentally Arming ISIS", *The Fiscal Times*, June 4, 2015.
http://www.thefiscaltimes.com/2015/06/04/Fog-War-US-Has-Armed-ISIS

Eric Schmitt, "CIA Said to Aid in Steering Arms to Syrian Opposition", *The New York Times*, June 21, 2012.
http://www.nytimes.com/2012/06/21/world/middleeast/cia said-to-aid-in-steering-arms-to-syrian-rebels.html?pagewanted=all&_r=1&.

Erica Wenig, 4 Issues With The Pentagon's Plan To Train Syrian Rebels Against ISIS, The Daily Caller News Foundation, 05.09.2015.

Ernesto Londoño and Greg Miller, CIA begins weapons delivery to Syrian rebels, *The Washington Post*, September 11. 2013.
https://www.washingtonpost.com/world/national-security/cia-begins-weapons delivery-to-syrian-rebels/2013/09/11/9fcf2ed8-1b0c-11e3-a628 7e6dde8f889d_story.html?utm_term=.a48c45621699

Evan F Kohlman, The Afghan-Bosnian Mujahideen Network in Europe, Swedish National Defence College (www.fhs.se).
www.aina.org/reports/tabmnie.pdf

Express Web Desk, Army Chief Bipin Rawat: Those displaying Pak, ISIS flags in Kashmir to face harsh action, *The Indian Express*, February 17, 2017.
http://indianexpress.com/article/india/army-chief-bipin-rawat-those-not supporting-our-operations-will-be-treated-as-workers-of-terrorists/

Faisal Irshaid, "ISIS, ISIL, IS or Daesh? One group, many names", BBC Monitoring, December 2, 2015.
http://www.bbc.com/news/world-middle-east-27994277.

Farah Douglas and Stephen Braun, "The Merchant of Death", *Foreign Policy*, No 157 (Nov-Dec, 2006).

Farah Douglas, Terrorist Responses to Improved US Financial Defenses (Testimony before the US House of Representatives, Committee on Financial Services, Subcommittee on Oversight and Investigations, February 16, 2005).

Fehim Taştekin, Contributor for Al-Monitor, Turkish Military Says MIT Shipped Weapons to al-Qaeda, Al-Monitor, Jan 16, 2015.
https://www.usnews.com/news/articles/2015/01/16/turkish-military-says-mit shipped-weapons-to-al-qaeda

Feroz Ahmed, *Ethnicity and Politics in Pakistan*, Karachi: Oxford University Press, 1998.

Foreign Policy, http://foreignpolicy.com/2014/06/11/exclusive-israel-is-tending-to wounded-syrian-rebels/.

Frontline, India's Most Wanted, 2002.

Garikai Chengu, "America Created Al-Qaeda and the ISIS Terror Group", *Global Research*, December 16, 2015.
http://www.globalresearch.ca/america-created-al qaeda-and-the-isis-terror-group/5402881.

Geo News, Pakistan arrests JeM militants after Pathankot airbase attack, January 13, 2016, https://www.geo.tv/latest/9329-Pakistan-arrests-Jaish-e-Mohammad members-after-Indian-airbase-attack.

Geoffrey Kambere, Puay Hock Goh, Pranav Kumar, Fulgence Msafir, "The Financing of Lashkar-e-Taiba", *CTX*, Vol 1, No 1, globalECCO.

Gil Feiler, The Globalization of Terror Funding, Mideast Security and Policy Studies, The Begin-Sadat Center for Strategic Studies Bar-Ilan University, Ramat Gan, 52900, Israel, September 2007.

Global Research, "Global Warfare: We're going to take out 7 countries in 5 years: Iraq, Syria, Lebanon, Libya, Somalia, Sudan and Iran", January 30, 2017.
http://www.globalresearch.ca/we-re-going-to-take-out-7-countries-in-5-years iraq-syria-lebanon-libya-somalia-sudan-iran/5166.

Hassan Abbas, "Is the NWFP Slipping Out of Pakistan's Control?",

Terrorism Monitor (Jamestown Foundation), Vol 5, No 22 (November 26, 2007), pp 9-12.
www.jamestown.org/terrorism/news/uploads/TM_005_022.pd.

Havocscope: Global Black Market Information.
http://www.havocscope.com/tag/arms-trafficking/.

Heath Druzin, "Fearing post-2014 environment, Afghans buy up weapons," *Stars and Stripes*, December 5, 2012.

Hein Kiessling, *Faith, Unity, Discipline: The ISI of Pakistan*, C Hurst & Co Publishers Ltd, 2016.

Helen Barnett, UK terror warning: 1600 Brits join ISIS terrorists – and 500 are back on our streets, April 27, 2015.
http://www.express.co.uk/news/uk/571468/UK-terror-warning-1600-Brits-join ISIS-terrorists-and-500-are-back-on-our-streets.

Hillary Clinton, https://www.youtube.com/watch?v=Dqn0bm4E9yw.

Hillel Fradkin, Husain Haqqani and Eric Brown (editors), "Current Trends in Islamist Ideology", Washington, DC: Hudson Institute, 2005.

Hindustan Times, JeM's Azhar lives freely in Pakistan, govt never detained him: Report, April 26, 2016.
http://www.hindustantimes.com/world/pakistan-didn-t detain-masood-azhar-after-pathankot-attack-report/story QlXZi7xMlPtaPNF1ZVg1 NJ.html.
http://satp.org/satporgtp/countries/india/states/jandk/terrorist_out fits/index.html.

Huffington Post, The (Sangeetha Nair), The Spectre Of Radicalised Minds Is Back To Haunt Kerala, Via Internet, Courtesy Of The ISIS, 22.1.2017.
http://www.huffingtonpost.in/2016/12/30/the-spectre-of-radicalised-minds-is-back to-haunt-kerala-via-in/.

Husain Haqqani, Pakistan: Between Mosque and Military (Washington, DC: Carnegie Endowment for International Peace, 2005).

________, Pakistan: Between Mosques and Military. Washington: Carnegie Endowment for International Peace, 2005.

Ibrahim Kazerooni and Rob Prince, "Humanitarian Intervention: Destroying Nations to Save Them", *Foreign Policy in Focus*, October 16, 2013.
http://fpif.org/humanitarian-intervention-destroying-nations-save/

IMF (M El Qorchi, S Maimbo, and JF Wilson), "Informal Fund Transfer

Systems: An Analysis of the Informal Hawala System", 2003.

India Today, Atir Khan, "Pakistan deploys special army commandos to secure Dawood Ibrahim", November 2, 2015.
http://indiatoday.intoday.in/story/pakistan deploys-special-army-commandos-to-secure-dawood-ibrahim/1/514062.html

________, Jitendra Bahadur Singh, "22 Kerala men receiving training at ISIS terror camp in Afghanistan, NIA tracks missing youths", January 5, 2017.
http://indiatoday.intoday.in/story/kerala-islamic-state-national-investigation agency/1/850064.html

________, "ISI promised Dawood Ibrahim protection, shelter if he invested 30% of his earnings to fund terror: Sources", August 27, 2013.
http://indiatoday.intoday.in/story/isi-promised-dawood-ibrahim-protection-shelter if-he-invested-30percent-of-his-earnings-to-fund-terror-sources/1/304061.html

Indian Express, The, "China snubs India again, blocks proposal at UN to list Masood Azhar as terrorist", December 30, 2016.
http://indianexpress.com/article/india/china-united-nations-masood-azhar-jem terrorist-india-4451956/

Inigo Gilmore, "Weapons stolen by Israeli soldiers arm Palestinians", *Daily Telegraph*, July, 22, 2003.

International Crisis Group, "Pakistan: Karachi's Madrasas and Violent Extremism", March 29, 2007.

InvestmentWatch, "Assange Reveals that the West is Behind ISIS and Ukraine Crisis", March 29, 2015.
http://investmentwatchblog.com/assange-reveals-that-the-west-is-behind isis-and-ukraine-crisis/

http://anonhq.com/assange-reveals-wes

Iran English Radio, IRIB World Service, September 09, 2014.
http://english.irib.ir/voj/commentaries/item/195569-isis-atrocities-and-the-us-vested-interests

Isambard Wilkinson, "Lashkar-e-Taiba: The group accused of Mumbai attacks", Telegraph.co.uk, November 30, 2008.

Ivan Eland, "Excessive US Military Action Overseas Breeds Anti-US Terrorism", Director of Defense Policy Studies, Cato Institute.

Jack Losh, "Did the Islamic State Go Shopping For Weapons in Ukraine?", Vice.com, December 1, 2015.

https://news.vice.com/article/did-the-islamic-state go-shopping-for-weapons-in-ukraine

Jack Moore, Amnesty International: "'Reckless Arms Trading' Fuels ISIS War Crimes in Iraq, Syria", *Newsweek*, 12/8/15.
http://europe.newsweek.com/reckless arms-trading-fuels-isis-war-crimes-iraq-and-syria-amnesty-report-401853?rm=eu

Jacob N Shapiro and C Christine Fair, "Why Support Islamist Militancy? Evidence from Pakistan", *International Security*, 34 (Winter): 79-118, 2009-2010.

Jacob N Shapiro and David A Siegel, "Underfunding in Terrorist Organizations", *International Studies Quarterly*, Vol 51, No 2, 2007, p 408.

Jamaat-ud-Dawa, *"Hum Kyon Jihad Kar Rahen Hain?"* [Why Are We Waging Jihad?] Lahore: Dar-ul-Andulus, 2004.

James Bamford, "The Shadow Factory: The NSA from 9/11 to the Eavesdropping of America", *Anchor*, 2009.

James Corbett, Corbett Report, "Breaking: US Troops Deploying on Jordan-Syria Border", December 11, 2011.

James Fallows, "Declaring Victory", *The Atlantic*, September 2006 Issue.
https://www.theatlantic.com/magazine/archive/2006/09/declaring-victory/305124/

Jaques Leslie, "The True Cost of Hidden Money: A Piketty Protégé's Theory on Tax Havens", *The New York Times*, June 15, 2014, p A19.

Jasna Lazarevic, "Guided Light Weapons Reportedly Held by Non-State Armed Groups (1996-2007)", Unpublished background paper, Geneva: Small Arms Survey. February 2008.

Jay Syrmopoulos, "Media Blacks Out Pentagon Report Exposing US Role in ISIS Creation", The Free Thought Project, *Mintpress News*, June 3, 2015.
http://www.mintpressnews.com/media-blacks-out-pentagon-report-exposing-u-s role-in-isis-creation/206187/.

Jayashree Bajoria, Profile: "Lashkar-e-Taiba (Army of the Pure) (aka Lashkar-e-Tayyiba, Lashkar-e-Toiba; Lashkar-i-Taiba)", Council on Foreign Relations, January 14, 2010.
http://www.cfr.org/pakistan/lashkar-e-taiba-army-pure-aka lashkar-e-tayyiba-lashkar-e-toiba-lashkar—taiba/p17882.

Jean-Charles Brisard, "Terrorism Financing, Roots and Trends of Saudi Terrorism financing", Report prepared for the President of the Security Council of the United Nations, 19 December 2002.

Jeremy Binnie and Christian Le Miere, "In the Line of Fire: Could Mumbai Happen Again?", *Jane's Intelligence Review*, January 2009.

Jerry Harris, *The Dialectics of Globalization: Economic and Political Conflict in a Transnational World*, Cambridge Scholars Publishing, 2006.

John Bellamy Foster, Hannah Holleman and Robert McChesney, "The US Imperial Triangle and Military Spending", Monthly Review.org, October 1, 2008, p 1.

John J Mearsheimer, "Why the Ukraine Crisis is the West's Fault", *Foreign Affairs*, September/October 2014 Issue.
https://www.foreignaffairs.com/articles/russia fsu/2014-08-18/why-ukraine-crisis-west-s-fault
And Ukraine and NATO Expansion
https://www.youtube.com/watch?v=fhILmIvBe6o&feature=you tube.com

———, "The Tragedy of Great Power Politics", Norton, 2001.

John K Cooley, *Unholy Wars: Afghanistan, America and International Terrorism*, Pluto Press, 1999.

John L McClellan, Senator, Remarks of, Cong. Rec. S9609, daily ed., 6.4.1974.

John Roth, Douglas Greenburg, Serena Wille, Monograph on Terrorist Financing, National Commission on Terrorist Attacks.
http://www.9-11commission.gov/

Jonathan Broder, "The ISIS Creation Myth", *Newsweek*, 12.6.15.
http://www.newsweek.com/2015/07/03/isis-george-w-bush-barack-obama 342613.html

Jonathan Figel, "Pakistani-Jamal-ud-Da'wah: The Saudi Wahabbi Influence".
http://www.islamdaily.org/wahabism/6987.Pakistanjamat-ud-awal-thesaudi wahabbi-influence.htm/

Jonathan Grant, "Merchants of Death: The International Traffic in Arms", *Origins*, Vol 6, Issue 3, December 2012, Ohio State University and Miami University.
http://origins.osu.edu/article/merchants-death-international-traffic-arms

Joseph Goebbels, speech in Munich (March, 1933)

Joseph Holliday, Institute for the Study of War, "The Struggle for Syria in 2011", December 2011.

Joshua Partlow and Kamran Khan, "Charity Funds Said to Provide Clues to Alleged Terrorist Plot", *The Washington Post*, 15 August, 2006.

Juan Miguel del Cid Gomez, "A Financial Profile of the Terrorism of Al-Qaeda and Its Affiliates", *Perspectives on Terrorism*, Vol 4, No 4, October 2010, p 17.

Julian E Barnes and Adam Entous, "US to Give Some Syria Rebels Ability to Call Airstrikes", *Wall Street Journal*, February 17, 2015.
https://www.wsj.com/articles/u s-to-give-some-syria-rebels-ability-to-call-airstrikes-1424208053

K Alan Kronstadt and Bruce Vaughn, "Terrorism in South Asia", CRS Report for Congress No RL32259 (Washington DC: Congressional Research Service, August 31, 2005).
fpc.state.gov/documents/organization/52750.pdf.

K Alan Kronstadt, "International Terrorism in South Asia", CRS Report for Congress No RS21658 (Washington DC: Congressional Research Service, November 3, 2003).
fpc.state.gov/documents/organization/26047.pdf.

Karin Brulliard, "Pakistan's Top Military Officials Are Worried about Militant Collaborators in Their Ranks", *The Washington Post*, May 17, 2011
http://www.washingtonpost.com/world/pakistani-military-worried-about collaborators-in-itsranks-officials-say/2011/05/27/AGgN1o CH_story.html

Kashmir Herald, Kanchan Lakshman and Ajaat Jamwal, J&K: Financing the Terror.
http://www.kashmirherald.com/main.php?t=OP&st=D&no=382

________, "Maulana Masood Azhar", Vol 1, No 8, January 2002.
http://kashmirherald.com/profiles/masoodazhar.html

Kathy Gilsinan, "The Confused Person's Guide to the Syrian Civil War: A brief primer", *The Atlantic*, Oct 29, 2015.
https://www.theatlantic.com/international/archive/2015/10/syrian-civil-war-guide isis/410746/.

Katrin Kuntz, :The Dutch Teen Who Maps the Jihadists", Spiegel Online.
http://www.spiegel.de/international/world/how-thomas-van-linge-mapped-islamic state-a-1048665.html

Khaled Ahmed, *Sleepwalking to surrender: Dealing with terrorism in Pakistan*, Penguin Books.

Khurshid Ahmad, "Amrika: Muslim Dunya ki Bey-Itminani" (America and Unrest in the Muslim World), (Islamabad: Institute of Policy Studies, 2002) (in Urdu).

Kiko Itasaka, "In Afghanistan, insider attacks begin with a trip to the market", NBC News, October 6, 2013.

Kurth Cronin, Audrey; Huda Aden; Adam Frost; Benjamin Jones, "Foreign Terrorist Organizations", Congressional Research Service, 6 February 2004.

Laura Lump (ed), *Running Guns, The Global Black Market in Small Arms*, London: Zed Books Ltd, 2001.

Lawrence G Potter, "Islam and Politics: Egypt, Algeria and Tunisia, Great Decisions" (New York: Foreign Policy Association, 1994), pp 71-72.

Lawrence Lifschultz, "The Heroin Empire", *Newline*, July 1989, p 73.

Leonard Schonberg, *Morgen's War* (2005) p 218.

"Less than Half of Pakistani Public Supports Attacking Al Qaeda, Cracking Down on Fundamentalists", World Public Opinion.org, October 31, 2007.
www.worldpublicopinion.org/pipa/ articles/home_page/424.php?lb =hmpg1&pnt=424&nid=&id

Louise Ridley, "Islamic State Receiving Weapons from Eastern Europe in 'Rapid' New Supply Chain Says Arms Expert", *The Huffington Post*, September 11, 2016.
http://www.huffingtonpost.co.uk/entry/islamic-state-weapons-eastern-europe conflict-armament-research_uk_57d2b66be4b0ced6a09927fd

Mahmood Mamdani, *Good Muslim, Bad Muslim: Islam, the USA and the Global War Against Terror*, Permanent Black, 2002.

Majid Khadduri, *War and Peace in the Law of Islam*, Lawbook Exchange Ltd, 2010, p 56.

Maliha Zulfacar, *Afghan Immigrants in the USA and Germany: A Comparative Analysis of the Use of Ethnic Social Capital*. Kulturelle Identitat und politische Selbstbestimmung in der Weltgesellschaft, LIT Verlag, p 33, 1998, ISBN 9783825836504.

Margaret Parton, "Invaders Flee Vale of Kashmir Before India's Advancing Army", *NY Herald Tribune*, Nov 11, 1947.

http://cojs.org/cojswiki/Invaders_Flee_Vale_of_Kashmir_Before_India's_Advancing_Army,_NY_Herald_Tribune,_Nov._11,_1947.

Mariam Abou Zahab and Olivier Roy, *Islamist Networks: The Afghan-Pakistan Connection*, London: C Hurst & Co, 2004.

Mariam Abou Zahab, "I Shall be Waiting at the Door of Paradise: The Pakistani Martyrs of the Lashkar-e-Taiba (Army of the Pure)", *The Practice of War: Production, Reproduction and Communication of Armed Violence*, eds. Aparna Rao et al (New York: Berghahn Books, 2007).

Mark Hanrahan, "Battle Against ISIS In Mosul: Iraqi Forces Advance on Airport", NBC News, February 21, 2017.
http://www.nbcnews.com/storyline/isis terror/battle-against-isis-mosul-iraqi-forces-advance-airport-n723496.

Mark Mazzetti and Eric Schmitt, "CIA Outlines Pakistan Links with Militants", *The New York Times*, July 30, 2008.

Mark Mazzetti and Ali Younes, "CIA Arms for Syrian Rebels Supplied Black Market, Officials Say", *The New York Times*, June 26, 2016.
https://www.nytimes.com/2016/06/27/world/middleeast/cia-arms-for-syrian rebels-supplied-black-market-officials-say.html?_r=0

Mark Pieth (ed), *Financing Terrorism*, Kluwer Academic Publishers, Dordrecht, 2002.

Mark Urban, *War in Afghanistan*, Macmillan Press Ltd, p 271.

Matthew Brunwasser, "Gallery of International Arms Dealers Victor Anatoliyevich Bout – The Embargo Buster: Fueling Bloody Civil Wars", Frontline World.

Matthew Levitt, "Stemming the Flow of Terrorist Financing: Practical and Conceptual Challenges", *Fletcher Forum of World Affairs*, Winter/Spring 2003, Vol 27, No 1.

Maulana Masood Azhar, Ma'arka (The Struggle); Faza'il Jihad (The Virtue of Jihad); Tuhfa-e-Saadat (The Gift of Virtue), (Karachi: Idara AI-Khair, 2001) (all in Urdu).

Meir Amit Intelligence and Terrorism Information Center (ITIC) at the Israel Intelligence Heritage and Commemoration Center (IICC), "Lashkar-e-Taiba, A Pakistani Islamic Organization", December 21, 2008.

_______, "ISIS: Portrait of a Jihadi Terrorist Organization", November 2014.

Michael Bhatia and Mark Sedra, *Afghanistan, Arms and Conflict: Armed groups, disarmament, and security in a post-war society*, Routledge, 2008.

Michael Chossudovsky, "America's 'Global War on Terror', Al Qaeda and the Islamic State (ISIS): A Review", *Global Research*, November 16, 2015.

http://www.globalresearch.ca/americas-global-war-on-terror-al-qaeda-and-the-islamic-state-isis/5434057.

_______, "The Globalization of War: America's "Long War" against Humanity", 2015.

_______, "Syria: Who is Behind the Protest Movement? Fabricating a Pretext for a US-NATO 'Humanitarian Intervention'", Centre for Research on Globalization, May 3, 2011.

_______, "US 'Military Aid' to Al Qaeda, ISIS-Daesh: Pentagon Uses Illicit Arms Trafficking to Channel Enormous Shipments of Light Weapons into Syria", *Global Research*, October 5, 2016.

http://www.globalresearch.ca/u-s military-aid-to-al-qaeda-routine-ship ments-of-weapons-to-syrian-freedom fighters/5548960

_______, "9/11 Analysis: From Ronald Reagan and the Soviet-Afghan War to George W Bush and September 11, 2001", *Global Research*, September 09, 2010.

Michael Freeman, "Introduction to Financing Terrorism: Case Studies" in Michael Freeman, *Financing Terrorism: Case Studies*, Farnham: Ashgate, 2012, p 3.

Michael Kaplan, "How ISIS Acquires Weapons: Islamic State Benefits from Region Overflowing with American, Russian Made Arms", *International Business Times*, 11.17.15.

http://www.ibtimes.com/how-isis-acquires-weapons-islamic state-benefits-region-overflowing-american-russian-2188758.

Michael Scheuer, *Frontline*, "Al Qaeda's New Front: Interviews: Michael Scheuer".

http://www.pbs.org/wgbh/pages/frontline/shows/front/interviews/scheuer.html

_______, *Imperial Hubris*, Dulles, Virginia, Brassey's, Inc, 2004, p 9, ISBN 0-965-51394-7.

Mohammad Amir Rana, "Jammat-ud-Dawa has No Global Network or Ambitions: Mujahid", *Daily Times*, May 25, 2004.

_______, *The Seeds of Terrorism* (London: New Millenium, 2005).

_______, *A to Z of Jehadi Organizations in Pakistan, Mashal*, Lahore, 2004.

_______, trans Saba Ansari, *The A to Z of Jehadi Organizations in Pakistan* (Lahore: Mashal, 2004).

Mohammad Yousaf and Mark Adkin, *Afghanistan: The Bear Trap: The Defeat of a Superpower*, Casemate Pub, 2001.

Muhammad Mustafa Khan 'Maddah', *Urdu-Hindi Shabdkosh*, Uttar Pradesh Hindi Sansthan, Lucknow, Seventh edition, 1992.

Muhammad Yousaf, *Silent Soldier: The Man Behind the Afghan Jihad*, Jang Publishers, 1991.

Muzamil Jameel, "Explaining the History of Masood Azhar's Jaish-e-Mohammad, the Mystery of its Re-emergence", *The Indian Express*, January 5, 2016.
http://indianexpress.com/article/explained/in-fact-history-of-masood-azhars-jaish the-mystery-of-its-re-emergence/

NYPD Intelligence Division, "Mumbai Attack Analysis", December 4, 2008.

Nabeelah Jaffer, "The secret world of ISIS brides: 'U dnt hav 2 pay 4 Anything if u r wife of a martyr'", *The Guardian*, June 24, 2015.
https://www.theguardian.com/world/2015/jun/24/isis-brides-secret-world-jihad western-women-syria

Nadjma Yassari, *The Sharīʿa in the Constitutions of Afghanistan, Iran, and Egypt*, Tübingen: Mohr Siebeck, p 49, 2005, ISBN 3-16-148787-7.

Najam Sethi, "Why was Daniel Pearl Killed", *Friday Times*, March 4, 2002.
http://mea.gov.in/articles-in-indian media.htm?dtl/15752/Why+was +Daniel+Pearl+killed.

NDTV, "US Strikes Syrian Military Targets in First Direct Assault on Bashar al Assad's Government", April 7, 2017.
http://www.ndtv.com/world-news/us-strikes syrian-military-targets-in-first-direct-assault-on-bashar-al-assads-government-1678386

New America Foundation, cited in "Out of the Blue" in *The Economist*, July 30, 2011, http://www.economist.com/node/21524916.

New Eastern Outlook, "The Mystery of ISIS' Toyota Army Solved", 9.10.2015.
http://journal-neo.org/2015/10/09/the-mystery-of-isis-toyota-army-solved/

Newsweekpakistan.com, "After Six Years, Masood Azhar Almost Resurfaces", March 23, 2014.
http://newsweekpakistan.com/in-plain-view/.

Nicholas Howenstein, "The Jihadi Terrain in Pakistan: An Introduction to the Sunni Jihadi Groups in Pakistan and Kashmir", Pakistan Security Research Unit, Bradford University, Research Report No 1, 2008. http://spaces.brad.ac.uk:8080/download/attachments/748/resrep1.pdf

Nicholas Marsh, "Two Sides of the Same Coin? The Legal and Illegal Trade in Small Arms", *Brown Journal of World Affairs*, Vol 9 (2002), pp 217-228.

Nirodbhusan Roy, *Niamatullah's History of the Afghans* (n.d., reprint, Lahore: Sang-e-Meel Publishers, 2002.

Noam Chomsky, "Chomsky: Paris attacks show hypocrisy of West's outrage", CNN, January 20, 2015. http://edition.cnn.com/2015/01/19/opinion/charlie-hebdo-noam chomsky/

________, cited in "Urban Terrorism: Introduction', Urban Terrorism essays and Articles at eNotes. http://www.enotes.com/urban-terrorism-article

________, "Noam Chomsky on How the Iraq War Birthed ISIS and Why US Policy Undermines the Fight Against It", March 2, 2015, Full transcript on democracynow.org. https://www.democracynow.org/2015/3/2/noam_chomsky_on_how_the_iraq

Olaf Caroe, *The Pathans: 500 BC-AD 1957*, Macmillan and Co, London, 1958.

"Operation Cyclone", Wikipedia. https://en.wikipedia.org/wiki/Operation_Cyclone

Pakistan Times, Hafiz Mohammed Saeed. https://www.pakistantimes.com/topics/hafiz-mohammad-saeed/.

Pakistan's failure to keep a check on terrorism funding to be discussed at Paris meet, *Financial Express*, February 17, 2017.

"Pakistan's Tribal Areas: Appeasing the Militants", Asia Report No 125 (Islamabad/Brussels: International Crisis Group, December 11, 2006), pi. www.crisisgroup.org/library/documents/asia/ south_asia/125_pakistans_tribal_areas_appeasing_the_militants.pdf

"Pakistani Army ran Muslim extremist training camps: Anti-terrorist expert". Daily News and Analysis, 14 November 2009.

"Paragliding part of LeT training camp: Jundal", *Hindustan Times*, New Delhi, June 29, 2012.

https://web.archive.org/web/20130617024138/http://www.hindustan times.com/In ia-news/NewDelhi/Paragliding-part-of-LeT-training-camp-Jundal/Article1 880615.aspx

Patrick B Johnson and Anoop Sarbahi, "The Impact of US Drone Strikes on Terrorism in Pakistan", *RAND Corporation*, 25 February 2012.

Patrick Cockburn, "If this battle for Mosul ends in defeat for ISIS, we shouldn't feel too optimistic about what comes next", *Independent*, March 3, 2017.
http://www.independent.co.uk/voices/isis-mosul-iraq-caliphate-islamic-state-a7608981.html.

_______, "Iraq crisis: How Saudi Arabia helped ISIS take over the north of the country", *Independent*, July 12, 2014.
http://www.independent.co.uk/voices/comment/iraq-crisis-how-saudi-arabia helped-isis-take-over-the-north-of-the-country-9602312.html

Paul Allan Schott, "Reference Guide to Anti-Money Laundering and Combating the Financing of Terrorism", The World Bank, 2006.

Paul Rivlin, "Money makes the world go round", *Iqtisadi*, Vol 4, No 9 (Sept 28, 2014), The Moshe Dayan Center for Middle Eastern and African Studies.
http://dayan.org/iqtisadi-vol4-no-9-sept-28-2014

Pete Papaherakles, "Is 'IS' a CIA-Mossad Creation?", *American Free Press*, August 28, 2014.
http://americanfreepress.net/is-is-a-cia-mossad-creation/

Phillip Killicoat, "Weaponomics: The Global Market For Assault Rifles", World Bank Policy Research Working Paper 4202, April 2007.

Praveen Swami, "Behind terror attack, a reborn jihad empire", *The Indian Express*, January 3, 2016.
http://indianexpress.com/article/india/india-news-india/behind terror-attack-a-reborn-jihad-empire/.

_______, *India, Pakistan and the Secret Jihad: The Covert War in Kashmir, 1947-2005*, London: Routledge, 2007.

_______, "No one arrested, we are still in business, says Jaish-e-Mohammad", *The Indian Express*, January 15, 2016.
http://indianexpress.com/article/india/india news-india/no-one-arrested-we-are-still-in-business-says-jaish-e-muhammad/

________, "Using fictitious names, Lashkar operates bank accounts in Pakistan", *The Indian Express*, February 8, 2017.

PRI (Public Radio International), "This one Toyota pickup truck is at the top of the shopping list for the Free Syrian Army – and the Taliban", April 1, 2014. https://www.pri.org/stories/2014-04-01/one-toyota-pickup-truck-top-shopping-list free-syrian-army-and-taliban
Proc Home-Judl, Sept-Dec 1872, p 3252.

Proceedings of the Trial of Muhammad Bahadur Shah, Calcutta, 1895, pp 176 77.

Rachel Ehrenfeld, *Funding Evil: How Terrorism Is Financed – and How to Stop It*, MultiEducator, Inc. New Rochelle, NY, 2011.

Rachel Stohl, "Fighting the Illicit Trafficking of Small Arms", *ISAIS Review*, Vol XXV, No 1 (Winter-Spring 2005), Project Muse.

________, "The Tangled Web of Illicit Arms Trafficking", https://www.americanprogress.org/wp-content/uploads/kf/Terrorin Shadows Stohl.pdf

Rachel Stohl and EJ Hogendoorn, "Stopping the Destructive Spread of Small Arms: How Small Arms and Light Weapons Proliferation Undermines Security and Development", Center for American Progress, March 10, 2010.

Rajesh Ahuja, "Prayer, Weapons and Maps: A Day in a Pakistan Jihad Camp", *Hindustan Times*, September 3, 2015.
http://www.hindustantimes.com/india/prayer-weapons-and-maps-a-day-in-a pakistan-jihad-camp/story-grvVtXo8QpJ13UtGelW0UL.html

Richard Cumings, "US: Lockheed Stock and Two Smoking Barrels", CorpWatch, Jan 16, 2007.

Richard Skaff, "The Military-Industrial Complex: A Capitalist System Run Amok", *Global Research*, Centre for Research on Globalization, Dec 14, 2012.

Robert J Bunker, "Fighting Irregular Fighters: Defeating Violent Non-State Actors", *Parameters*, Vol 43, No 4, Winter 2013-2014, p 64.

Robin Thomas Naylor, *Satanic Purses: Money, Myth and Misinformation in the War on Terror*, Montreal: McGill-Queen's University Press, 2006.

Rodrigue Tremblay, "US Covert Support to the Islamic State (ISIS) as a Means to Creating Chaos and Destroying Syria", *Global Research*, September 16, 2015.

http://www.globalresearch.ca/us-covert-support-to-the-islamic-state-isis-as a-means-to-creating-chaos-and-destroying-syria/5476356

Rohit Honawar, "Jaish-e-Mohammed", IPCS Special Report, No 4, November 2005, Institute of Peace and Conflict Studies, New Delhi.

Ronald W Cox, "The Military-Industrial Complex and US Military Spending After 9/11", *Class, Race and Corporate Power*, Vol 2: Iss 2, Article 5, 2014. http://digitalcommons.fiu.edu/classracecorporatepower/vol2/iss2/5

RT.com, "Moscow objective to defeat ISIS, US objective to defeat Assad – George Galloway to RT", December 11, 2015. https://www.rt.com/uk/325559-galloway russia-us-syria/

________, "Turkey is key supplier of weapons, military hardware to ISIS – Russian envoy to UN", April 1, 2016. https://www.rt.com/news/338038-isis-weapons turkey-churkin/

________, "Western ISIS adventurism, Israel behind Hamas – new Assange revelations", March 24, 2015. https://www.rt.com/news/243445-assange-west islamists-us/.

Ryan Clarke, "Lashkar-i-Taiba: The Fallacy of Subservient Proxies and the Future of Islamist Terrorism in India" (2010) from the Strategic Studies Institute website. http://www.strategicstudiesinstitute.army.mil/pubs/display.cfm?pubid =973

Saeed Shah, "Terror group builds big base under Pakistani officials' noses", McClatchy newspapers, 13 September 2009.

Sayyid Abul Ala Maudoodi, "Jihad fi Sabilillah" (tr Prof Khurshid Ahmad, ed Huda Khattab, UKIM Dawah Centre).

Schroeder, Matt, "Appendix 14A, Global Effort to Control MANPADS", *SIPRI Yearbook 2007*, Armament, Disarmament and International Security, Oxford: Oxford University Press, pp 623-639, 2007.

Scott Shane, "The War in Pashtunistan", *The New York Times*, December 5, 2009. http://www.nytimes.com/2009/12/06/weekinreview/06shane.html

Seth G Jones, "Pakistan's Dangerous Game", *Survival*, 49:1 (2007), pp 18-26.

Seth Moulton, "Syrian refugees are not the problem in ISIS fight", *The Boston Globe*, November 23, 2015. https://www.bostonglobe.com/opinion/2015/11/23/seth moulton-syrian-refugees-are-not-problem-isis fight/OU0sY6eIx6mMfHjHE jwpFO/story.html

Seumas Milne, "Now the truth emerges: how the US fuelled the rise of ISIS in Syria and Iraq", *The Guardian*, June 3, 2015.
https://www.theguardian.com/commentisfree/2015/jun/03/us-isis-syria-iraq

Seymour Hersh, "Sy Hersh Reveals Potential Turkish Role in Syria Chemical Strike That Almost Sparked US Bombing", *Democracy Now*.
https://www.democracynow.org/2014/4/7/sy_hersh_reveals_potential_turkish_role

Seymour M Hersh, "The Redirection: Is the Administration's new policy benefitting our enemies in the war on terrorism?" Annals of National Security, March 5, 2007 Issue, *The New Yorker*.
http://www.newyorker.com/magazine/2007/03/05/the-redirection

Shashank Shantanu, "US move for a UN ban on Jaish-e-Mohammed chief Masood Azhar blocked again by China", *India Today*, February 7, 2017.
http://indiatoday.intoday.in/story/us-moves-un-for-ban-on-pathankot-attack plotter-masood-azhars-china-again-puts-a-hold/1/876966.html

Shuja Nawaz, *Crossed Swords: Pakistan, Its Army and the Wars Within*, New York: Oxford University Press, 2008.

Shushant Sareen, *The Jihad Factory: Pakistan's Islamic Revolution in the Making* (India: Observer Research Foundation, 2005), 243.

Sibel Edmonds, Boiling Frogs Post, "BFP Exclusive – Developing Story: Hundreds of US-NATO Soldiers Arrive and Begin Operations on the Jordan-Syria Border", December 11, 2011.

———, "Syria – Secret US-NATO Training and Support Camp to Oust Current Syrian President", November 21, 2011.

———, "Syria Coverage Update: BBC Reporter was detained and prevented from covering US-NATO-Syrian Operations in Turkey!", December 15, 2011.

———, "US Media: Distorters of Reality and Gravediggers of Truth", December 3, 2011.

———, "War on Syria Cover-Up Update: Who is Breaking the Blackout?", December 9, 2011.

Small Arms Survey, "Guided light weapons reportedly held by non-state armed groups, 1998-2013".

———, Small Arms Survey 2003: "Development Denied" (Oxford: Oxford University Press, 2003).

Stephen Philip Cohen, "With Allies Like This: Pakistan and the War on Terror", in Adam Garfinkle, ed, *A Practical Guide to Winning the War on Terrorism* (Stanford: Hoover Institution Press, Stanford University, 2004), pp 103-116.

Stephen Tankel, "Lashkar-e-Taiba in Perspective: An Evolving Threat" (Washington, DC: New America Foundation, Counterterrorism Strategy Initiative Policy Paper, 2010).
http://www.carnegieendowment.org/files/Lashkar-e Taiba_in_Perspective.pdf

________, "Lashkar-e-Taiba: Past Operations and Future Prospects" (PDF), National Security Studies Program Policy Paper, Washington, DC: New America Foundation, 27 April 2011.

________, "The Long Arm of Lashkar-e-Taiba", PolicyWatch 1631, Policy Analysis, The Washington Institute, February 17, 2010.
http://www.washingtoninstitute.org/policy-analysis/view/the-long-arm-of-lashkar-e-taiba

Steve Coll, *Ghost Wars: The Secret History of the CIA, Afghanistan, and bin Laden, from the Soviet Invasion to September 10, 2001* (New York: Penguin Books, 2005).

________, "Zawahiri's record suggests he will struggle", *Frontline*, PBS, 2 May 2011.

Steven Chovanec, The West Created and Perpetuates The Syrian Civil War, Mintpressnews, March 24, 2015.
http://www.mintpressnews.com/MyMPN/the west-created-perpetuates-the-syrian-civil-war/

Stuart Taylor, Jr, "The Big Snoop: Life, liberty, and the Pursuit of Terrorists", Brookings Essay.

Sudha Ramchandran, "India Tackles Terror Financing", *Terrorism Monitor*, Vol 15, Issue 1, Jan 2017, Jamestown Foundation.

Suhasini Haider, "China's move to block ban against Azhar came just before deadline", April 2, 2016, *The Hindu*.
http://www.thehindu.com/news/national/Chinas-move-to block-ban-against-Azhar-came-just-before-deadline/article14215314.ece

Sutirtho Patranobis, "China blocks India's move to ban Jaish chief Masood Azhar again", *Hindustan Times*, October 2, 2016.
http://www.hindustantimes.com/india news/china-extends-veto-on-

india-s-move-for-un-blacklisting-of-jaish-chief masood-azhar/story-Ut9sxWSJGQJb5Rc70cIweM.html.

Syed Saleem Shahzad, "Pakistan, the Taliban and Dadullah", Pakistan Security Research Unit, Brief Number 3, Department of Peace Studies, University of Bradford, March 1, 2007.
http://spaces.brad.ac.uk:8080/ download/attachments/748/Brief3 finalised1.pdf

Tara Kartha, "Light Weapons Proliferation and Regional Instability in Central Asia", *Strategic Analysis*, Vol XIX, No 9, 1996, pp 1278.

Terrence McCoy, "How the Islamic State evolved in an American prison", *The Washington Post*, November 4, 2014.
https://www.washingtonpost.com/news/morning-mix/wp/2014/11/04/how-an american-prison-helped-ignite-the-islamic-state/?utm_term =.0bd47edac9d6

"The Balance, War on Terror Facts, Costs and Timeline".
https://www.thebalance.com/war-on-terror-facts-costs-timeline-3306300

The Diplomat, Franz J Marty, "The Taliban's New Plan for Capturing Kunduz", March 28, 2017.
http://thediplomat.com/2017/03/the-talibans-new-plan-for-capturing-kunduz/

The Guardian, Ivan Angelovski in Belgrade, Miranda Patrucic in Sarajevo and Lawrence Marzouk in London, "Revealed: the £1bn of weapons flowing from Europe to Middle East".
https://www.theguardian.com/world/2016/jul/27/weapons flowing-eastern-europe-middle-east-revealed-arms-trade-syria

________, Martin Chulov in Beirut, Fazel Hawramy in Irbil and Spencer Ackerman in New York, "Iraq army capitulates to ISIS militants in four cities", June 12, 2014.
https://www.theguardian.com/world/2014/jun/11/mosul-isis-gunmen-middle-east-states

________, "WikiLeaks cables portray Saudi Arabia as a cash machine for terrorists", October 1, 2015.
http://www.mintpressnews.com/wikileaks-cables-portray-saudi-arabia-as-a-cash-machine-for-terrorists/210038/

The Hindu, "Anjuman plot to invade India", July 21, 2000.
http://www.thehindu.com/2000/07/21/stories/01210007.htm

_______, "Highlights of Union Budget", February 1, 2017.
http://www.thehindu.com/business/budget/Highlights-of-Union-Budget-2017 18/article17127298.ece

The Investigative Project on Terrorism, "Jaish-e-Mohammed (JeM)", Profile, Chapter 8; Foreign Terrorist Organizations, Country Reports on Terrorism 2005, US Department of State, April 30, 2006.
http://www.investigativeproject.org/profile/134/jaish-e-mohammed-jem

The Telegraph, Ashley Kirk, "Iraq and Syria: How many foreign fighters are fighting for ISIL?", March 24, 2016.
http://www.telegraph.co.uk/news/2016/03/29/iraq-and-syria-how-many-foreign-fighters-are-fighting-for-isil/

The Times of India, "China blocked US move to get Masood Azhar banned by UN", Feb 8, 2017.
http://timesofindia.indiatimes.com/india/china-blocked-us-move-to-get masood-azhar-banned-by-un/articleshow/57029498.cms

_______, "JeM chief Masood Azhar under house arrest", December 9, 2008.
http://timesofindia.indiatimes.com/world/pakistan/JeM-chief-Masood-Azhar under-house-arrest/articleshow/3811634.cms?

Thomas J Biersteker and Sue J Eckert (eds), *Countering the Financing of Terrorism*, Routledge, 2008.

Thomas Young, "40 years ago, Church Committee investigated Americans spying on Americans", Brookings, May 6, 2015.
https://www.brookings.edu/blog/brookings now/2015/05/06/40-years-ago-church-committee-investigated-americans-spying-on americans

Tim Lister, "Why ISIS is winning and How to reverse gains".
http://www.mycentx.com/news/why-isis-is-winning-and-how-to-reverse-that-success/82816313

Timothy McGrath, "Watch this English-speaking ISIS fighter explain how a 98 year-old colonial map created today's conflict", *Los Angeles Daily News*.
http://www.dailynews.com/general-news/20140702/watch-this-english-speaking isis-fighter-explain-how-a-98-year-old-colonial-map-created-todays-conflict

Tom Cooper Air Combat Information Group, I Indo-Pakistani War, 1947-49, October 29, 2003.

Tom Keatinge, "Breaking the Banks: The Financial Consequences of Counterterrorism", *Foreign Affairs*, June 26, 2014.

Tory Cartalucci, "How the US Supports the Islamic State (ISIS): One 'Accidental Airdrop' vs Billions in Covert Military Aid", *Global Research*, June 25, 2016.
http://www.globalresearch.ca/how-the-us-supports-the-islamic-state-isis-one accidental-airdrop-vs-billions-in-covert-military-aid/5409449

———, "Is Washington Financing Terrorism? Islamic State (ISIS) Mercenary Admits Getting Funds from US", *Global Research*, January 31, 2015.
http://www.globalresearch.ca/is-washington-financing-terrorism-islamic-state isis-mercenary-admits-getting-funds-from-us/5428594

———, Land Destroyer, "Syrian Conflict Escalates"; "It's Official: 'Arab Spring' Subversion is US Funded"; and "Syria: Intervention Inevitable".
http://landdestroyer.blogspot.in/2011/04/syrian-conflict-escalates.html

———, "Logistics 101: Where Does ISIS Get Its Guns?", *Global Research*, February 20, 2016.
http://www.globalresearch.ca/logistics-101-where-does-isis get-its-guns/5454726

Trevor Timm, "The US decision to send weapons to Syria repeats a historical mistake", *The Guardian*, September 19, 2015.
https://www.theguardian.com/commentisfree/2015/sep/19/us-weapons-to-syria repeats-historical-mistake

Tyler Durden, "Officials Admit ISIS, Like Al-Qaeda, was a Creation of US Foreign Policy", *ZeroHedge*, August 17, 2015.
http://www.zerohedge.com/news/2015-08-17/officials-admit-isis-al-qaeda-was creation-us-foreign-policy

"Unfulfilled Promises: Pakistan's Failure to Tackle Extremism", Asia Report No 73 (Islamabad/Brussels: International Crisis Group, January 16, 2004).
www.crisisgroup.org/library/documents/asia/south_asia/073_unfulfil_promises_pakistan_extr.pdf

UNODC, "The Opium Economy in Afghanistan: An international Problem", Vienna, 2003.

US embassy cables: "Hillary Clinton says Saudi Arabia 'a critical source of terrorist funding'", *The Guardian*, 5 December 2010.

———: "Lashkar-e-Taiba terrorists raise funds in Saudi Arabia", *The Guardian*, 5 December 2010.

US State Department, Chapter 6: "Foreign Terrorist Organizations", May 20, 2013.
http://www.state.gov/j/ct/rls/crt/2012/209989.htm

Vappala Balchandran, "Black Money And Terror: Quality of counter-terrorism, not currency crackdown, will prevent terrorism", *The Indian Express*, Nov 23, 2016.
http://indianexpress.com/article/opinion/columns/demonetisation-pm-modi-black money-terror-funding-corruption-4390492/

Vicky Nanjappa, "Revealed: How hawala funds terror in Kashmir", OneIndia News, Jan 17, 2017.

Vishwas Kumar, "Exclusive: How Jaish-e-Mohammad is funding terrorists in J&K: An assessment of JeM operations by the Indian intelligence agencies", *India Today News*, Jan 18, 2016.

Washington's Blog, "The Syrian Chemical Weapons Attack Was a False Flag By Turkey and ISIS", December 15, 2015.
http://www.washingtonsblog.com/2015/12/syrian-chemical-weapons-attack-false flag-turkey-isis.html

WikiLeaks, Craig Whitlock, *The Washington Post*, "US Secretly Backed Syrian Opposition Groups", cables released by WikiLeaks show, April 17, 2011.

William Colby, Testimony, House Select Committee on Intelligence, p 122, 8.4.1975.

William Hartung and Rachel Stohl, "Hired Guns", *Foreign Policy*, May/June 2004.

William Hartung, and Michelle Ciarrocca, "The Military-Industrial Think Tank Complex", *Multinational Monitor*, Jan-Feb 2003, 17-20.

World Bank Working Paper, "New Technologies, New Risks? Innovation and Countering the Financing of Terrorism", 2010.

Yaniv Barzilai, *102 Days of War: How Osama bin Laden, al Qaeda and the Taliban Survived 2001*, Potomac Books, Inc, p 97, 2014.

Yaqut al-Hamawi, "Mu'jam al-Buldan" (Dictionary of Countries) [Gazetteer], Beirut, Dar Beirut, 1957, Vol 4, Al-Taibah.

Yoginder Sikand, "The Islamist Militancy in Kashmir: The Case of the Lashkar e-Taiba", in *The Practice of War: Production, Reproduction and Communication of Armed Violence* (eds), Aparna Rao et al (New York: Berghahn Books, 2007).

Z Hussain, *Frontline Pakistan: the struggle with militant Islam*, Columbia University Press, New York (2007); pp 66.

Zachary Laub and Jonathan Masters, Council on Foreign Relations: "Islamic State in Iraq and Greater Syria," June 12, 2014, updated August 8, 2014. http://www.cfr.org/iraq/islamic-stateiraq-syria/p14811

Zahid Hussain, "Freed Militant Surfaces", abcnews.com, 2000-01-05. https://web.archive.org/web/20000901092056/http://abcnews.go.com/sections/wor d/DailyNews/militants000105.html

Zee News, "23 Indians joined ISIS to fight in Iraq and Syria, 17 belong to southern states: Report", December 29, 2015.
http://zeenews.india.com/news/india/23 indians-joined-isis-to-fight-in-iraq-and-syria-17-belong-to-southern-states report_1839650.html

Index